The Future of Pension Management

For David: the rule of 3
is a powerful tool used in
the book!

With best wishes,

Keith

The Wiley Finance series contains books written specifically for finance and investment professionals as well as sophisticated individual investors and their financial advisors. Book topics range from portfolio management to e-commerce, risk management, financial engineering, valuation and financial instrument analysis, as well as much more. For a list of available titles, visit our Web site at www.WileyFinance.com.

Founded in 1807, John Wiley & Sons is the oldest independent publishing company in the United States. With offices in North America, Europe, Australia and Asia, Wiley is globally committed to developing and marketing print and electronic products and services for our customers' professional and personal knowledge and understanding.

The Future of Pension Management

Integrating Design, Governance, and Investing

KEITH P. AMBACHTSHEER

Published by John Wiley & Sons, Inc., Hoboken, New Jersey.
Published simultaneously in Canada.

For general information on our other products and services or for technical support, please contact our Customer Care Department within the United States at (800) 762-2974, outside the United States at (317) 572-3993 or fax (317) 572-4002.

Wiley publishes in a variety of print and electronic formats and by print-on-demand. Some material included with standard print versions of this book may not be included in e-books or in print-on-demand. If this book refers to media such as a CD or DVD that is not included in the version you purchased, you may download this material at http://booksupport.wiley.com. For more information about Wiley products, visit www.wiley.com.

Library of Congress Cataloging-in-Publication Data is available:

ISBN 978-1-119-19103-2 (Hardcover)
ISBN 978-1-119-19100-1 (ePDF)
ISBN 978-1-119-19102-5 (ePub)

Cover Design: Wiley

Printed in the United States of America.
10 9 8 7 6 5 4 3 2 1

The reasonable man adapts himself to the world.
The unreasonable one persists in trying to adapt the world to himself.
Thus all progress depends on the unreasonable man.

George Bernard Shaw
Man and Superman, 1903

Contents

Preface   xi

PART ONE
Touchstones

CHAPTER 1
Improved Pension Designs and Organizations: Gateways to a More
Functional Capitalism   3

CHAPTER 2
Pension Plans for the Masses: Good Idea or Pipe Dream?   11

CHAPTER 3
Does Institutional Investing Have a Future?   17

CHAPTER 4
Thomas Piketty's *Capital in the 21st Century*: Its Relevance to
Pension Fund Management   25

PART TWO
Pension Design

CHAPTER 5
Why We Need to Change the Conversation about Pension Reform   33

CHAPTER 6
On the Costing and Funding of Defined-Benefit Pensions: Separating
Fact and Fiction   41

CHAPTER 7
Defining Defined-Ambition Pension Plans: Conclusions from an
International Conversation   49

CHAPTER 8
What Are Target-Benefit Plans and Why Should You Care?   55

CHAPTER 9
Designing 21st-Century Pension Plans: We're Making Progress!   61

PART THREE
Pension Governance

CHAPTER 10
How Effective Is Pension Fund Governance Today?: Findings from a
New Survey   69

CHAPTER 11
The Evolving Meaning of Fiduciary Duty: Is Your Board of Trustees
Keeping Up?   81

CHAPTER 12
Pension Organizations and Integrated Reporting: Improving
Stakeholder Communications   87

CHAPTER 13
Measuring Value-for-Money in Pension Organizations: A New Look   93

CHAPTER 14
Measuring Value for Money in Private Markets Investing: Why
Investors Need a Standard Protocol   101

CHAPTER 15
How Pension Funds Pay Their Own Investment People   107

CHAPTER 16
Investment Beliefs and Organization Design: Are They Aligned in Your
Organization?   127

CHAPTER 17
Norway versus Yale—or versus Canada?: A Comparison of
Investment Models   133

CHAPTER 18
Does Culture Matter in Pension Organizations?   141

PART FOUR

Pension Investing

CHAPTER 19
Are Investment Returns Predictable? 151

CHAPTER 20
Investment Returns in the 21st Century 157

CHAPTER 21
Long-Termism as the Dominant Investment Paradigm 163

CHAPTER 22
Investing for the Long Term I: From Saying to Doing 169

CHAPTER 23
**Investing for the Long Term II: How Should We Measure
Performance?** 177

CHAPTER 24
Investing for the Long Term III: Does It Produce Better Outcomes? 183

CHAPTER 25
Are Alphas and Betas Bunk? 189

CHAPTER 26
Risk Management Revisited 195

CHAPTER 27
From an Unknown to a Known: Managing Climate Change Risk 201

Conclusion 207

Notes 209

About the Author 219

Index 221

Preface

I thought my third book on pension management, *Pension Revolution*, published in 2007, would be my last. To their credit, Bill Falloon and his Wiley colleagues changed my mind. How? By featuring that 2007 book at the CFA Institute's 2015 Annual Conference in Frankfurt. To my surprise, attendees were lining up to buy an eight-year-old book on a revolution in pension design, management, and investing!

THE EVOLVING PENSION REVOLUTION

A lot of things have happened in the pensions world in the past eight years, many foreseen in the 2007 book, some not. On the pension design side, the traditional defined benefit (DB) and defined contribution (DC) formulas are converging into hybrids with names such as "defined ambition" (DA) and "target benefit" (TB). The Netherlands and Australia offer good examples of these shifts. The former is transforming its traditional DB plans into DA plans, while the latter is transforming its traditional DC plans into TB plans. At the same time, pension coverage is expanding in some countries through government initiatives. The United Kingdom is leading the way with its National Employment Savings Trust (NEST) initiative, while the United States and Canada are designing their own strategies to expand workplace pension coverage.

On the pension-governance front, the process of reconciling the opposable needs for boards of trustees to be both representative and strategic continues to slowly move in the right direction. There is a growing understanding that it is not a question of "either-or," but rather how to get *both* ingredients into board composition. Why both? Because pension boards need legitimacy to be trusted, and at the same time, need to be strategic to produce value-for-money outcomes for their stakeholders. This strategic mindset addresses tough issues such as organization design and culture, investment beliefs, incentives, and stakeholder communication and relations. Behind these governance imperatives lies the broader question of organizational autonomy. Unnecessary legal constraints are increasingly seen as value-for-money destroyers in pension organizations.

Pension investing has been changing for the better, too, starting with serious re-examinations of investment beliefs. There is growing evidence the leadership of the global pensions sector is beginning to see its job as transforming retirement savings into wealth-producing capital. There are a number of factors at play here. One is the simple reality that good investment returns are increasingly difficult to come by. Another is a growing understanding of the zero-sum nature of short-horizon active management. Yet another is that both logic and empirical evidence support the idea that long-horizon active management should, and actually does, produce higher long-term returns than either passive or short-horizon active management. However, saying is one thing, doing another. For many pension organizations, there is still a sizable aspiration–implementation gap to be closed.

THREE "UNREASONABLE" MEN

In that moment at the Frankfurt conference, I recognized that the significant pension revolution developments of the last eight years in pension design, governance, and investing should be chronicled in a coherent, integrated manner, and that I was well placed to do that job. However, I would not be doing it alone. A good deal of the necessary insight and inspiration would come from three "unreasonable" men, as defined by George Bernard Shaw ("...all progress depends on the unreasonable man...").

Dutch Nobel Prize winner Jan Tinbergen's Two Goals/Two Instruments principle offers a way out of the long-standing affordability-versus-safety dilemma in pension design. Achieving both goals effectively will require two instruments, not one. Father of modern management principles and practices Peter Drucker asserts that pension organizations are not exempt from governance effectiveness dictates. Ineffective governance will produce poor outcomes for the pension organization's stakeholders. The 20th century's most influential economist John Maynard Keynes makes a clear distinction between dysfunctional short-term "beauty contest" investing and wealth-producing long-term investment processes. Yet, ironically, many boards continue to choose the former over the latter. Readers will encounter these three "unreasonable" men and their ideas many times through this book's 27 chapters.

There are other "unreasonable" people who deserve mention as contributors to the ideas and their implementation set out in this book. Nobel Prize winner George Akerlof's "asymmetric information" insight figures prominently in my thinking about the design of pensions systems and organizations, as does the life-cycle theory of personal finance set out by Nobel Prize winners Robert Merton and Paul Samuelson. Former Dean of University of

Toronto's Rotman School of Management Roger Martin's work on integrative thinking and the creative resolution of opposable ideas has also played an integral role in the structure and tone of this book.

Many more people have contributed to this book in one way or another, including colleagues, clients, family, and friends. I thank you all, but mention only two by name. My wife and partner, Virginia Atkin, once again provided the inspiration and encouragement to write this book, while also ensuring I was not consumed by it. My editor Christina Verigan skillfully guided my original manuscript of the book into this much improved final version.

Keith Ambachtsheer
Toronto, Canada
January 2016

One

Touchstones

*Literally: Stones used to test the quality of precious metals.
Metaphorically: Tests to assess the value or merits of a claim
or idea.*
—Adapted from the *Oxford English Dictionary.*

CHAPTER 1

Improved Pension Designs and Organizations

Gateways to a More Functional Capitalism

*" ... with the separation between ownership and management
which prevails today ... and with the development of organized
investment markets ... a new factor of great importance has
entered in ... which sometimes facilitates investment ... but
sometimes adds greatly to the instability of the system ... "*

*" ... it might have been supposed that competition between
expert professionals ... would correct the vagaries of ignorant
individuals left to themselves ... it happens however that their
energies and skill are mainly occupied otherwise ... largely
concerned with foreseeing changes in conventional valuations a
short time ahead ... "*

*" ... the measure of success attained by Wall Street ... regarded
as the institution of which the proper social purpose is to direct
new investments into the most profitable channels in terms of
future yield ... cannot be claimed as one of the outstanding
triumphs of laissez-faire capitalism ... if I am right in thinking that
its best brains have in fact been directed towards a different
object ... "*

—Excerpts from John Maynard Keynes, *The General Theory
of Employment, Interest, and Money* (1936), Chapter 12.

A "GATEWAYS" LECTURE IN LONDON

Some time ago, I was invited by the UK's ShareAction organization to give
a lecture in the Houses of Parliament. It provided an opportunity to place
Keynes' insights on faux vs. functional capitalism, Peter Drucker's on the

special role of retirement savings in shaping capitalism, and Jan Tinbergen's on aligning pension goals and instruments in a 21st-century setting. These insights lead to the critical conclusion that the over-$30 trillion pension fund sector is by far the largest investor class with a fiduciary duty to invest across generations. Thus it is the leading institutional investor class with a clear motivation to, in Keynes' words, "direct new investments into the most profitable channels in terms of future yield."

The lecture, which I called the "Gateways" lecture, acknowledged that capitalism faces strong headwinds today as reflected in issues such as aging populations, physical limits to growth, bubbles and financial crises, a growing rich–poor divide, and continuing alignment of interest challenges between corporate managers and owners. Also, the traditional defined-benefit (DB) and defined-contribution (DC) pension designs both mitigate against pension funds playing the wise intergenerational investor role we would like them to play. Their ability to play this role is further hampered by the generally weak governance and organizational structures of these funds.

The good news is that there is no need to invent either better pension designs or stronger organizational structures. Logic and research have already identified them. Further, here and there, they already exist in practice. Our collective challenge is to vastly accelerate the process of moving these better ways into widespread practice around the globe. In the end, it is a question of what Peter Drucker would call effective leadership.

SETTING THE STAGE

The Gateways lecture had four parts:

1. A quick sweep through 400 years of capitalism
2. An equally quick assessment of the challenges facing capitalism in the 21st century
3. The special role pension funds should and could play to address these challenges
4. Getting pension funds to actually *do* this on a large scale

Capitalism is an economic system in which the means of production are privately owned and operated for profit, usually in competitive markets. Many consider the Dutch East Indies Company, founded in 1602, as the prototype of the first modern corporation, complete with key features such as limited liability for shareowners and the ability for them to buy or sell their shares on the stock exchange. However, it was the 19th-century industrial revolution that transformed capitalism into the dominant economic system it continues to be today.

At first, its major owners were not institutions, but powerful individuals with names such as Carnegie, Rockefeller, Getty, Vanderbilt, Ford, and JP Morgan. With their passing, and after the deeply traumatic experiences of WWI, the Great Depression, WWII, and the drawing of the Iron Curtain across Europe, we witnessed the birth of "institutional capitalism" with insurance companies, mutual funds, and pension funds becoming the dominant owners of the means of production.

Before we diagnose the ills of today's version of capitalism and discuss possible remedies, we should reflect for a moment on its central role in the remarkable transformation of the still-largely agrarian societies of the 18th century into the post-industrial societies of the developed world today. As just one indication of this remarkable transformation, global GDP per capita grew roughly 50 percent in the seven centuries from 1000 to 1800, compared to a 20-fold (2,000 percent!) increase in GDP per capita for the developed world in the 19th and 20th centuries, while at the same time significantly reducing the number of hours people worked, as well as eliminating forced labor for children and for the aged.[1]

ADDRESSING CAPITALISM'S 21ST-CENTURY CHALLENGES

However, with our entry into the 21st century, most of us are painfully aware that capitalism is facing strong headwinds today. For example:

- Physical limits to continued economic growth in such forms as carbon emissions, pollution, water usage, and food production
- Aging populations and very modest economic growth prospects in the developed world
- Preferences by collective electorates and individual family units to maintain or enhance public services and private living standards through borrowing rather than through current taxes and earnings
- Increased frequency of bubbles and crises in financial markets
- A growing societal have–have not divide in both perception and reality
- Continued alignment-of-interests challenges between corporate managers and corporate owners[2]

The question before us is what the over-$30 trillion global pension fund sector can do to ameliorate some of these headwinds, while at the same time fulfilling its mission to provide retirement income security to hundreds of millions of beneficiaries.

I believe it is within our reach to move capitalism in a direction that is more wealth-creating, more sustainable, less crisis-prone, and more legitimate than the "headwinds" capitalism of today. And why specifically pension funds? Because they are the only global investor class which has a fiduciary duty to invest across generations. In determining their investment strategies, pension funds are duty-bound to be even-handed between the financial needs of today's pensioners and those of young workers, whose retirement years lie 30, 40, even 50 years ahead of them.

However, this transformation to pension fund capitalism will not be easy for two reasons:

1. It requires the redesign of pension systems so these systems *themselves* become more sustainable and intergenerationally fair.
2. It requires the redesign of pension fund organizations so that they *themselves* become more effective and hence more productive stewards of the retirement savings of young workers and pensioners alike.

These two pre-conditions are essential and will take hard work to bring about.

SUSTAINABLE PENSION DESIGNS

The designs of traditional DC and DB plans are both problematical:

- **Traditional DC plans** force contribution rate and investment decisions on participants that they cannot and do not want to make. Also, little thought is given to the design of the post-work asset decumulation phase. As a result, DC plan investing has been unfocused, and post-work financial outcomes have been and continue to be highly uncertain. This raises fundamental questions about the effectiveness and sustainability of this individualistic pension model.
- **Traditional DB plans** lump the young and the old on the same balance sheet, and unrealistically assume they have the same risk tolerance, and that property rights between the two groups are clear. These unrealistic assumptions have had serious consequences. Over the course of the last decade, aggressive return assumptions and risk-taking, together with falling asset prices, falling interest rates, and deteriorating demographics, have punched gaping holes in many DB plan balance sheets. Unfocused responses have ranged the full spectrum, from complete de-risking at one end, to piling on more risk at the other.

Fortunately, there is a growing understanding of these traditional DC and DB design faults, and of the problems they have caused and will continue to cause plan participants in the years ahead. There is also the beginning of an understanding of what must be done to address these design faults.

The Dutch economist Jan Tinbergen won the first Nobel Prize in Economics for his proposition that the number of policy goals must be matched by the number of policy instruments. This proposition has direct application to pension system design. Pension systems have two goals:

1. Affordability for workers (and their employers)
2. Payment security for pensioners

Thus it follows plan participants need two instruments: first, a long-horizon (LH) return compounding instrument to support the affordability goal; and second, an asset-liability matching instrument to support the payment security goal.

Logically, younger workers should favor using the first instrument, and pensioners the second. Over the course of their working lives, plan participants should transition steadily from the first to the second. There continues to be considerable resistance to adopting this more transparent, robust "two goals–two instruments" pension model. Some continue to defend traditional DB models for emotional rather than rational reasons; others continue to defend the *caveat emptor* philosophy of traditional DC plans because they profit from it.

In concluding these comments about pension design, let me be clear about why the two goals–two instruments design feature is critically important to pension funds' ability to reshape capitalism. Without the existence and legitimacy of highly focused, well-managed, long-horizon return-compounding instruments, pension funds *cannot* the play the wise intergenerational investor role that we have cast them in.

EFFECTIVE PENSION FUND ORGANIZATIONS

Such investment instruments are a necessary condition for a pension sector-led transition to a more functional form of capitalism. However, they are not enough. Something else is required. We must also have pension organizations that can effectively construct and manage the two needed implementation instruments. Fortunately once again, we know what such pension organizations look like. They have five success drivers:

1. Aligned interests with pension plan participants
2. Strong governance
3. Sensible investment beliefs

4. Right scale
5. Competitive compensation

Unfortunately, there are only a handful of pension organizations on the planet today that score well on all five counts. Instead:

1. Most pension organizations employ many layers of agents in the execution of their mission. The greater the number of layers of agents employed, the greater the likelihood that principal–agent problems will arise with their attendant costs.
2. Ideal boards of trustees are passionate about the cause, and also understand the purpose of the governance function as distinct from the executive function in the complex business of pension management. While most actual pension boards pass the first test, they do far less well on the second.
3. Actual investment behavior suggests many pension funds do not have sensible investment beliefs. John Maynard Keynes pointed out the distinction between short-horizon "beauty contest" investing and genuine long-horizon wealth-creating investing way back in 1936. Yet even today, the former dysfunctional investment style continues to dominate the wealth-creating latter.[3]
4. Effective pension organizations need scale to afford the requisite resources to be successful and to drive down unit costs. Yet, far too many funds continue to be too small to attain either of these two critical success drivers.
5. Executing long-horizon wealth-creating investment strategies success-fully requires a special breed of investment managers working inside pension organizations. Yet, because these people are not cheap, this requirement is usually discarded in favor of hiring far more expensive people outside the organization. Why? Because their cost can be buried by only reporting net returns to plan stakeholders.

Again, let me be clear about the bottom line of all this. Without the existence and legitimacy of pension organizations willing and able to create and execute long-horizon wealth-creating investment mandates, they cannot play the wise intergenerational investor role we have cast them in.

OPENING UP A SECOND FRONT

Many people around the world are working hard on the pension fund trans-formation project I describe here, including the ShareAction organization. Its research publications, advocacy campaigns, and engagement strategies have had a measurable impact on UK decision makers, elected officials, regulators, pension trustees, business executives, and investment managers in their understanding that retirement savings should not be invested based on short-term profit considerations. Instead, they should be based on the longer-term, sustainable wealth-creation potential of prospective investments.

And ShareAction is not alone in this quest. As just two further examples, the Principles for Responsible Investing (PRI) project is rapidly globalizing the responsible investing movement around the world. The Rotman International Centre for Pension Management (ICPM) project is documenting the drivers of sustainable pension systems and of effective pension organizations, and translating them into actionable implementation strategies—and this list could go on.

Having said that, I do believe the time has come to accelerate the implementation of the pension fund transformation project by opening up a second front. We must develop explicit strategies to move from saying to doing at a faster pace. To that end, in pension design space, the Dutch have publicly acknowledged that the traditional DB plan is dead, but that does not mean moving to traditional DC plans. Similarly, the Australians have publicly acknowledged that their traditional DC plans need "income-for-life" back-ends. Serious searches for middle ways between traditional DB and DC designs are underway, and I am betting better ways will be found and implemented.

In pension delivery space, my colleague David Beatty at the Rotman School of Management advocates a "measure, disseminate, and celebrate" strategy: Measure what should be managed, disseminate results widely, and celebrate successes publicly. Two quick examples of the "M-D-C" strategy:

1. **CEM Benchmarking Inc.** has been measuring the cost-effectiveness of pension organizations since 1991. Research using the resulting databases is validating the "5 success drivers" model.[4]
2. **Ontario Teachers' Pension Plan** was explicitly designed with the five Drucker success drivers in mind in the late 1980s. It, too, began operations in 1991. Over 20 years later, OTPP has accumulated investment and pension administration track records unequalled anywhere in the world. It is most encouraging that the growth in other large pension institutions, both in Canada and elsewhere, adopting OTPP's "5 success driver" formula is beginning to accelerate.[5]

In closing, I leave you with a vision.

A VISION

Imagine workers around the world covered by pension arrangements that secure retirement income at affordable contribution rates. Imagine tens of trillions of dollars managed under truly long-horizon, wealth-creation investment mandates by hundreds of "5 success drivers" pension organizations like OTPP. I put it to you that if we could achieve that vision, we would not just create sustainable income streams for millions of current and future pensioners. We would also transform today's "headwinds" capitalism into a more sustainable, wealth-creating version, less prone to generate the financial bubbles and crises of the last decade, and more legitimate in the eyes of a skeptical public.

CHAPTER 2

Pension Plans for the Masses

Good Idea or Pipe Dream?

"An ambitious idea for a universal retirement program introduced by Senator Tom Harkin is being welcomed for advancing a national debate on ways to improve retirement security...."
—From *Pensions & Investments*, February 3, 2014

THE LOOMING RETIREMENT SAVINGS CHALLENGE

Through a multi-decade series of political and private sector co-missions and omissions, the majority of private sector workers in the United States, Canada, and the United Kingdom do not participate in a workplace pension plan today. A growing body of studies in all three countries suggests that, as a result, a significant proportion of these workers and their families face the prospect of material declines in living standards in their post-work years in the coming decades.

These projections have raised a profound public policy question. What, if anything, should the governments of these countries do about this looming challenge? There is a growing consensus in all three countries that doing nothing is no longer a defensible option. But what to do? That is the question this chapter addresses. It does so by providing brief updates of the state of the pension reform debate in each of the three countries, documenting the surprisingly similar solutions that are emerging, and raising questions about the remaining gaps between intent and implementation.

THE USA RETIREMENT FUNDS INITIATIVE

The headline in the cited *Pensions & Investments* article about Senator Harkin's USA Retirement Funds Act was a pleasant surprise. It read: "Harkin's plan called a good start despite some hurdles."[1] America's financial services industry has a history of vigorously defending its turf against any government initiative it perceives might intrude on it. Has the industry turned altruistic? Or is the Harkin initiative not seen as a threat to its financial interests? These are surely intriguing questions.

Cleverly, the acronym USA in the tabled pension legislation stands for Universal, Secure, Adaptable. The preamble to the Act asserts that its passage "would tackle the retirement crisis head-on by ensuring that the 75 million working people without a retirement plan would drastically increase retirement savings through automatic enrollment, while reducing the cost of retirement by up to 50 percent. And unlike 401(k) plans, USA Retirement Funds would shield workers from market volatility and other risks by utilizing a shared risk design."

Here is the essence of the proposal:

- **Universal Coverage:** Every working American will have access to a retirement plan through automatic enrollment and payroll deduction: mandatory participation for employers with more than 10 employees; voluntary participation by smaller employers, their employees, and the self-employed.
- **Employer Responsibility:** Because a USA Retirement Fund would be approved by the Department of Labor and overseen by an independent Board of Trustees, employers would not have any fiduciary responsibilities in selecting, administering, or managing the pension arrangement. Their only obligation would be to enroll their employees and ensure that employee contributions are duly processed.
- **Contributions:** The employee default contribution rate would be 6 percent of pay up to a maximum of $10,000 per year. They could choose to contribute more, less, or opt out altogether. Employers would be able to contribute up to $5,000 per year per employee, provided contributions are made uniformly for all employees.
- **Pension Providers:** USA Retirement Funds would be managed by independent entities, but these organizations would be approved and overseen by the Department of Labor. Each Fund would be governed by a board of qualified trustees able to represent the interests of employees, retirees, and employers as fiduciaries. Management costs would be controlled through achieving significant economies of scale.

- **Transparency and Fund Democracy:** The Funds would be required to regularly disclose their investment policies and returns, their procedures for providing lifetime income, their operating costs, and their conflict-of-interest policy. They will provide participants regular estimates of their pension benefits in retirement. They will practice democracy by permitting participants to petition the trustees to remove service providers, to comment on management and administration of the Fund, and approve or disapprove of trustee compensation.
- **Plan Design:** The goal of each Fund is to provide its participants with a cost-effective stream of income in retirement and reduce benefit level volatility for those approaching retirement. There will be a requirement to protect participants from longevity risk (i.e., the risk of outliving one's savings), with spousal protection and survivor benefits. The inherent risks will be borne collectively by large groups of employees and retirees. They will not be underwritten by employers.
- **Portability:** Participants can change to another Fund once a year. They would be allowed to roll their 401(k) or IRA balances into the Fund of their choice.
- **Integration with Other Retirement Plans:** The Funds are not intended to replace already-existing retirement plans, but to supplement them.

Taking all these features together, this proposal surely ranks 10-out-of-10 on the bold scale. It also raises many questions, starting with "who is going to invest the human and financial capital required to build expert pension organizations capable of meeting the Act's specifications?"

Can Individual States Lead the Way?

The only plausible answer that comes to mind is individual states. In fact, 14 individual American states have taken, or are contemplating taking, some kind of action on private sector retirement security. For example, California passed legislation in 2012 to create a state-sponsored payroll deduction IRA for employees of small private sector firms. Massachusetts has passed similar legislation for small not-for-profits. Ohio, Arizona, Wisconsin, and Washington are preparing legislation. Maine, Vermont, and Minnesota are contemplating doing so. Oregon, Maryland, and Connecticut have created task forces to make recommendations on the issue.

It is noteworthy, and not surprising, that none of these state initiatives is even close to being operational. Creating an expert, cost-effective pension organization from scratch is a hugely challenging, time-consuming, risky, expensive proposition. Americans contemplating doing so would do well to look north of the 49th parallel and east across the Atlantic before proceeding much further.

CANADA'S PENSION REFORM JOURNEY

I proposed a Canadian solution to its looming retirement savings crisis in 2008 called the Canada Supplementary Pension Plan (CSPP).[2] It had many similar features to the design specifications embedded in the USA Retirement Funds Act. For example:

- Universal access for all Canadian workers without a workplace pension plan through automatic enrollment with an opt-out option; employers not offering a qualifying pension plan are required to enroll their employees in the CSPP.
- Target pension (including the pillar one Old Age Security [OAS] and Canada Pension Plan [CPP] pensions) set at 60 percent of final gross earnings over a 40-year work period.
- A default contribution rate consistent with the target pension, with an employee–employer split of 50–50. Under a set of assumptions I believe to be reasonable, this default contribution rate is in the 6 percent of pay area, split evenly between employees and employers. Both have options to contribute more or less than their default portion.
- The CSPP should not harm low-income workers who will already achieve 100 percent income replacement through the combination of CPP, OAS, and Guaranteed Income Supplement (GIS). For example, this could be done by exempting the first $25,000/year from any CSPP deductions.
- A default investment policy based on participant age and a deferred annuitization option for older workers and retirees.
- CSPP investment, administration, and communication functions managed at low cost (e.g., 50 bps or lower) by an arms-length expert pension agency with strong governance and management functions.

This proposal was well received at the time, but was superseded by two competing alternative proposals: first, enhancing the benefits of the mandatory Canada Pension Plan (CPP); and second, creating new voluntary Pooled Registered Pension Plans (PRPPs).

To break this ongoing stalemate, the Province of Ontario announced in its 2014 budget that it would create its own pension plan for workers without one (the Ontario Retirement Pension Plan or ORPP), and has created an advisory panel to advise it on plan design.[3] The return in October 2015 of a Liberal government in Ottawa makes it possible that Ontario's ORPP initiative will evolve into a Canada-wide program. As a result, my 2008 CSPP proposal is back on the table in Canada, with one important new dimension. That dimension is the fact that the United Kingdom decided to proceed with a pension plan for its uncovered workers in 2007.

THE UK PENSION JOURNEY

The UK Pensions Commission chaired by Lord Turner produced its first report in 2004 and a follow-up report in 2005. The Commission's four key findings were that 9 million UK workers were under-saving for retirement, the UK pension system was overly complex, UK longevity was rising while its birthrate was falling, and UK institutional arrangements for managing pensions were inadequate. A key recommendation was a new earnings-related pension provision which relied on the automatic enrollment of employees either into a new National Pensions Savings System or into existing company pension schemes, but with the right to opt out, and with a requirement for employers to make matching contributions.

The recommendation was accepted by the UK Government in 2006. In 2007, the arms-length Personal Accounts Delivery Authority (PADA) with an independent Board of Directors was created to "provide expert advice to the Government to develop the practical implementation of the new pension policy."[4] PADA was transformed into the operating entity National Employment Savings Trust (NEST) in 2010. UK legislation requiring employers to enroll their employees in a pension plan with certain minimum features went into effect in 2011. Under that legislation, NEST began enrolling workers on a beta-test basis and had workers from 100 different employers participating in the plan by the end of March 2012.

At this time of writing, NEST has auto-enrolled some 2 million UK workers without a pension plan, and has some £500 million under management. Under the same legislation, an additional two million workers have been auto-enrolled in other qualifying plans offered by commercial providers chosen by the employers of these workers. Around 8 percent of all enrolled workers exercised their option to dis-enroll themselves. Perhaps not surprisingly, most were higher-income workers close to retirement. Looking ahead, NEST faces the daunting task of auto-enrolling millions of additional UK workers over the course of the next few years.[5]

On the financial side, the creation of PADA and then NEST was made possible by a loan provided by the UK Government. The loan agreement signed in 2011 allows for NEST to borrow up to £650 million by 2020, although with ongoing changes in the policy and economic environment, this number will be kept under review. On the revenue side, NEST is charging its participants a 0.3 percent per annum management fee on assets under management, as well as a 1.8 percent one-off charge on contributions to recover the start-up costs. Together, the two charges are, for the average member, equivalent to about 0.5 percent of assets per annum.

LESSONS FOR THE USA AND CANADA

The unfolding UK pension reform story provides the American and Canadian national and provincial/state governments with critically important insights in how they should proceed down the pension reform path from here. For example:

- Are they prepared to explicitly choose a middle way to pension reform with the basic design features of the USA Retirement Funds Act and my 2008 CSPP proposal, which is now being implemented in the UK in the form of NEST? Arguably, these features combine the best elements of traditional DC and DB plans (e.g., a target pension, clear property rights, no intergenerational wealth shifting, lifetime income, opt-out option).
- Are they prepared to require employers not already offering a qualifying pension arrangement to enroll their employees in a qualifying arrangement?
- Are they prepared to appoint expert task forces charged with designing and creating effective implementation strategies that would finalize the design of and administer a provincial or state pension plan?
- Will they find acceptable ways for commercial vendors to participate in these newly created markets for pension services?

If the answer to these questions is yes, there are three success drivers that should be kept in mind: first, a viable, explainable vision to address the pension coverage problem; second, the political will to see it through; and third, a properly resourced, effectively led effort to implement it.

In this context, the NEST story is instructive for three reasons:

1. **It Confirms Three Success Drivers:** The Turner Commission defined the problem and a solution for fixing it; the UK Government of the day committed to transforming the "on paper" solution into an actual solution, and the UK Government created a properly resourced, effectively led effort that successfully managed the transformation.
2. **Getting It Right Takes a Long Time:** The Turner recommendations were accepted by the UK Government in 2006. PADA was created in 2007. NEST became operational in 2011.
3. **Good Governance Is Key:** The NEST organization continues to demonstrate that a collective mix of skill, experience, and "greater good" mindsets is essential to overcoming the many landmines and roadblocks the organization experienced on the road to turning vision into reality.

So are pension plans for the masses a good idea or a pipe dream? In the end, it all depends on the power and clarity of the political vision, and on the will and the resources required to successfully implement it.

CHAPTER 3

Does Institutional Investing Have a Future?

"How can we allow people of varying abilities and financial sophistication to express preferences for investments without making them vulnerable to salespeople selling 'snake oil'?"
—George Akerlof and Robert Shiller in *Animal Spirits* (2009)

A TALK IN TOKYO

In a recent keynote speech in Tokyo, I addressed the question: Does institutional investing have a future? Not to keep you in suspense, the answer was "Of course it has." But there was an important caveat. A significant proportion of institutional investment services on offer today cannot meet a reasonable "value for money" test. Following, I set out the argument for this view, provide evidence supporting its validity, use logic and empirical evidence to lay out a better way, and indicate how that better way can be realized.

The argument for the "no value for most of the customers" reality follows logically from the two key facts:

1. Markets for investment management services are asymmetrical. Most sellers know more about what they are selling than most buyers know about what they are buying.
2. Sellers take advantage of this situation by not competing on price, but on less tangible factors such as hope, quality, and building strong distribution channels.

Nobel Prize-winning economist George Akerlof pointed out many years ago that in markets with these characteristics, customers will pay too much for too little. Conversely, sellers will be paid too much relative to the economic value of the product or service they provide.[1]

THE COST OF ACTIVE INVESTING

How much do the customers in fact pay for institutional investment services? Professor Ken French answered this question in his 2008 presidential address to the American Finance Association. Focusing specifically on the U.S. stock market, he estimated the annual investment costs (management fees and trading costs) paid by investors over the 1991–2006 period. As a specific example, the total cost of investing in U.S. stocks in 2006 amounted to 77 basis points, or $115 billion dollars. Of that $115 billion, French estimated that the total cost would have been about $15 billion (10 bps) if the entire pool had been passively managed, leaving the remaining $100 billion (67 bps) as the incremental cost of active management to investors in that year.[2]

The question Professor French's work allows us to pose is this: "What *value* did that incremental $100 billion in active fees and trading costs create for participants in pension, mutual, and hedge funds in 2006?" The correct economic answer is "price discovery." In other words, with zero active management, stock prices would have no economic basis. Thus the economics-based question becomes: How much money *should* be spent on active fees and trading costs in order to maintain "fair value" pricing in the U.S. stock market? The economics-based answer of course is: up to the point where an incremental dollar spent does not have a sufficient incremental expected economic payoff.

In this context, is Professor French's $100 billion estimate for 2006 likely to be the right amount to be spending if the goal is price discovery in the U.S. stock market as we defined it earlier? In my view, not likely. I show below that the price discovery job could likely get done at one-tenth of that cost. In short, recognizing the likelihood that similar "too-high-cost" processes are at work in other asset class markets in the United State as well as around the world, we conclude that hundreds of billions of dollars are likely drained out of the pockets of retail investors and workers each year for which there is no economic *quid pro quo*.

NEW EVIDENCE FROM THE PENSION FUND SECTOR

Most of the hundreds of $billions in annual "value losses" likely hit mutual fund investors. That is where the informational asymmetry between buyers and sellers is the greatest. However, two recent studies indicate pension fund beneficiaries are not immune from them, either:

1. "Investment Horizons: Do Managers Do What They Say?" (published by the Investor Responsibility Research Center Institute and Mercer Consulting, February 2010) finds that most active managers investing pension assets have higher turnover rates than anticipated. When asked why they seemed to be engaged in self-defeating "short-termism," the managers cited volatile markets, adversarial hedge fund trading, mixed signals from clients, and short-term incentive systems. Interestingly, many seemed to recognize the negative consequences of what they were doing, but felt they were locked into these value-destroying behavior patterns.
2. "Absence of Value: an Analysis of Investment Allocation Decisions by Institutional Plan Sponsors" (Stewart et al., *Financial Analysts Journal*, Nov–Dec 2009) finds that "plan sponsors are not acting in their stakeholders' best interests when they make rebalancing or reallocation decisions concerning plan assets." Investment strategies that plan sponsors allocate new money to tend to underperform after the money is allocated. Strategies that they withdraw money from tend to outperform after the money is withdrawn. The measured cost of these faulty rebalancing decisions ran into the hundreds of $billions over five-year periods for the funds they examined.

In short, there seems to be measurable decision-making dysfunction in the pension fund sector, too.

HOW SHOULD INSTITUTIONS INVEST?

All this begs the question: How *should* institutions such as pension funds invest? In the *Financial Analysts Journal* article, "Beyond Portfolio Theory: The Next Frontier," I noted that traditional investment theory had sidestepped this question.[3] To derive elegant solutions, the messy "real world," with its "animal spirits," informational asymmetry, agents willing to take advantage of it, and complex organizational structure challenges, was simply assumed away. As a result, "rational" investment decisions could be derived solely from a universe of investment opportunities, their return distributions and co-variances, and the degree of investor risk aversion.

The article introduced real-world considerations such as "animal spirits," agents, and organizational behavior into the equation. Thus traditional investment theory became Integrative Investment Theory:

$$\text{Client/Beneficiary Value} = F\ \{A,\ G,\ IB,\ R, IMPL\}$$

Where: A = Agency considerations such as potential misalignment of interests between client/beneficiaries and the organizations providing investment services.

G = Governance quality considerations that recognize that bad fund governance is likely to lead to bad investment outcomes.

IB = Investment Beliefs going beyond just specifying return distributions and their co-variances. IB also asks what *predictive power* those specifications are likely to have, and how behavioral issues such as "short-termism" should be addressed.

R = Risk management should go well beyond specifying return distributions and understanding investor risk aversion (although that is no mean task!). It should also delve deeply into what risk really means, how it is being borne, and how it is best measured.

IMPL = Implementation is a "real-world" issue that cannot be ignored: To outsource or not? To use derivatives or not? To pay performance-based compensation or not? All critically important questions.

Empirical research confirms that all five of these considerations can materially impact client/beneficiary value creation for better...or for worse.

For example, research using mutual fund databases and the CEM Benchmarking Inc. pension fund database confirms that mutual fund investors endure significantly higher agency costs than pension fund beneficiaries.[4] Good governance in pension funds has been shown to be a source of return value-added,[5] as have investment beliefs that incorporate realities such as the 10–20 year animal spirit mood swings in investor mindsets (i.e., from pessimism to optimism and back again). On the implementation side, funds with low cost structures generally outperform funds with high cost structures (adjusted for differences in investment policies). Internal management generally outperforms external management (for similar mandates, on a net excess return basis).[6]

Implicit in the latter two IMPL findings is that scale matters. Fund management and pension administration are both activities that can greatly benefit from economies of scale. Take, for example, the finding from the CEM database that internal management generally outperforms external management. Cost differentials are a major driver here, especially in private markets areas such as real estate, infrastructure, and private equity. However, avoiding the heavy external "2 and 20" haircut by going in-house is only an option for pension funds that can staff up to place tens of $billions in these market segments themselves. Scale really does matter.

FROM THEORY TO PRACTICE: THE CASE OF ONTARIO TEACHERS' PENSION PLAN

It is one thing to design the ideal investment institution on paper; it is another to actually create and manage one. Has it been done in the real world, and do the actual value creation results match expectations? The question would be best answered by pitting a large sample of "ideal" funds against a large sample of "non-ideal" funds over a multi-decade evaluation period. Unfortunately, we are still decades away from being able to perform such tests. Funds that have the ideal design set out previously are few, and those with multi-decade performance records are fewer still. However, the prior chapter noted that we do have the instructive case of Ontario Teachers' Pension Plan (OTPP). I was involved in its early design phase in the late-1980s, and have watched OTPP achieve significant scale since its inception in 1991 to this day.

The 1987 Ontario Government Task Force study "In Whose Interest?" set out the ideal design for OTPP. CEO Claude Lamoureux recounted the actual startup of the organization, and its evolution through to his retirement in 2007, in an article in the *Rotman International Journal of Pension Management*.[7] Lamoureux writes that OTPP's golden rules have been:

- Get the best Board members you can.
- Do not engage in politics: the organization's only goal is to deliver good pensions at an affordable price.
- Hire the best people possible and agree on clear goals.
- Reward them so that incentives and goals are aligned.
- Ensure the organization has the right resources to get the job done.
- Run the investment program as a team effort.
- Treat plan members and employees the way you would want to be treated.
- Give people real responsibilities and don't be afraid to take risks.
- Listen to plan members, employees, and the Board.
- Communicate constantly and clearly.
- Never give in to the temptation, as Keynes put it, "to fail conventionally rather than succeed unconventionally."

A sequel article by colleagues Bob Bertram and Barbara Zvan explains how OTPP's incentive compensation scheme evolved over time.[8]

And what about performance? On the investment side, OTPP has outperformed its policy benchmark portfolio by a highly material 2 percent per annum over its 20+ year history. On the pension administration side, its initial Quality Service Index score in 1993 was 8.1. The score rose steadily through the 1990s, broke through 9.0 in 2002, and has remained above 9.0 since.[9]

"IDEAL" INVESTMENT ORGANIZATIONS AND THE COST OF INVESTING

What impact would a world filled with "ideal" investment organizations have? Let's conduct a thought experiment, starting with Professor French's finding that the cost of managing the aggregate $15T U.S. equity portfolio was 77bps or $115B in 2006. Let's create 150 ideal investment institutions of $100B each to manage that aggregate portfolio. They all start with a passive strategy, each holding 1/150 of the market portfolio. This only requires a small staff and very little transaction costs. Assume each spends 2.5bps, or $25M per annum. Thus, together the 150 institutions spend $375M per annum.

Now one of the institutions notices that there is no price discovery in the market (i.e., no active management). It hires some security analysts who have a field day selling overvalued stocks and buying undervalued ones. This institution starts to outperform the other 149, which now also begin to hire analysts. When should this hiring process stop? When the marginal cost of an additional analyst has no expected net payoff. With how many analysts might that point be reached? We don't know. But let's assume that each of the 150 institutions hires 100 analysts and pays each of these analysts a base of $250,000 per annum. That adds $25M to the operating cost of each institution. Total cost goes from $25M to $50M per annum. Let's add an additional $25M for trading, travel, administration, and other expenses, pushing the annual cost for each institution to $75M, or 7.5bps.

Should 15,000 motivated, professional security analysts with $trillions of capital behind them be able to establish fair value pricing in the U.S. equity market? I would think so. If I am right, and if the optimal $75M annual investment cost per institution is in the ballpark, we can calculate to optimal cost to society of price discovery in the U.S. equity market. If the 150 institutions spend $75M each, that optimal cost works out to about $11B per annum, or 7.5bps in relation to the $15T market portfolio. That is one-tenth of the actual 77bps or $115B spent in 2006. If that same ratio holds in other securities markets, the potential reductions in unnecessary costs by ideal institutions rise to the hundreds of $billions per annum.

And that is not all. These ideal institutions have already discovered that some of their investee corporations have their own unnecessary agency and governance costs. Chapter 1 noted that collaborative strategies between ideal institutions can reduce these corporate agency and governance costs. As a result, the societal benefits from this ideal institutional investment structure rise even higher.

GETTING FROM HERE TO THERE

Market forces did not create OTPP, and will not create the 150 ideal investing institutions described in the thought experiment. Only public-interest entities can create such organizations. Democratically elected governments are an obvious, but not sole example. Industry associations could also do it, as could organized labor. Even better, they could do it together. With so much to be gained, why are public-interest entities doing so little to capture these benefits?

CHAPTER 4

Thomas Piketty's *Capital in the 21st Century*

Its Relevance to Pension Fund Management

"To put it bluntly, the discipline of economics has yet to get over its childish passion for mathematics, and for purely theoretical and often highly ideological speculation at the expense of historical research and collaboration with other social sciences. The obsession with mathematics is an easy way of acquiring the appearance of scientificity without having to answer the more complex questions posed by the world we live in."

—Thomas Piketty, 2014

THE PIKETTY PHENOMENON

It has been quite some time since a book on economics has created the global buzz of French academic economist Thomas Piketty's *Capital in the 21st Century* (Belknap Harvard, 2014). The quote above from the book's introductory chapter immediately resonated. Almost 700 pages later, I found him true to his word. His book is indeed full of serious historical research and multidisciplinary thinking. As promised, it is blissfully light on mathematics and does indeed address complex questions about the world we live in.

So what is causing the global buzz for the book? Both the medium and the message. The medium is relentlessly didactic: proposition → historical research → application to proposition → conclusion. To keep the reader engaged, the historical research is not just data-driven. For example, Piketty makes liberal use of Jane Austin's and Balzac's novels to convey the meaning and conceptions of capital and wealth in 19th-century England and France. In the end, he reaches three broad conclusions:

1. **Future distributions of societal wealth and income are not pre-determined:** The paths of these distributions over time are deeply political, and not determined by economic laws.
2. **The dynamics of wealth distribution reveal powerful mechanisms pushing toward divergence:** There are no natural self-correcting mechanisms to prevent destabilizing, divergence forces from gaining the upper hand.
3. **The risk of a continuing divergence in the distribution of societal wealth toward inequality is great enough to justify political action:** For example, a progressive annual tax on capital could be one way to avoid an endless de-egalitarian spiral, while preserving incentives for continued innovation and productivity gains.

While these conclusions are profound and have broad sociopolitical implications, it is Piketty's intellectual and historical journey to their discovery that makes his work especially noteworthy for people working in the pension design, governance, and investing spaces. This chapter explains why.

THE R > G INEQUALITY

The engine driving Piketty to his conclusions is the R > G inequality. R is the average annual rate of pre-tax real return on capital, including profits, dividends, interest, rents, expressed as a percentage of its total value; and G is the real growth rate of the economy. In calculating the behavior of R over the last three centuries in France and the UK, Piketty finds that R averaged about 5 percent in the pre-WWI era, climbed to a higher rate (in the 8%+ area) over the course of the almost 60-year WWI–1970 period, and then began descending to lower rates, to the 4 percent area today. On the global G side, Piketty shows there was very little G pre-1700, and annual rates of 0.5 percent for 1700–1820, 1.5 percent for 1820–1913, and 3.0 percent for 1913–2012.

These growth rates become 0.1, 0.9, and 1.6 percent respectively on a per-capita basis, after subtracting population growth. Looking ahead, with falling population growth, G will decline below 3 percent and eventually stabilize in the 1.5 percent area if the 20th-century rate of productivity growth can be maintained in the 21st century.

The point is that for much of recorded history, R has exceeded G, a situation likely to continue in the future. Piketty points out that this R > G situation embodies the potential for inherited wealth to grow faster than output and income. That in turn implies that inherited wealth will concentrate further with the passage of time. This dynamic is re-enforced to the degree the savings rate rises as the concentration of wealth becomes more extreme. Importantly, there are no market imperfections at work here, and no self-correction processes short of political measures such as a direct or indirect progressive tax on wealth.

THE LAWS GOVERNING WEALTH CONCENTRATION

To help readers grasp these important conclusions, he sets out some key definitions and relationships:

- **National Income (I):** The sum of a country's capital income (profits, dividends, rents, royalties, interest, etc.) and labor income (wages, salaries, bonuses, etc.).
- **Savings Rate (S):** The proportion of national income not consumed.
- **Capital (C):** All forms of wealth that individuals (or groups of them) can own and can be transferred or traded through the market.
- **Capital/Income Ratio (C/I):** The value of a country's capital stock divided by the flow of annual national income. The C/I in developed countries is currently in the 5–6 range.
- **First Fundamental Law of Capitalism:** The share of national income going to capital is (R × C/I). So with R = 5 percent and C/I = 6, the share of national income going to capital is 30 percent, with the other 70 percent going to labor. If C/I and/or R change, the relative national income shares of capital and labor will change.
- **Second Fundamental Law of Capitalism:** In the long run, a country's C/I ratio will be determined by the ratio of its savings rate S and its growth rate G (i.e., by S/G). So a low S and a high G combine to produce a low C/I ratio (e.g., 8%/4%=2). Conversely, a high S and a low G combine to produce a high C/I ratio (e.g., 15%/1.5%=10).

These concepts help explain Piketty's primary concern with capitalism in the 21st century: the implications of plausibly moving from a relatively low S/high G economy to a relatively high S/low G economy. For example, today's situation can be roughly approximated as R=5, S=10, G=2, and C/I=5, implying a 30 percent to 70 percent national income split between capital and labor. What if S and G move to plausible 12 percent and 1.5 percent rates respectively? This means the C/ I ratio will start to rise (Second Law), heading for 12%/1.5% = 8. If R remains at 5 percent, this means the 30 percent to 70 percent national income split between capital and labor will shift toward 40 percent to 60 percent (First Law). Politically, such a 10-point income shift from labor to capital would surely be seriously problematic. It seriously confirms Piketty's call for action now to deal with the very real possibility that wealth and income concentration will increase materially in the decades ahead.

WHAT IS THE R STORY?

Piketty develops his pre-WWI estimate of a reasonably stable R = 5% experience for France and the UK based on actual estimates of C and the income accruing to capital starting in the 18th century. He sees the almost 60-year WWI–1970 period as an anomaly driven by the impact of two world wars with a depression in between. It was a period marked first by rising taxes, falling capital prices, and physical capital destruction (1914–1945), setting the stage for an extended period (1946–1970) of capital reconstruction, high economic growth, rising capital values, and high R experience.

Piketty's R calculations suggest that this anomalous period is now well behind us, and that, if anything, R experience is now falling below the R = 5% experience of the 18th and 19th centuries, with an R = 4% now more realistic. Readers will see that I come to a similar conclusion in Chapter 20, where I suggest that we have been living in a "mature capitalism" era for some time already, and that one of its defining features is a materially lower R than we experienced during the post-WWII capital reconstruction/high economic growth era. Specifically, I calculate a prospective equities-long TIPS real return spread of 5 percent to 1 percent (pre-tax, pre-expense) in that chapter. That estimate is consistent with Piketty's average R calculation (across all forms of capital) in the 4 percent area today.

In passing, he offers a good primer of how to think about R prospects today. Most of today's pool of capital is geared toward providing real estate services (housing and commercial) and toward the production of goods and providing a broad range of non–real estate services. Thus, capital returns take the forms of rents (imputed or actually paid), profits (collected directly or indirectly), and interest (depending on how the various forms of capital are financed). Future R prospects depend on innovation and productivity gains on one hand, and on relative scarcity (or surplus) of capital on the other. An added thought here is that there can also be relative scarcity and surplus within a national (or international) capital pool. It seems today, for example, that judging by their cash hoards, corporations are finding it challenging to find new investments that pass their cost-of-capital hurdle rates. At the same time, most countries are experiencing material infrastructure capital deficits.

HOW IMPORTANT ARE PENSION FUNDS IN THE GLOBAL SCHEME OF THINGS?

Pension people have the general view that pension funds are major players in the global wealth leagues. In other words, there is a perception that the estimated current $36T of dedicated pension assets is one of the largest asset pools in the world.[1] Is it? Piketty's order-of-magnitude numbers throw interesting light on this question. Consider this:

- Total Global Capital (4.5B Adults): $350T
- Total Global Capital/Adult: $78K
- Top 0.1% (4.5M Adults): $59T (17% of Total Global Capital)
- Top 0.1%/Adult: $13M
- Next 0.9% (39.5M Adults): $116T (33% of Total Global Capital)
- Next 0.9%/Adult: $2.9M
- Next 49% (2.2455B Adults): $175T (50% of Total Global Capital)
- Next 49%/Adult: $79K
- Bottom 50% (2.25B Adults): negligible[2]

Clearly, the globe's wealth is far from evenly distributed. For example, the top 1 percent of global wealth owners own 50 percent of all global capital ($175T). Suddenly, the $36T global pension assets pool doesn't seem that massive any more. Wikipedia provides a more complete picture of global institutional asset holdings by key categories. Table 4.1 tells the story. Note that the value of pension assets ($36T) is about the same as private wealth assets ($33T), with insurance assets and mutual fund assets not far behind at $24T each. The values of sovereign wealth funds and endowment and foundation assets are much smaller at $5T and $1T.

Linking the Table 4.1 institutional asset distribution back to Piketty's global wealth distribution, it seems reasonable to infer that the pension

TABLE 4.1 Global Asset Values for Major Institutional Investment Categories

Category	Asset Value (in Trillions)
Private Wealth	$ 33
Pension Funds	$ 36
Insurance Companies	$ 24
Mutual Funds	$ 24
Sovereign Wealth Funds	$ 5
Endowments/Foundations	$ 1
Total	$123

Sources: Data compiled by the author from Towers Watson, Bloomberg, and IMF.

and mutual fund pools ($60T together) is mainly "next 49 percent" (i.e., middle-class) wealth. In contrast, most of the $33T of institutionally managed private wealth assets is part of the much larger $175T wealth pool of the "top 1 percent." In the context of Piketty's wealth concentration story, the distinction is important. Most of the middle-class $60T is "life-cycle" wealth in the sense that savings inflows into these sectors are largely matched by savings outflows to support pre- and post-work consumption of the next 49 percent. In contrast, most of the $175T belonging to the top 1 percent is legacy wealth in the sense that it will not be spent, but inherited by either the heirs of the top 1 percent or other designated recipients.

A related issue is the "wealth is power" reality. Their $175T gives the top 1 percent a vast amount of power. How will they use it? In the interest of the public good? Or to achieve other, less noble goals? And what about the $60T of largely next 49 percent wealth managed by pension and mutual funds? There is certainly a lot of potential power here as well. For example, it almost matches the $69T mid-2015 market capitalization of total listed global equities according to Marketwatch.com.

Throughout this book, we point to an important distinguishing feature between pension and mutual funds. Pension funds have a more clearly defined duty to manage the wealth in their care with a long-term fiduciary mindset. Thus, the members on pension fund boards and management teams are the logical people to create and lead processes that ensure the assets in their care are managed with long-term, wealth-creation strategies in mind.

PIKETTY'S CONTRIBUTIONS

So what should we make of the Piketty phenomenon? Two things come to mind. In the broad sociopolitico-economic scheme of things, Piketty provides a clear, non-ideological framework for discussing the future direction of capitalism. In contrast to the fiduciary capitalism vision led by pension funds set out in this book, Piketty describes the mechanics of an inheritance-driven patrimonial capitalism outcome fueled by the R > G inequality. It will take strong, concerted political action to derail the arithmetic that leads to such an outcome.

More specifically in the pensions sector, Piketty reminds us that we must now find our way in a 21st century where R and G will likely be lower than in the anomalous post-WWII high R/high G period. This reality should be reflected in our cost and funding calculations for future pension provision. At the same time, as Peter Drucker wrote four decades ago in his book, *The Unseen Revolution,* the fiduciary imperatives of the pensions sector make pension funds the best "lead wagon" candidates to steer capital toward a path that produces long-term economic outcomes beneficial to all.[3]

Pension Design

A design is the preliminary conception of an idea that is to be carried into effect by action; the process, practice, or art of devising, planning, or constructing something according to functional criteria, including economic and sociopolitical dimensions.

—Adapted from the *Oxford English Dictionary* and Sjaak Brinkkemper's *Method Engineering* (1996)

CHAPTER 5

Why We Need to Change the Conversation about Pension Reform

"Pension envy and pension bashings is counterproductive. Pension plans can work. They were not built to accommodate so many graying and long-living boomers. An unsteady market can no longer make up for these structural failures. But none of these weaknesses need to be fatal if we repair them now ..."
— Jim Leech and Jacquie McNish in *The Third Rail: Confronting Our Pension Failures* (2013)

DEBATING PENSIONS IN WASHINGTON D.C.

I was recently asked to share my thoughts on pension reform with 125 federal and state legislators, their officials, and a cadre of pension lobbyists representing a broad range of the political spectrum in Washington D.C. The talk title was "Public Sector Pension Design: Changing the Conversation." The essence of the message was that as long as the pension reform debate in the U.S. and elsewhere continues to be framed in stark terms—defined-benefit (DB) versus defined-contribution plans (DC)—it will continue to be a dysfunctional one with, in the end, only losers and no winners. Truly moving the pension reform yardsticks requires that we stop this stark either/or framing, and move on to more constructive conversations about what we are trying to do, and how to get from here to there.

To practice having this kind of conversation, I split the 40 minutes allotted for the talk in half, with the first 20 minutes devoted to setting out the key elements of any constructive conversation about pension reform. The second 20 minutes would be devoted to practicing having such a conversation with a very specific rule: Nobody would be allowed to utter either "DB" or "DC" during the entire conversation. This chapter sets out what, in my view, the key ideas and words of such a conversation need to be, and reports on how the actual Washington conversation turned out.

A NEW BOOK ON PENSION REFORM

Just before the Washington event, I had penned a review of a new book on pension reform for Canada's national newspaper, *The Globe and Mail*.[1] Serendipitously, as the quote above from the book confirms, authors Jim Leech and Jacquie McNish closely echo the "changing the conversation" theme of the Washington talk. *The Third Rail* starts by connecting the future of pensions to its past. To fix the future, we need to understand how we got to today. Next, the authors deftly juxtaposition the need for collectivity in good pension design on the one hand, with the imperative of individual leadership to make that collectivity work on the other.[2]

To make their point, we follow the travails of a Canadian city councilor, an American state treasurer, and a Dutch pension regulator. All three of these pension reform heroes endure not just denial, but actual hostility as they point to the fragility and non-sustainability of the pension arrangements under their watch. These dramatic scenes underscore the book's fundamental message: Fixing creaking, out-of-date pension arrangements can be dangerous, and takes a good deal of political courage.

To their credit, Leech and McNish do not advocate a one-size-fits-all pension solution in their book. But they do advocate collective pension designs that can benefit from good governance, economies of scale, and the sensible pooling of risks. They also point to the challenge of making good collective pension designs work in the real world. It is a fundamental human temptation to favor the present at the expense of the future. So, for example, we did not save the pension surpluses that emerged in the late 1990s for a rainy day. Instead, we spent them on enriching pension benefits and taking contribution holidays. Are we now acknowledging the resulting pension deficits that have emerged over the course of the last decade? No, in many cases the true sizes of these deficits continue to be hidden by making unrealistically optimistic asset return assumptions. In short, the authors tell us, to be sustainable, retirement income systems must be designed and managed with intergenerational fairness foremost in mind.

CHANGING THE PENSION REFORM CONVERSATION

So back to Washington. How did I propose to change the conversation about pension reform from dysfunctional to constructive? By reflecting on the implications of five pension design realities:

1. All good pension systems have three common features (more on this to follow).
2. All pension systems have embedded risks that need to be understood and managed.
3. Some of these risks have an *intergenerational* dimension.
4. Pension plan sustainability requires intergenerational fairness.
5. Achieving this fairness has plan *design* implications.

Each of these realities received a brief exposition, starting with the three common design features of all good pension systems. Such systems are:

1. **Inclusive:** All workers are provided a fair opportunity to provide for their retirement.
2. **Fit-for-Purpose:** The system is purposefully designed to start paying a target pension for life on a target retirement date. However, it should also have the flexibility to make course corrections along the way.
3. **Cost-Effective:** Retirement savings are transformed into pension payments by "value for money" pension organizations.

Surely no rational person would disagree with these three features? So far, so good.

A FIT-FOR-PURPOSE PENSION FORMULA

Leaving the "inclusive" and "cost-effective" pension design features for another day, the Washington talk focused on constructing "fit-for-purpose" pension formulas. Again, a logical three-step protocol follows:

1. **Set a Pension Target:** A typical target might be 65 percent of average pay, inflation-indexed.
2. **Cost that Pension Target:** This requires projections of working life length, post-work longevity, amount of pillar one state pension payments (e.g., old age pension, Social Security, etc.), and the investment return on pension contributions.

Two Types of Risks:

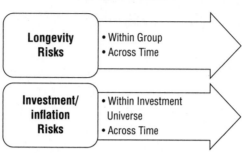

FIGURE 5.1   Pension Risks to Be Considered
Source: KPA Advisory Services Ltd.

3. **Identify Associated Risks and Their Possible Mitigation:** The major
   uncertainties relate to longevity (i.e., how long will I live?) and the
   net real return on pension contributions (i.e., what is a reasonable
   long-term return projection after expenses and adjusted for inflation?).

Arguably, step 3 is the most challenging. Figure 5.1 makes the important
point that both longevity and real return risks have a within-group/within-
time-period dimension, and they also have across-time-period dimensions.
The within-group/within-time-period risks are easily pooled and diversified;
the across-time risks are not.

INTERGENERATIONAL FAIRNESS

This difficulty to pool risks across time is a critically important point. The
argument is often made that traditional DB plans are capable of pooling
across-time longevity risk (i.e., the risk that the whole group lives longer
than expectations) and across-time real return risk (i.e., the risk that real
return experience is below expectations for multiple time periods). These
asserted key beneficial features in traditional DB plans do not square well
with either logic or the facts. On the logic side, the next generation is typically not at the DB plan bargaining table. Hence, they typically have no
voice to press their interests. As a result, succeeding generations usually end
up being the residual risk bearers in traditional DB plans without receiving
any compensation for the "privilege."

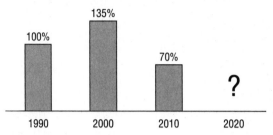

Intergenerational Risk Asymmetry in Action:

Typical U.S. Public Sector DB Plan Funded Status

FIGURE 5.2   The Intergenerational Fairness Problem
Source: KPA Advisory Services Ltd.

This logic is confirmed by facts. Have a look at Figure 5.2. It displays the time path of the funded ratio of a typical U.S. public sector DB plan over the course of the last 20+ years. Remember how we talked ourselves into a "new era" paradigm as the last decade of the 20th century rolled on? As it ended, most DB plan funded ratios were well over 100 percent. Did we treat these balance sheet surpluses as rainy-day funds to see the plan through the coming lean years? We did not. Predictably, we spent the surpluses on benefit increases and contribution holidays. After all, was this not a new era of outsized economic growth rates and stock market returns? Was taking on more risk not synonymous with earning even higher returns?

A decade later we know that the answers to these turn-of-the-century rhetorical questions were "no" and "no." On top of these stark economic realities, red-faced actuaries are now confessing they have been underestimating increases in retiree longevity for quite some time. So today the search is on for the magic bullet that will transform today's 60 to 80 percent funded ratios of U.S. public sector DB plans back to the 100 percent ratios of a full generation (i.e., 20+ years) ago. Mindful of the third rail problem so well-described by Leech and McNish, many people in leadership positions today continue to search for some easy way out. Let's stretch the unfunded liability amortization period out to 30 years. Let's turn the risk dial up even higher and hope for the best. Note that all of these "solutions" effectively pass the problem on to the next generation once again.

WHERE TO GO FROM HERE?

Given the current poor state of affairs in many public sector DB plans, it should come as no surprise that people on the radical right of the political spectrum want to do away with this type of pension arrangement altogether. This would be a tragedy. We agree with authors Leech and McNish when they write: "None of these weaknesses need to be fatal if we repair them now."

It seems to me the place to start these repairs is to ditch the dysfunctional DB/DC language. Political leaders in the UK, the Netherlands, Denmark, and Australia have already done so. They now speak of defined-ambition (DA) pension plans. In North America the term *target benefit* (TB) plan tends to be used. Vigorous debates are taking place on how to best design and implement DA/TB plans. In our view, a good DA/TB pension plan has five critical features:

1. **A Target Income-Replacement Rate:** How much post-work income is needed to maintain an adequate standard of living?
2. **A Target Contribution Rate:** Given realistic assumptions about working life length, longevity, and net real investment returns, how much money needs to be set aside to achieve the pension target?
3. **No Intergenerational Wealth-Shifting:** The plan design is tested for intergenerational fairness.
4. **Long-Horizon Wealth-Creation Capability:** The pension delivery organization has the capability to acquire and nurture healthy multi-decade cash flows (e.g., streams of dividends, rents, tolls) through a well-managed long-horizon investment program.
5. **Payment-Safety Purchase Capability:** Plan members can acquire payment-for-life income streams at a reasonable price.

In addition, the pension delivery organization creates a plan participant default option where plan contributions are automatically directed to the individually owned units in the long-horizon wealth-creation program until participants reach an age (say 50), at which point they begin to slowly acquire payment-safety instruments over the remaining period of their working lives. The pension delivery organization has excellent financial planning and communication skills and infrastructure to guide participants through this financial life-cycle journey.

The Washington talk ended with the DA/TB plan delivery organization example displayed in Figure 5.3. It bears close resemblance to an actual large industry pension plan/delivery organization based in the U.S. that has successfully operated with the five critical DA plan features set out previously

A U.S. Example:

A Large-Scale DA Pension System

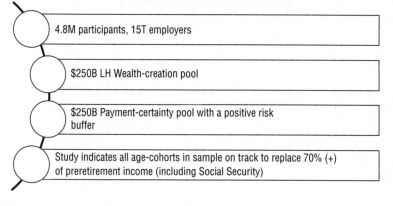

- 4.8M participants, 15T employers
- $250B LH Wealth-creation pool
- $250B Payment-certainty pool with a positive risk buffer
- Study indicates all age-cohorts in sample on track to replace 70% (+) of preretirement income (including Social Security)

FIGURE 5.3 A DA Plan Delivery Organization
Source: KPA Advisory Services Ltd.

for over 60 years. Remarkably, as has usually been the case when we pose the "do you know the organization?" question, very few people come up with the right answer. Can you?[3]

CHANGING THE CONVERSATION

There is of course a pension elephant in the room we have not yet mentioned in this chapter: getting from here to there. The three cited pension heroes in *The Third Rail* learned first-hand how difficult it is to persuade pensioners and older workers to reduce their traditional DB plan pension income claims in the name of plan solvency and intergenerational fairness. In the New Brunswick and Rhode Island cases, it took undeniable evidence of looming bankruptcies, which would lead to even larger pension cuts. In the Netherlands case, it took tough legislation legally requiring that pension guarantees be backed by large-enough asset pools to ensure that pensions promised would become pensions paid without resort to pension bailouts paid for by the next generation. Very large doses of leadership will continue to be required to repair the current weaknesses on both traditional DB and DC plans, and in meeting the needs of workers with no pension plan at all.

Miraculously, the 20 minutes of polite post-talk conversation in Washington was conducted without a single utterance of the DB and DC words. Even better, the DA/TB model triggered plenty of curiosity and some good questions. Maybe the beginning of a new conversation?

CHAPTER 6

On the Costing and Funding of Defined-Benefit Pensions

Separating Fact and Fiction

"An incomplete agency game is one where not all parties are represented at the bargaining table."
—Woody Brock, SED Client Memo, August 2013

UNCONVENTIONAL WISDOM NEEDED

The goal of this chapter is to foster progressive, productive discussions about the costing and funding of pension arrangements. Such discussions are critical to sorting out the many pension reform challenges discussed in the previous chapter. The reasons for these challenges, guided by conventional wisdom, are well known: aging populations, extended retiree longevity, fragile economies, fiscal imbalances, and disappointing returns on retirement savings. Unfortunately, conventional wisdom cannot solve such current pension finance problems as inadequate savings rates, investment policy confusion, and inadequate asset accumulations in relation to accumulated liabilities.

Solving these problems will require unconventional wisdom. A good example of such unconventional wisdom is Woody Brock's game theory–based observation that parties not represented in a pensions bargaining game are likely to receive the short end of the bargaining stick.[1] A related factor is fuzzy property rights. Just as incomplete agency bargaining leads to asymmetric pension design outcomes, so do incompletely defined pension property rights eventually lead to adversarial win–lose pension conflicts.

In theory, pension legislation and regulations should not permit pension bargains to be struck without knowledgeable, un-conflicted agents representing *all* of the key parties (i.e., including future workers and taxpayers). Similarly, pension arrangements lacking clear property rights for *all* the key parties (i.e., including future workers and taxpayers) should be deemed illegal, and not allowed to come in force. In practice, the fiduciary duties of evenhandedness and loyalty notwithstanding, this self-evident logic has seldom been applied. In the United State, Detroit's bankruptcy offered a stark example of the consequences of incomplete pension contracts with unclear property rights.

COMPLETE PENSION CONTRACTS

The simplest complete pension contract is a defined-contribution (DC) plan where an employer commits to deposit a known percentage of pay into retirement accounts owned separately by each of its employees. Under what conditions is a defined-benefit (DB) plan contract equally complete? Consider the following simplified example: Benefits are based on an explicit accrual formula (e.g., 1.5 percent of annual earnings) and on an explicit retirement date (e.g., age 65); and they are fully inflation-indexed.

- Benefits are costed and funded based on the actual market-based, risk-free, real yield curve, and on mortality tables that conservatively project continuous increases in plan member longevity.
- Plan contributions are invested in a laddered, default risk–free, inflation-linked bond portfolio that matches the term structure of accrued pension liabilities, thus immunizing the pension plan balance sheet.

In financial economics terms, this DB plan contract is as fully defined as the earlier DC contract. Plan members know the terms of the accrual formula, and there is complete certainty (at least as complete as possible in a world with known and unknown unknowns) that the terms of the pension contract will be honored. The biggest unknown may be the ability of the employer to continue to be an employer in the years ahead.

INCOMPLETE PENSION CONTRACTS

This simplified complete DB plan contract allows us to examine ways in which DB contracts can be incomplete. Possibly the most common path to incompleteness is to adopt a risk-taking investment policy with an expected asset return that is higher than the risk-free return of the asset–liability matching immunization strategy (the latter is under 1 percent based on the current TIPS real yield curve). Such a choice triggers two things:

1. It exposes the DB balance sheet to asset–liability mismatch risk. This risk has to be borne. If the pension contract is not clear about who the balance sheet risk bearers are, it is incomplete.
2. It opens up the possibility of reducing the DB plan's funding requirements and lowering reported total compensation costs. This in turn raises important questions about whether the plan leads to "ex-ante" wealth transfers between plan stakeholders, and whether all plan stakeholders are being fairly treated.

While both of these implications seem self-evident, there continues to be a good deal of resistance to serious examinations of their consequences. They do *not* mean that retirement savings should never undertake investment risk. Instead, they mean that how, and by whom, investment risk is borne should be clearly spelled out.

THE RISK-FREE ARBITRAGE TEST

To test the fairness of a financial contract, financial economists have devised a risk-free arbitrage test. The principle is simple: For a financial contract to be fair, neither party should be able to manipulate it in a way that shifts wealth from one party to the other on a risk-free basis. Consider the following example:

- There are two one-year investments: One is risk-free offering a 2 percent return. The other offers a 4 percent expected return, but with a range of possible outcomes, including the material possibility of an actual return outcome less than 2 percent.
- An employer guarantees to make a pension payment of $102 one year from now, which must be funded today. In Case 1, the employer writes a check for $100 and invests the money in the risk-free bond, which pays the required $102 one year from now. In Case 2, the employer writes a check for only $98, and invests the $98 in the risky investment. Has the employer saved $2 of pension costs? It depends.
- The Case 2 answer is "yes" if the investment actually earns 4 percent or better. What if it doesn't? Somebody has to make up the shortfall. Who? Logically, the employer who saved the $2 in pension funding. The $2 savings covers return outcomes under 4 percent down to 2 percent.
- What if the actual return was, say, 0 percent? Now the original $98 is still $98 one year later, and the employer needs to reach in its own pocket to make up the $4 difference between that $98 and the $102 pension payment owed. Even lower actual returns require even greater "own pocket" makeups.

- All this is fair if the employer is the same person(s) today and one year from now. What if they are not? Then next year's employer is underwriting the risks taken by this year's employer.

You have just witnessed a case of risk-free arbitrage in action. In Case 2, the Year 1 employer arranged its financial affairs in a way that it passed $2 of employment costs on to the Year 2 employer without taking any risk (i.e., it contributed $98 rather than $100). This simple example can be generalized in many different ways. Think, for example, of public-sector DB pension plans operating over multiple decades. Future generations of taxpayers (and workers in shared-risk plans) are underwriting the risk that pension plans being funded with a 4% (or higher) net real return assumption today will not actually earn those returns in the decades ahead.

THE CASE OF PERS

Back in 2005, I wrote a case study to facilitate the understanding of the incomplete contract problem, and how it might be addressed. Alyson Green had just been appointed CEO of the U.S.-based Public Employees' Retirement System (PERS) pension plan. At first, she was comforted to learn that the plan was 100 percent funded, with assets and liabilities both at $50B. She paid little attention to the fact that the $50B liability estimate was calculated using a net real return discount rate of 4 percent, which was justified by the historical return earned with the PERS 60–40 asset-mix policy.[2]

Then she attended a Rotman ICPM Discussion Forum on the financial economics of DB plans like PERS. The key thing she learned was that, applying the principles of financial economics, calculating the risk-free value of PERS' inflation-indexed liabilities requires using the market-based TIPS yield curve. What were the implications of using a 2 percent (i.e., the 2005 long TIPS yield) liability discount rate rather than the 4 percent used in PERS' most recent liability calculation? As representatives of the Dutch pension fund PGGM were at the Forum demonstrating their new ALM model, she soon had her answer: The PERS liability would be $74B rather than the reported $50B, and the PERS funded ratio 68 percent rather than 100 percent.

Verbalizing what she had just learned, the PERS 4 percent net real return projection was just one point in a range of possible future return outcomes. It was not a certainty. The $24B difference between the $50B PERS liability calculation and the $74B risk-free calculation could be thought of as the cost of eliminating balance sheet uncertainty. In the absence of somebody writing a $24B check, who is bearing this underperformance risk currently embedded in the PERS balance sheet? Whoever it is, do they know they are bearing this risk? Are they being compensated for bearing it? If not, is that fair?

Solving the PERS Balance Sheet Problem

Actually, it didn't seem fair to Alyson that the $24B bet should unknowingly be underwritten mainly by future generations of workers and taxpayers. She wondered how the PERS balance sheet problem could be solved? Historically, the 15 percent of pay contribution rate had been shared 50–50 between employers and employees. What if the contribution rate was increased to 20 percent of pay, with both parties paying an additional 2.5 percent? Based on this, and a number of other assumptions, the PGGM model projected PERS' finances out 15 years into the future, and then converted the outcomes to present values.

The results displayed in Table 6.1 indicated that even this material contribution rate increase would not solve the PERS intergenerational fairness problem. The estimated present value of the new liabilities accruing over the next 15 years is $71B versus only a $68B value for new contributions. So even a 20 percent contribution rate is insufficient to pay for future PERS pension benefits on a risk-free basis. The calculated option values indicate (a) that $32B would have to be paid to an insurer to buy a "put" option that would cover all potential balance sheet deficits that could exist 15 years from now; and (b) that today's "call" option value of all potential surpluses that could exist in 15 years is $5B. The $27B difference between the put and call option values is the updated cost of eliminating balance sheet uncertainty.

With the deemed impossibility of pushing contribution rates above 20 percent of pay, Alyson decided to look at the impact of reducing the pension guarantees embedded in the pension contract. What if, in addition to a 20 percent contribution rate, future benefit accruals were career-average rather than final earnings–based, and pensions-in-pay inflation adjustments were conditional on the existence of a balance sheet surplus to pay for them? The results in Table 6.2 indicate that moving from final earnings

TABLE 6.1 The Enhanced PERS Balance Sheet with Full Guarantees (20 percent contribution rate for the next 15 years)

Assets	Value (in Billions)	Liabilities	Value (in Billions)
Current pension fund	$50B	Current liabilities	$74B
Contributions	$68B	New liabilities	$71B
Option deficit	$32B	Option surplus	$ 5B

Source: PERS Case Study, Rotman ICPM, University of Toronto.

TABLE 6.2 The Enhanced PERS Balance Sheet with Reduced Guarantees
(20 percent contribution rate for the next 15 years)

Assets	Value (in Billions)	Liabilities	Value (in Billions)
Current pension fund	$50B	Current liabilities (without indexation)	$45B
Contributions	$68B	New liabilities (with conditional indexation on accrued and new benefits)	$50B
Option deficit	$ 1B	Option surplus	$24B

Source: PERS Case Study, Rotman ICPM, University of Toronto.

to career-average benefits and providing inflation protection only when
affordable would swing the PERS balance sheet from a $27M deficit to a
$23B surplus. The impact of the reduction in guarantees in option terms
can be seen by comparing Table 6.1 and 6.2 results. The put value of future
deficits falls from $32B to $1B, while the call value of future surpluses rises
from $5B to $24B. Now future generations of risk bearers would get a
better deal than the current generation, and that didn't seem fair, either.

FURTHER REFLECTIONS

These insights prompted further reflections on Alyson's part:

DB pension arrangements are far more complex than she had originally
thought. They seem to be complex puzzles, balancing the respective interests
of multiple stakeholder groups using a dynamic mix of contribution rate and
benefit changes, conditional on the actual evolution of the DB balance sheet.

Given the generally high discount rates in use, most younger and future
workers and taxpayers generally bear more risk than current older workers,
retirees, and taxpayers today, but are not rewarded for it. They are the put
issuers in most DB plans today.

The direction for pension contract reform is clear: toward understandable, explainable blends of complete contracts that are fairly priced on an
intergenerational basis. The simplest way to do that is to move to some form
of a defined-ambition/target-benefit (DA/TB) pension model explored in the
previous chapter.

Simplifying DB pension arrangements and making them more attractive
for younger and future workers and taxpayers will be very challenging work
because of the "it's not in my interest to understand why" problem. DB plan

stakeholders who currently have the financial upper hand will not relinquish it easily.

And what about the hundreds of pension professionals who have actually discussed and debated the PERS case study over the last decade? What conclusions have they come to? The majority believed PERS has a serious problem requiring immediate attention for three reasons:

1. The $24B gap represents the current risk embedded in the PERS system. Everyone should be aware it is there.
2. There is a material probability that plan members will get lower pensions than expected, or pay more than expected. This fact must be disclosed.
3. Alyson Green must make her mark by raising these issues in her first board meeting. Waiting until later would be a strategic mistake.

However, a minority of case study participants took a more sanguine view:

- PERS is not insolvent. There is time to take a slow, deliberate approach to a solution.
- Things may turn out okay. Don't take an alarmist view.
- Having a funding target less than the economic cost of accrued pension promises (and hence the risk of underfunding) is just one part of any compensation arrangement between an employer and its employees. It may be offset by other considerations, and this reality should be made clear to all.

What is *your* view on what Alyson should do, dear reader?[3]

CHAPTER 7

Defining Defined-Ambition Pension Plans

Conclusions from an International Conversation

"Ambition is a strong desire to do or achieve something, typically requiring determination and hard work."
—Oxford Dictionaries Online

AN INTERNATIONAL CONVERSATION IN ROTTERDAM

Prior chapters noted that we must move beyond the tiresome debate between defined-benefit (DB) and defined-contribution (DC) models if we are going to design and implement pension arrangements suitable to 21st-century realities. Evidence that this is in fact happening was presented at a recent workshop held at Rotterdam's Erasmus University. In addition to the Netherlands, workshop participants came from Australia, Canada, Sweden, the United Kingdom, and the United States.

The Dutch pensions think-tank NETSPAR initiated the event in its role of providing thought-leadership in transitioning the second pillar of the Dutch pension system out of its current troublesome "collective DC" framework into a less complex, more functional defined-ambition (DA) version. NETSPAR invited a multi-country delegation of supporters of the International Centre for Pension Management (ICPM), based at the University of Toronto's Rotman School of Management, to participate in the workshop in order to broaden the range of perspectives on what 21st-century DA pension plans should look like. This chapter summarizes the workshop highlights and my take on its key conclusions.

ADDRESSING THE ADEQUACY-AFFORDABILITY-SAFETY CONUNDRUM

There was broad workshop consensus that the historical DC and DB narratives have both become increasingly problematic. On the DC side, serious adequacy and safety questions have come to the fore. For example, is the savings rate while working high enough to ultimately generate an adequate pension? Who invests the pension pot? How do people make their accumulated pension pot last their entire post-work life? On the DB side, employers are increasingly raising pension affordability questions, and withdrawing from their traditional role as pension risk underwriters.

The acceptance of these realities sets the stage for a fresh look at the adequacy-affordability-safety conundrum inherent in any pension arrangement. If 21st-century realities require that explicit trade-offs between these three desirable pension plan features must be made (i.e., "You can't have it all!"), who is in the best position to describe what those trade-offs really are? Who actually chooses among alternative trade-off possibilities? Who implements the choices made? And what should be the role of a 21st-century pension organization in addressing these questions?

In its 1994 report "Averting the Old Age Crisis," the World Bank proposed a three-pillar framework to address these questions.[1] Broadly speaking, pillar one constitutes a country's universal, tax-funded component; pillar two its employment-based pre-funded component; and pillar three its individual supplementary retirement savings component. In this context, the questions posed above relate to pillar two (i.e., employment-based) pension arrangements. A related, but different pension design question is: What are (and should be) the key features of a country's public/universal (i.e., pillar one) pension arrangement? Stating the obvious, adequacy-affordability-safety trade-offs should be considered in the joint context of the first and second pillars of a country's pension arrangements. For example, if a country's first pension pillar provides its citizens with 35 percent lifetime inflation-indexed income replacement up to some maximum ceiling, that is an important consideration in the design of any functional second pillar pension arrangement in that country.

DESIGNING 21ST-CENTURY DA PENSION PLANS

Constructive pension design discussions start from positions of agreement. For example, there was broad consensus at the workshop that pension plans should be designed with a clearly defined ambition in mind: the post-work maintenance of a person's or couple's standard of living. Such agreement sets the stage for a fresh look at how pension design could/should address the unavoidable affordability–safety trade-off question. In other words, what are the plan's key affordability drivers, what are its key risk control levers, and how is the opposable nature of these two desirable plan features best resolved? This question captures the essence of what the conversation in the room was all about. Two starting viewpoints emerged:

1. **Affordability** considerations should dominate the design of second pillar pension plans. This means an emphasis on the long-horizon return compounding of retirement savings. It is fair to say that the Anglo-Saxon participants leaned in this direction.
2. **Safety** considerations should dominate the design of second pillar pension plans. This means an emphasis on the efficient pooling of risks related to investments, inflation, and longevity. These considerations were foremost on the minds of the Dutch and the Nordics.

As the day progressed, the starting viewpoints began to soften. The "affordability" people began to think more about risk-management considerations, while the "safety" people began to think more about the affordability implications of buying safety in a low-interest-rate world.

A related design question that surfaced more than once is the appropriate degree of individual choice in pension plan design. While complete individualization may be impractical, a one-size-fits-all approach may be equally dysfunctional. Something in-between those extremes will likely be best. The QSuper story told by CEO Rosemary Vilgan illuminated all these points, which I will recap here.

THE QSUPER STORY

QSuper looks after the post-work income needs of 540K public sector workers and retirees in the Australian state of Queensland. It defines its fiduciary obligation to these people as overseeing "the accumulation of retirement assets and their transition to retirement income across the lifecycle." Its current asset base amounts to A$70B. Historically, like other Australian super funds, QSuper managed its DC plan assets with a standard equity-bond asset mix, into which 90 percent of plan participants defaulted. Australian super funds compete with each other via regularly published performance "league tables" which show the relative investment returns of the major funds.

Some years ago, QSuper came to the view that its actions and services fell short of a 21st-century interpretation of their fiduciary obligation to members. A multi-year transition plan was developed with the following five key elements:

1. **Move away from the traditional one-size-fits-all delivery model** to one that recognizes differences in member needs based on such factors as age. As members age, the proportion of their pension pots in safety assets automatically increases while the duration of these assets decreases.
2. **Move toward providing members with pension targets and regular progress reports** on where they stand in the accumulation phase of their journey toward their post-work pension target. Offer members tools and advice that guides them toward achieving their target.
3. **Upgrade the choices in the decumulation phase** of the lifecycle journey by including a longevity protection purchase option.
4. **Dynamically adjust the pension design default settings** based on the organization's best professional assessment of asset pricing conditions and other relevant socioeconomic considerations over time.
5. **Reset the asset management program** to focus on long-horizon wealth-creation in both public and private markets. Signal this intent by dropping out of participation in short-horizon performance league tables competition set up in super fund space.

Taken together, these five initiatives moved QSuper resolutely toward managing a state-of-the-art 21st-century DA pension plan in an Australian setting. In the process, the organization will have inverted its business model from one where organization needs dictate the design of member services to one where member needs dictate the design of the organization.

THE PFZW-PGGM STORY

The Dutch pension setting offers an interesting contrast to Australia's. While both countries pre-fund their mandatory second-pillar pension plans, and both countries are heading toward DA designs, they are coming from very different places. While the historical Australian context is DC, the historical Dutch context is DB. The DB designs of the 1980s and 1990s evolved into collective DC (CDC) designs with nominal guarantees after the bursting of the .com bubble. The salience of these guarantees was swept away by the global financial crisis, opening the window for a national debate on what the post-CDC design of Dutch second pillar pension plans should look like. The Rotterdam workshop made it clear that while the direction is "defined ambition," a broad consensus on its pension design implications has not yet been achieved.

The conversation reflected a growing recognition in the Netherlands that its second pillar plans need to shift their emphasis away from safety toward affordability. The PFZW-PGGM story summarized next illustrates this reality well. Pensioenfonds Zorg en Welzijn (PFZW) looks after the post-work income needs of 2.6M workers and retirees in the Dutch healthcare sector. Its current asset base stands at about $200B. PGGM was spun out of PFZW in 2008, and provides PFZW with its investment, pension administration, and communication needs. Three initiatives have signaled the evolution of PFZW-PGGM thinking over the course of the last few years:

1. **Increasing use of the term "defined ambition"** in various PFZW-PGGM communications to members, other stakeholders, and policy makers. The communications indicate the organization's belief that a well-designed DA plan is affordable, fair, inflation-linked, and sustainable in the face of future socioeconomic shocks, and provides members with clear property rights. The communications are also clear about the fundamental difference between an ambition and a hard guarantee.
2. **Increasing emphasis on addressing individual member needs and trust-building** is indicated by providing members with multimedia, interactive information and planning options. The design of these options is guided by both in-depth member surveys and the research findings of behavioral economics studies.
3. **Redirecting the investment program toward long-horizon wealth-creation and sustainability** through a multi-year project that started with setting out member affordability needs and PFZW Board responsibilities to ensure that the $200B asset portfolio is invested in ways responsive to those needs. This work is reflected in an investment framework that articulates PFZW's beliefs and principles regarding investment policy, its implementation, and the related requirements for effective governance and control.[2]

While all three initiatives are still works in progress, PFZW-PGGM's chosen direction is clear. It intends to lead in the design and implementation of 21st-century DA plans in the Netherlands. As in the case of QSuper, this means inverting its business model from one where organization needs dictate the design of member services, to one where member needs dictate the design of the organization.

LOOKING AHEAD: THREE 21ST-CENTURY CHALLENGES

My contribution to the workshop was to encourage participants to frame the pension challenges we face with integrative "and-and" mindsets, rather than with silo 'either-or' ones. With that framing in mind, we suggested that three 'and-and' challenges will require ongoing attention:

1. **The Pension Design Challenge:** Reconciling the opposable needs for affordability and safety while at the same time heeding Einstein's admonition "to keep things as simple as possible, but no simpler." This will require designing lifecycle-based member transition paths that first emphasize affordability and eventually safety, as people move through the working and post-work phases of their lives. The design of these paths should reflect the combined contributions of the first and second pension pillars, as well as the findings of behavioral economics research.
2. **The Pension Governance Challenge:** Reconciling the need for board legitimacy through representativeness on the one hand, with the need for boards to be able to think strategically, backed by requisite collective skill/experience sets on the other. Historically, the selection of board members has favored representativeness over skill/experience. This needs to change by mutual agreement among the appointing stakeholder groups. A key tool is a single board skill/experience matrix that all appointing stakeholder groups agree to respect.
3. **The Pension Investment Challenge:** Reconciling the opposable needs for plan member affordability and safety will require separate investment programs, one focusing on the affordability goal, and the other on the safety goal. The focus of the former is long-horizon wealth-creation by acquiring and nurturing long-horizon cash flows (e.g., dividend, rents, tolls) in public and private markets through individual member accounts with no guarantees. The focus of the latter is the matching of payment promises with safe assets of similar duration, and the pooling of longevity risk.

Reflecting back on his book, *The Unseen Revolution*, Peter Drucker observed there were no obvious answers to the many profound questions that would surely arise as the Boomer generation pushed pension design and management issues on to a very visible center stage around the globe. Innovative mindsets would be needed to address these profound questions. The NETSPAR-ICPM workshop provided living proof that innovative mindsets are indeed rising to the challenges of pension design, governance, and investing.

What Are Target-Benefit Plans and Why Should You Care?

A target is a goal to be achieved.
—Adapted from *Merriam-Webster's Dictionary*

WHY YOU SHOULD CARE

While Europeans have been talking about defined-ambition (DA) pension plans for some time now, the term has not caught on elsewhere. Instead, Americans and Canadians have begun to talk about target-benefit plans (or TB plans for short). As it is still early going in the conduct of these conversations, not surprisingly, the TB term still means different things to different people. This is a problem. Constructive conversations on the design and merits of TB plans require a common understanding as to what they are—and what they are not. The goal of this chapter is to foster that common understanding, which in turn should lead to more constructive conversations about pension plan design in general.

We start by deconstructing the TB plan term into its three components: plan, benefit, and target. The meaning of the "plan" in this context is straightforward. It is an arrangement meant to generate post-retirement income.

WHAT "BENEFIT" ARE WE TALKING ABOUT?

That gets us to the "benefit" question. It is best answered by a simplified example:

- Assume an average worker (John or Janet), who works 40 years at a pay $60K/year, lives 20 years after retirement and needs $40K/year to maintain his/her post-work standard of living.

- Assume $20K/year comes from a universal pillar one pension arrangement (e.g., Social Security, OAS/CPP, etc., depending on the country), leaving $20K/year to come from other sources.
- In our simplified example, this second $20K/year is the benefit the pillar two TB plan is supposed to deliver.

This answer logically leads to the next question: Where does this second $20K/year come from?

Financing the Benefit

The simple answer is that it comes from saving part of the $60K/year earnings. How much needs to be saved to finance 20 years of retirement? That depends on whether the retirement savings are invested, and what return they earn. Consider two cases: 0 percent and 4 percent:

- Assuming a 0 percent return, Janet or John will need to have accumulated $400K at retirement to fund the 20 payments of $20K/year. This means saving $10K/year over the 40 working years, or (about) 17 percent of pay.
- In contrast, with a 4 percent return, John or Janet will have to save about $3K/yr, or only 5 percent of pay. For clarity, we assume the money earns 4 percent in both the pre- and post-retirement periods. No wonder Albert Einstein called compound interest the eighth wonder of the world!

These calculations get us to understanding the "target" part of the TB plan term.

WHAT DOES "TARGET" MEAN IN A TB PLAN?

The "target" part of the TB term formally acknowledges two uncertainties in the TB plan financing calculations: First, we don't know how long Janet or John will *actually* live; and second, we don't know what the return on retirement savings will *actually* be. So the target part of the TB plan is aspirational: It is the benefit John or Janet will receive if the longevity and return expectations are in fact realized.

This aspirational element raises a fundamental question: Who will underwrite the shortfall risk between expected and actual longevity outcomes and between expected and actual investment return outcomes? This question has two answers: from the good old days and from here and now.

- In the good old days, the employer underwrote the shortfall risks in the form of traditional defined-benefit (DB) plans. At the time, this seemed like a reasonable thing to do. Workforces were relatively young and homogeneous, economic growth was robust, investment returns were strong, and regulatory and financial disclosure requirements were soft. But the good old days are gone.
- The here-and-now retiree populations are relatively larger, workforces are older and less homogeneous, economic growth is less robust, investment returns are weaker, and regulatory and financial disclosure requirements are harder.

Not surprisingly, employers are far less keen to be pension risk underwriters today. Now we understand the real meaning of the target part of the TB term. It helps make clear the distinction between the aspiration of a target benefit and the reality that employers are no longer willing to underwrite the risk that future investment returns might be lower than expectations and longevity experience higher than expectations.

WHERE DOES THAT LEAVE JANET AND JOHN?

If employers are no longer willing to underwrite the risks embedded in pillar two pension plans, where does that leave Janet and John? How you answer this question depends very much on how you see the world. There are two possible views:

1. If you believe that the Janets and Johns of world are rational, well-informed people, and that the markets for investment and annuity management services are complete and competitive, the logical conclusion is that they will be fine left to their own devices. They will do the kind of calculations set out earlier, decide on the right savings rate and investment program, and annuitize at least part of their accumulated retirement savings when the time is right.
2. The research-supported alternative view is that John and Janet are not always rational by economic theory standards, and not as financially literate as we would like them to be. This means that in the absence of membership in a traditional DB plan that takes care of all of the risks, Janet and John sure could use some help in securing that supplemental $20K/year pension they will need to maintain their post-work standard of living.

There are three possible (not mutually exclusive) forms that help could take: first, through a "shared risks" pension arrangement between an employer (or employers), employees, and retirees via employer-sponsored, jointly sponsored, or union-sponsored TB plans; second, through employer-specific solutions designed and implemented by the commercial financial services industry; or third, through collective solutions designed and implemented by governments and their agencies. We examine each form of help in turn.

Answer #1: Shared-Risk TB Plans at the Single/ Multi-Employer Levels

Shared-risk arrangements with plan members obviously do shift some of the risk (and possibly cost as well) away from the employer relative to the traditional DB arrangement. Following the logic set out in earlier chapters, the questions become: How much risk (and cost) is shifted? To whom? Based on what assumptions about future expectations and uncertainty about member longevity and investment return experience? Is the TB plan design sensitive to differing risk tolerances among plan members (e.g., young workers vs. retirees)? Are property rights clearly defined? Will TB plan trustees be able to demonstrate that their decisions (e.g., on investment policy) are evenhanded with a balanced view of all stakeholder interests? Is there an element of member choice in the design? Finally, is the arrangement *understandable* to the average plan participant?

The previous chapter noted that the Dutch are coming to the view that their current shared-risk collective DC plans are not meeting these tests, and in-depth studies have been launched on how to address these problems. There is a growing consensus in the Netherlands that it *is* possible to design shared-risk arrangements that can meet the clarity and fairness tests set out previously. They are recognizing that part of the solution is to separate the long-term wealth-creation investment and short-term payment-safety hedging functions into separate instruments, and to transition member participation in each instrument on an age-related basis over time. Designing and moving to such arrangements is becoming a national priority.[1]

Another part of the solution is the design and governance of pension organizations capable of effectively managing this kind of arrangement. As already noted, the Drucker pension organization has an arm's-length legal structure, strong governance and management functions, sensible investment beliefs, scale, and the capability and willingness to attract and retain the professional talent necessary to create value for plan stakeholders. We use the term "stakeholders" advisedly here. Shared-risk pension arrangements typically have multiple risk-bearing groups with multiple risk-bearing tolerances.

Answer #2: Commercial Solutions

Large commercial organizations offering investment and risk underwriting services are capable of designing and implementing effective group pension arrangements along TB plan lines. However, an additional challenge needs to be addressed here. The combination of asymmetric information between sophisticated sellers and unsophisticated buyers (think John and Janet), and the fact that commercial organizations have a duty to generate an adequate return on shareholder capital, can easily lead to high-cost, uneconomic pension arrangements for workers and retirees.

However, if they are willing to make the effort, employers and regulators can play a key role in ensuring that any such arrangement is in fact fit-for-purpose and cost-effective for their past, current, and future workers. Pension and securities legislation can also play important roles. Requiring clear, plain disclosure of all participant fees and their potential impact on future pension payments is one obvious example.

Answer #3: Government Initiatives

Chapter 2 noted that the most visible recent event in the government initiative category is the creation of NEST (National Employment Savings Trust) in the UK. Despite its good start, NEST's management has made it clear that multiple challenges still lie ahead, including enrolling millions more workers, raising contribution rates to ensure income replacement adequacy, and eventually designing and implementing an effective and understandable decumulation protocol for the post-work phase of the life-cycle of NEST participants.[2]

Chapter 2 also noted that Ontario's ORPP (Ontario Retirement Pension Plan) initiative offers an opportunity to build a simple, understandable shared-risk pension design that will not suffer from the complexities and fuzziness that would result from trying to integrate benefit enhancements into the CPP (Canada Pension Plan) as it exists today. In my view, Janet and John would be best served if, like NEST, the ORPP is set up as a cost-effective retirement savings plan, with the plan's decumulation details put in place by the time there were material accumulated ORPP assets to decumulate. With the recent election of a Liberal government at the federal level, these ideas may well go national. Another idea here is to involve Canada's financial services industry in developing a feasible "on time–on budget" solution. Chapter 2 also noted that a number of U.S. states are exploring these TB plan ideas.

SO WHAT ARE TARGET-BENEFIT PLANS?

So what should we make of all this in relation to the "What are TB plans?" question this chapter started with? It is that, if not explicitly, then implicitly, *all* pension arrangements are TB plans (or using the European term, DA plans). The hard work is creating versions that work for Janet and John, and for their employers, too.

CHAPTER 9

Designing 21st-Century Pension Plans

We're Making Progress!

"There is an urgent need to find a better balance between the individual orientation of a DC plan and a collective approach where there is some sharing of risks ...."
—Melbourne Mercer Global Pension Index, 2013

PENSION DESIGN IN THE 21ST CENTURY

Chapters 7 and 8 explored the possible meanings of defined-ambition (DA) and target-benefit (TB) pension plans. Two underlying messages were that regardless of the name we attach to a pension design, two features always deserve special attention:

1. How the plan uses the investment return on retirement savings to achieve pension adequacy and affordability
2. How the plan provides post-retirement income for life

To make these messages tangible and clear, readers met Janet or John in Chapter 8, who earned $60K/year over a 40-year career, and who need $40K/year to maintain their standard of living over their expected 20-year post-work lives. If half of this $40K/year comes from a universal pillar one pension, then ideally, the other half comes from an effective, efficient employment-based pillar two pension arrangement. So specifically, two important questions regarding the pillar two arrangement become:

1. How much do John or Janet (and/or their employer) have to contribute over 40 years to fund the expected 20 post-retirement payments of $20K/year from that plan?
2. What can be done to prevent Janet or John outliving their money?

The answer to the first question depends on the investment return on retirement savings. The pillar two plan will cost an expensive 17 percent of pay at a 0 percent return, and a much more affordable 5 percent of pay at a 4 percent return. Stating the obvious, generating a reasonably high investment return on retirement savings always has been, and always will be, a critical pension design success element. The answer to the second question depends on whether a mechanism exists where John or Janet can pool the risk of outliving their money with other plan participants. Without such a mechanism, Janet or John may materially lower their post-retirement standard of living to prevent outliving their money. We explore each of these two pension design questions in greater detail in this chapter.

THE HIGH HISTORICAL RETURNS MIRAGE

The 50-year (1965–2014) nominal returns on the S&P 500 and on a portfolio of 10-year U.S. Treasury Bonds were 9.8 percent and 6.7 percent respectively. Price inflation over this period averaged 4.2 percent, resulting in real return realizations of 5.6 percent and 2.5 percent, respectively. These outcomes led to apparently reasonable 8.5 percent nominal and 4.5 percent real return assumptions for the traditional 60–40 asset-mix policy. These return assumptions in turn have led to affordable contribution rate calculations to fund adequate, or even more than adequate Pillar 2 pension promises to the Johns and Janets of the 1980s, 1990s, and 2000s.

A key message of this book is that these 50-year return realizations are not the best estimates for the next 50 years. Most fundamentally, the experience of 3 percent real GDP growth and 4 percent inflation in most developed economies over the last 50 years is not a best estimate for the next 50 years. Current demographic and economic realities suggest that an experience of 2 percent GDP growth and 2 percent inflation is a more reasonable expectation.

And what about equity and bond return prospects? Chapter 4 has already asserted, and Chapter 20 will further assert, that the current S&P500 earnings yield of 5 percent offers a realistic long-term real equity return estimate at this time of writing. However, with lower GDP growth and lower inflation experience, materially lower nominal and real bond yield curves should be expected (e.g., more like 3.5 percent nominal and 1.5 percent real at the long end). All this leads to lower prospective return rules of thumb for a 60–40 asset mix than the historical 8.5 percent nominal and 4.5 percent real. Expectations of 5.5 percent nominal and 3.5 percent real are now more realistic.

Implications for Funding and Investment Policies, and for Plan Design

The simple logic of pension economics tells us that with lower investment return prospects relative to historical realizations, something has to give. Either current contribution rates and current investment policies will likely produce lower (or later) future pensions, or if current pension target levels are to be maintained in the future, either contribution rates will have to rise or asset mix policies will have to move to greater exposure to return/growth assets at the expense of safety assets. For example, under the assumptions set out above, the traditional 60–40 asset mix policy will have to move to 80–20 to produce a realistic 4.5 percent real return expectation.

This logic leads to two related questions: First, how should we think about the risk implications of moving from a 60–40 to an 80–20 asset mix policy? And second, what role can/should guarantees play in 21st-Century pension designs? The reflex response is that 80–20 is too risky for a pension investment policy. A more measured response is that it depends on the nature of the pension contract, and on the nature of the assets in the return/growth portfolio. If the pension contract requires that assets must exceed liabilities at all times, then 80–20 likely is a too risky asset mix policy. On the other hand, if no such requirement exists, and if the assets in the return/growth portfolio throw off a healthy, sustainable cash flow in the forms of interest, dividends, rents, and tolls, an 80–20 mix could well become a viable long-term investment policy.

Given the realities set out in this chapter, it makes good sense for risk underwriters of fully guaranteed pillar two DB plans to insist on reforming the nature of the DB contracts toward greater flexibility in any number of ways (e.g., conditional indexation, hybrid plans, greater risk sharing, etc.). The prior two chapters showed that whether such a plan is termed a DA plan or a TB plan is a matter of local convention.

RETHINKING INVESTMENT RISK SHARING

On the face of it, like motherhood, risk sharing seems like an unassailably good idea. In fact, that is not always the case. There is good risk sharing and bad risk sharing. Good risk-sharing arrangements are fair; bad ones are not. Probably the greatest debate in pension design today is whether investment returns with intergenerational risk sharing arrangements fall into the good or bad category. Specifically, are such arrangements fair or unfair?

Chapter 6 set out my stance on this question: While intergenerational risk-sharing arrangements related to investment returns can be fair in principle, they predictably lead to unfair outcomes in practice. Fairness requires that "good times" surpluses not be touched so that they can be used to offset "bad times" deficits. The most recent test of this principle was in the late 1990s/early 2000s period, a time when the extraordinary return experience of the 1980s and 1990s had led to large surpluses in most DB plans.

Were those surpluses saved to weather DB plans through the coming two-part bad times of the dot-com bubble and the global financial crisis? Predictably, they were not. Accompanied by prattle about new era economics by fiduciaries and experts alike, the surpluses were spent on increased benefits and lower contribution rates. Only independent, knowledgeable referees with very strong rulemaking and rule-enforcing powers can keep intergenerational investment risk-sharing arrangements fair.

In the absence of such wise, powerful rule-making/enforcement mechanisms, it is a far better, simpler thing to manage return/growth pension asset pools for plan participants as long-horizon, sustainable wealth-creation investment programs without any intergenerational risk-sharing or solvency-testing protocols attached to them. With little expected return help from safety assets in the future, the urgency to generate adequate returns from these return/growth pools has never been greater.

RETHINKING LONGEVITY RISK SHARING

In contrast to investment risk sharing, pooling the risk of outliving one's life expectancy falls more easily into the good category. Why? Because it can be set up as a fair arrangement, with all participants in a safety/longevity pooling vehicle agreeing to contribute identified amounts of capital into the vehicle, which they continue to own through individual capital accounts. There is, however, a "side deal" in the safety/longevity-pooling vehicle: In the case of a participant death, the capital remaining (or at least a significant portion of it) in his/her individual account is reallocated to the accounts of the still-alive participants. Thus the still-alive participants receive two types of periodic returns on their capital in the pool: an investment return and a return for being still alive.

The investment return earned by participants in the safety/longevity-pooling vehicle is straightforward: It is their share of the return on the underlying (likely low-risk) investment portfolio over the measurement period. The still-alive return comes from the capital reallocation side deal. This return is redistributed to the pool survivors according to a formula based on (a) the amount of capital they have in the pool, and (b) the participant mortality rate, which can vary by age, gender, and possibly other factors. The result is a fair capital transfer mechanism from deceased pool participants to the surviving pool participants. Pool participants living well beyond their life expectancy will receive most of their retirement income from this still-alive return component.

Giving credit where it is due, I thank David Knox, Lans Bovenberg, and Don Ezra for sharing and discussing these ideas with me. The essence of their message is that longevity risk can be efficiently pooled without having to use the traditional (and to many people, unattractive) life annuity mechanisms with their risk capital requirements and their regulatory and distribution costs. In the alternative approach, safety/longevity pool participants continue to have clear property rights to their contributed capital. What has been added to the mix is a longevity risk-pooling feature along the lines previously set out.[1]

UPDATING THE TINBERGEN PENSION MODEL AND ITS APPLICATIONS

This chapter updates the 21st-century pension model we have been advocating for some 10 years now. The model has had various names over time, most recently The Tinbergen Pension Model for reasons explained in Chapter 1. Its key feature is the "2 goals–2 instruments" rule for pension design: (1) a return/growth instrument that generates sustainable high returns over extended periods of time; and (2) a safety/longevity pooling instrument that provides a predictable stream of post-work pension payments for life. The key message of this chapter is that safety/longevity pooling instrument designs do not require converting accumulated retirement savings into nontransparent, likely expensive, inflexible life annuities.

The chapter ends by returning to the question of how this updated Tinbergen pension model can best help Janet and John achieve their financial retirement goals. It is unrealistic to assume that they will figure it all out by themselves. For example, a target pillar two pension will have to be determined and costed. An auto-default accumulation/decumulation glide path will have to be designed. An information protocol that regularly informs them about how they are doing relative to their target will also have to be designed. This protocol should also offer suggestions on how to get back on track if needed.

So who is going to be John and Janet's partner in making this pension model work for them? The prior chapter listed three (not mutually exclusive) possibilities:

1. **The Single or Multi-Employer Context:** With sufficient scale and motivation, a single employer or labor union could sponsor this kind of pension plan. In a broader context, groups of employers/employees in both the private and public sectors could also move their pension plan designs in this direction. These groupings could be industry- or geography-based. There are indications that both Dutch and Australian multi-employer plans are in fact doing so.

2. **Commercial Financial Services Providers:** The apparent lack of appetite in the commercial financial services industry to lead the innovative thinking needed to attach the kind of safety/longevity pooling instrument we describe here to their traditional DC plan offerings is surprising. The Mercer LIFETIMEPLUS initiative cited in Endnote 1 suggests this may now be changing.

3. **National/Regional Government Initiatives:** Happily, such initiatives are already underway in the national/regional government sectors. An example is the NEST initiative in the UK described in previous chapters. As a result, today, millions of UK workers who were without a pillar two pension plan now have one, or will soon have one. Ontario's ORPP initiative has put Ontario workers on a similar track. This initiative could well go national across Canada. Finally, these kinds of initiatives are also being explored in the United State at both the national and state levels.

The goal of this section of the book has been to indicate that the topic of 21st-Century pension design is alive and well. Progress is indeed being made on a number of fronts. Are you doing your part?

PART Three

Pension Governance

"*Governance relates to processes of interaction and decision-making among persons involved in a collective endeavour. The degree of formality depends on the internal rules of the organization.*"
    —Mark Bevir, *Governance: A Very Short Introduction* (2013)

CHAPTER 10

How Effective Is Pension Fund Governance Today?

Findings from a New Survey

"We need to move from long-term investing solutions to actions.... First, we need to address the issue of governance of financial institutions."

—Angel Gurria, Secretary General, OECD

A NEW SURVEY ON GOVERNANCE

As the OECD's Secretary General Angel Gurria points out, effective financial organizations require effective governance. This reality has motivated my involvement in pension governance research going back some 25 years. This chapter summarizes the findings of my most recent research project on pension fund governance in collaboration with John McLaughlin.[1] The project was launched by sending out a survey in mid-2014 to 180 CEOs of major pension organizations around the world. Two months later we began analyzing the 81 completed surveys, comparing the 2014 responses to those provided in identical surveys in 1997 and 2005. Before reporting the new study results, this chapter offers a brief summary of earlier research findings going back to 1992.

PRIOR PENSION GOVERNANCE RESEARCH FINDINGS

Anthropologists William O'Barr and John Conley caused quite a stir in 1992 with their book, *Fortune and Folly: The Power and Wealth of Institutional Investing*.[2] After observing the behavior of nine major U.S. pension funds over a two-year period, they concluded that the aim of the funds appeared to be focused more on responsibility deflection and blame management than on good governance and creating value for fund stakeholders. This observed behavior is very much in line with Keynes' 1936 remark about investment committees that "worldly wisdom teaches that it is better for reputation to fail conventionally than to succeed unconventionally ...."[3]

A 1995 study in which I was involved surveyed 50 senior U.S. pension fund executives on what they estimated the "excellence shortfall" to be in their organization. In other words, if the known barriers to excellence could be lifted out of their organizations, by how much might long-term investment performance improve? The median response was 66 bps. When asked to identify the sources of excellence shortfall, respondents most frequently cited poor decision-making processes, inadequate resources, and a lack of focus and clarity of mission.[4] Studies by Clark et al. in the UK (2006 and 2007) and by Clapman et al. in the United State (2007) confirmed the presence of these challenges in many pension organizations.[5]

An article by Clark and Urwin in *Rotman International Journal of Pension Management*[6] (RIJPM) made these key observations about boards of pension organizations:

- Understanding human behavior and cognitive biases is an important element in designing effective board governance structures.
- Board members must be collegial, representative, and make a collective commitment to understand and fairly balance stakeholder interests.
- In reality, boards often suffer from unacknowledged differences in individual decision-making styles, lack focus, and are overwhelmed by the range of issues they must deal with.
- In this context, the board chair role is critically important. The chair must ensure there is a clear link between stakeholder expectations and the organization's culture, its strategic plan, and how it executes that plan. Most importantly, this person must command strong personal respect.

An article by Ambachtsheer, Capelle, and Lum in that same RIJPM issue[7] describes a pension fund governance survey first carried out by the authors in 1997, and repeated in 2005. Its key findings and conclusions are set out next.

Understanding the Pension Governance Deficit

The survey posed two open-ended questions to pension fund CEOs. One was about board priorities; the other was about organizational priorities. It also asked participants to rank 45 statements about governance, management, and operational effectiveness in their organizations. They were asked to indicate their disagreement/agreement with each statement on a scale from 1 (total disagreement) to 6 (complete agreement). Each statement was crafted so that the higher the assigned number, the greater the perceived effectiveness. The survey elicited 80 responses in 1997 and 81 in 2005 from diverse groups of pension organizations by type, size, and geography.

Table 10.1 sets out the CEO responses to the board and managerial priorities questions in the 2005 survey. They saw big challenges for Board governance in three areas: agency/context issues, board effectiveness issues, and investment/risk management issues. The biggest managerial challenge is strategic planning and its execution. Table 10.2 provides greater detail about each of these four perceived challenge areas. Note that while, on the one hand, the four areas are distinct, they are also the four key pieces of a larger pension governance and management puzzle. They revolve around the following questions:

- How clear are pension boards about the pension contracts they are overseeing and about the fiduciary duties of loyalty and evenhandedness that oversight involves?
- Does the board understand the difference between board governance and management accountability for achieving clearly agreed-on organizational goals? Can the board ask the right questions about strategy and its execution?
- Has the organization worked out a set of well-articulated investment beliefs that both the board and management understand and truly believe in? Is it clear which stakeholders are bearing what risks?
- Does the organization have the necessary resources to execute its strategic plan? If not, what are the blockages and what is the plan for removing them?

TABLE 10.1 Pension Fund Oversight and Management: What Really Matters?

Issue Question	Proportion of Responses
1. What are the more important oversight issues?	
a. Agency/context issues	44%
b. Governance effectiveness issues	36%
c. Investment beliefs/risk management issues	20%
2. What are the more important management issues?	
a. Strategic planning/management effectiveness	73%
b. Agency/context issues	15%
c. Investment beliefs/risk management issues	12%

Source: Rotman International Journal of Pension Management, Fall 2008.

TABLE 10.2 Pension Fund Governance and Management: Specific Challenges

Challenges and Associated Tasks

1. **Agency/Context Issues**
   a. Balancing stakeholder interests
   b. Understanding the legal/regulatory environment

2. **Oversight effectiveness issues**
   a. Appropriate skill/knowledge set for the board
   b. Clear delegation to management

3. **Investment beliefs/risk management issues**
   a. Understanding context-based risk and its management
   b. Informed investment beliefs and their relevance
   c. Shift to risk budget-based investment process

4. **Strategic planning/management effective issues**
   a. Resource planning, organization design, and compensation
   b. Clear delegation from the board
   c. Effective information technology (IT) systems

Source: Rotman International Journal of Pension Management, Fall 2008.

The relevance and importance of these questions is reinforced by the outcomes of the scoring process of the 45 survey statements. Table 10.3 compares the six lowest-scoring statements in 1997 and 2005. Note they are almost identical, and that, directly or indirectly, all six relate to board effectiveness problems. Specifically, they point to board selection and evaluation difficulties, to ineffective delegation to management, and to difficulties attracting and retaining top talent into the organization.

Recommendations for Action

Based on these findings, the article identified six opportunities for fixing the documented governance deficit that still existed in many pension organizations in the middle of the first decade of the 21st century:

1. **Redesign pension contracts** to eliminate any existing incompleteness, over-complexity, and/or unfairness problems. This is usually not something boards themselves can do, but their views will likely be carefully listened to by the contracting parties.
2. **Create a board skill/experience matrix** to reflect the reality that while pension boards need to be seen to be representative and hence legitimate, that is not enough. They must also possess the requisite collective skills and experience to be an effective governance body.

TABLE 10.3 The Six Lowest Scoring Statements in 1997 and 2005

Ranking	1997	2005	Ranking
40	Compensation levels in our organization are competitive.	Compensation levels in our organization are competitive.	40
41	My board of governors does not spend time assessing individual investment managers or investments.	My board of governors does not spend time assessing individual investment managers or investments.	41
42	My board of governors examines and improves its effectiveness on a regular basis.	My board of governors examines and improves its effectiveness on a regular basis.	42
43	Our fund has an effective process for selecting, developing, and terminating members of the board of governors.	I have the authority to retain and terminate investment managers.	43
44	I have the authority to retain and terminate investment managers.	Our fund has an effective process for selecting, developing, and terminating members of the board of governors.	44
45	Performance-based compensation is an important component of our organization design.	Performance-based compensation is an important component of our organization design.	45

Source: Rotman International Journal of Pension Management, Fall 2008.

3. **Initiate a board self-evaluation protocol** in order to identify and address weaknesses.
4. **Ensure clarity between board and management roles** because lack of clarity causes organizational gaps, compressions, and a great deal of frustration.
5. **Adopt a high-performance stance** throughout the organization and ensure it has the necessary human and technical resources to turn the aspiration into reality.
6. **Make board effectiveness a regulatory requirement** since it would be a simple matter for pension regulators to require that pension organizations annually disclose the steps they are taking to ensure that an effective governance function is in place.

A significant outcome of this work was the establishment of the week-long Rotman-ICPM Board Effectiveness Program (BEP) for pension and other long-horizon investment organizations in 2011. Its curriculum covers all six of the action opportunities in the previous list. The program has been offered seven times at this time of writing, resulting in 229 BEP graduates from 67 different organizations and 12 countries.[8]

DESCRIPTION OF THE 2014 SURVEY AND RESPONDENTS

Table 10.4 compares the demographics of the 2014 responding organizations with those of 1997 and 2005. Note that the 2014 responding group was considerably larger, less corporate, and more geographically diverse than the 1997 and 2005 groups.[9] Aggregate assets amounted to about USD $5 trillion. Figure 10.1 indicates that the people who completed the survey were generally senior, long-tenured pension organization executives.

2014 SURVEY FINDINGS ON GOVERNANCE

The earlier 1997 and 2005 surveys listed 45 statements about the governance, management, and operational effectiveness in their organizations. The 2014 survey was reduced to the 23 statements directly related to governance effectiveness. In the analysis that follows, the 2014 responses to these 23 statements were compared to the 1997 and 2005 responses to the same 23 statements.

TABLE 10.4 Demographics of the 1997, 2005, and 2014 Responding Groups

Survey Respondents	1997	2005	2014
Number of Respondents	80	81	81
United States	54%	44%	29%
Canada	46%	41%	28%
Europe		11%	31%
Asia, Australia, New Zealand		4%	14%
Public Sector	24%	41%	60%
Corporate	63%	38%	19%
Other	14%	21%	21%
Median Plan Size Billion USD	2.1	3.7	22.7

Source: KPA Advisory Services Ltd.

FIGURE 10.1 Demographics of the People Completing the 2014 Survey
Source: KPA Advisory Services Ltd.

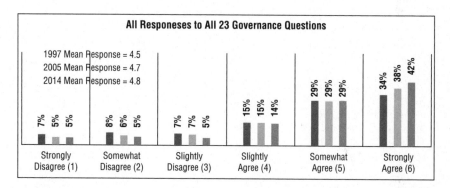

FIGURE 10.2 The Response Distributions in 1997, 2005, and 2014
Source: KPA Advisory Services Ltd.

Figure 10.2 displays the distribution of responses to the 23 governance statements in 1997, 2005, and 2014. The general bias toward high rather than low scores is a common phenomenon with this type of survey design. However, note that the average ranking marginally increased over the 17-year period (i.e., from 4.5 to 4.7 to 4.8), possibly indicating a marginal improvement in the effectiveness of pension boards over this period.

Table 10.5 compares the five highest-scoring statements in 2014 (i.e., indicating the highest satisfaction levels) with the five lowest-scoring statements (i.e., indicating the lowest satisfaction levels). Readers are invited to draw their own conclusions from Table 10.5. It seems to me there are elements of contradiction in these two sets of survey responses. For example, how is it possible for senior executives in pension organizations to, on the

TABLE 10.5 Areas of Highest vs. Lowest CEO Satisfaction

Highest Scores in Latest Survey	Mean Score 2014 Rank	Lowest Scores in Latest Survey	Mean Score 2014 Rank
My governing fiduciaries do a good job of representing the interests of plan stakeholders.	1	I have the authority to retain and terminate investment managers.	19
Developing our investment policy required considerable effort on the part of myself and the governing fiduciaries and it reflects our best thinking.	2	Compensation levels in our organization are competitive.	20
There is a clear allocation of responsibilities and accountabilities for fund decisions between the governing fiduciaries and the pension investment team.	3	My governing fiduciaries have superior capabilities, relevant knowledge, experience, intelligence, and skills necessary to do their work.	21
My governing fiduciaries hold me accountable for our performance and do not accept subpar performance.	4	Our fund has an effective process for selecting, developing, and terminating its governing fiduciaries.	22
My governing fiduciaries approve the necessary resources for us to do our work.	5	Performance-based compensation is an important component of our organizational design.	23

Source: KPA Advisory Services Ltd.

one hand, say they are getting the resources necessary to do their job, but on the other, say that compensation levels in the organization are uncompetitive? Similarly, how is it possible for senior executives in pension organizations to say that their boards hold them accountable for results, but on the other hand, that they meddle in operational matters (e.g., the hiring and firing of investment managers)?

Table 10.6 compares the five lowest-scoring statements in 1997, 2005, and 2014. Remarkably, they were the same five each time. To us, they offer the clearest indication of where the challenges with governance in the pensions field continue to lie, and the consequences they continue to lead to.

TABLE 10.6 The Five Lowest-Scoring Statements in 1997, 2005, and 2014

Lowest Scores over Three Surveys	Mean Score 1997 Rank	Mean Score 2005 Rank	Mean Score 2014 Rank
Compensation levels in our organization are competitive.	18	18	20
My governing fiduciaries examine and improve their own effectiveness on a regular basis.	20	20	17
I have the authority to retain and terminate investment managers.	22	21	19
Our fund has an effective process for selecting, developing, and terminating its governing fiduciaries.	21	22	22
Performance-based compensation is an important component of our organizational design.	23	23	23

Source: KPA Advisory Services Ltd.

Specifically, inadequate selection processes for board members continue to lead to ineffective board oversight protocols, which in turn continue to lead to board meddling in operational matters, and to inadequate resourcing in such key functional areas as investing.

Table 10.7 assesses the regional variations in how the 23 statements were ranked. The clear message here is that the European respondents scored a number of governance statements materially lower than their counterparts in North America and the Pacific Rim. At the other end of the spectrum, pension organizations in Canada, Australia, and New Zealand were more likely to feature a performance-based element in their compensation arrangements.

Additional Insights on Governance from Respondent Comments

In addition to ranking the 23 governance statements, survey participants were asked to address the question: "What do you see as the most important governance questions facing your board at this time?" This is what they told us:

Board Composition and Skills

- "Our board members should be more experienced and have more skills and intelligence."
- "Getting timely board appointments..."

TABLE 10.7 Regional Variations in Governance Quality*

Regional Variation from Mean Response to Questions	Europe	Canada	USA	Asia Australia New Zealand	All Plan Mean Response
Performance-based compensation is an important component of our organizational design.	–	+		+	3.7
My governing fiduciaries set a clear, appropriate, understandable, and well-communicated framework for values and ethics.	–				5.1
My governing fiduciaries set clear, appropriate, understandable and well-communicated standards for our organizational performance.	–				4.9
My governing fiduciaries do a good job of balancing over-control and under-control.	–				4.8
I have the necessary managerial authority to implement long-term asset mix/balance sheet risk policy within reasonable limits.	–		+		5.0
There is a clear allocation of responsibilities and accountabilities for fund decisions between the governing fiduciaries and the pension investment team.				–	5.4

*A plus sign indicates a response more than 0.5 above the mean. A minus sign indicates a response more than 0.5 below the mean.
Source: KPA Advisory Services Ltd.

- "Board turnover: too much among beneficiary reps and legislative reps. Too little among appointed investment experts. Control rests with state legislature."
- "Too much board turnover (due to term limits). Too much staff turnover (due to retirements). Even though policies are well documented, the loss of institutional memory and continuity has the potential for negative outcomes..."

- "The most important issue in governance...is illiteracy in committee members regarding pension fund management. Governance is in place but hardly operational..."
- "Selection of pension committee members with sufficient investment expertise..."
- "Education of board members..."
- "Getting new governing fiduciaries up to speed on pensions, pension investing, and fiduciary management (80 percent turnover)..."
- "...ensuring ongoing Board capacity for increasing oversight and risk management functions..."
- "...securing the ability of the board to actually handle the (increasing) responsibilities allocated to the board through regulatory changes..."

Board Process

- "The board spends too much time on administrative issues and individual approvals of investments and not enough time on overall strategic positioning of the portfolio and longer-term macro risks and opportunities for the fund and the business."
- "...blessed with a...truly outstanding group..., but they are collectively flying just above the tree tops instead of a higher fiduciary altitude. ... time is largely spent at the deal and manager level..."
- "Refused to delegate manager hiring and firing..."
- "...(management) can terminate while (board) investment committee retains managers."
- "Time management: spending more time on interviewing and meeting with investment managers versus strategic business decisions..."
- "Staying purposefully high level/strategic in their decision making and understand/be comfortable with the importance of clear delineation of responsibilities between the board and the organization...."
- "The board spends too much time on administrative issues and individual approvals of investments and not enough time on overall strategic positioning of the portfolio and longer-term macro risks and opportunities for the fund and the business."

Compensation

- "The design and implementation of market-competitive compensation plans to attract and retain high-caliber investment and senior management talent. As (a public entity we are) subject to restraint legislation and policies affecting compensation and business-related expenses."
- "Alternative compensation models: no appetite to review or discuss these."

These respondent comments strongly reinforce the insights extracted from the survey statement rankings.

MAJOR GOVERNANCE CONCERNS REMAIN

In the end, while there is some evidence of improvement in the governance of pension organizations since 1997, the key 2014 survey finding is that the major concerns about how board members are selected and trained, about the effectiveness of board oversight processes, and about the ability to attract and retain key executive and professional skills remain. Much remains to be done to materially raise the effectiveness of the governance function in pension organizations.

CHAPTER 11

The Evolving Meaning of Fiduciary Duty

Is Your Board of Trustees Keeping Up?

"Years of focus on the duty of prudence by fiduciaries has generated myopic investment herding behaviors, undermined intergenerational pension equity, and disrupted attention to the duty of loyalty and impartiality . . . ."
—From "Reclaiming Fiduciary Duty Balance" by Hawley, Johnson, and Waitzer (*Rotman International Journal of Pension Management*, 2011)

"The duty of impartiality requires fiduciaries to consider and balance the divergent interests of beneficiaries . . . including the intergenerational implications of their decisions . . . ."
—From "Reconnecting the Financial Sector and the Real Economy: A Plan for Action" by Waitzer and Sarro (*Rotman International Journal of Pension Management*, 2014)

PENSION BOARDS LAG COURTS IN INTERPRETING 21ST-CENTURY FIDUCIARY DUTY

One of the most important, and possibly most underappreciated research projects funded by the Rotman International Centre for Pension Management (ICPM) over the course of the last four years was on the evolving meaning of "fiduciary duty" for boards of pension organizations in the 21st century. This work was conducted by legal scholars Jim Hawley, Keith Johnson, Doug Sarro, and Ed Waitzer. Their work led to the two articles in the *Rotman International Journal of Pension Management* (RIJPM) quoted earlier.[1] The two quotes capture the essence of their message: Pension boards lag "the trajectory of the law" in their understanding of their fiduciary duties. Boards have some serious catchup work to do.

This chapter summarizes the conclusions of the ICPM fiduciary duties project, and sets out a work plan for pension boards that want to keep up with the evolving meaning of fiduciary duties in the 21st century, rather than suffering the regret of having to play catchup in possibly unpleasant circumstances a few years down the road.

WHY NOW?

Why now? The authors point to four "inflection point" catalysts that argue for proactive action by the boards of pension organizations now, rather than reactive action later:

1. **The Growth of Pension Funds:** Collectively, the global pension fund sector has become a major global financial force, with assets somewhere in the $30T–40T range. The growing sovereign wealth fund and the foundation/endowment fund sectors add materially to these numbers. Collectively, these massive asset pools represent the multigenerational financial interests of hundreds of millions if not billions of beneficiaries. Collectively, the investment decisions of these pools directly impact both how the global financial markets work, and how the global real economy works. With their scale and necessarily long-term perspective to understand and meet the retirement income needs of their members, pension organizations should be highly motivated to ensure they understand and are in fact fulfilling their fiduciary duties.

2. **The Pervasive Influence of Agents and Emphasis on the Short-Term:** While the investment policy documents of pension organizations tend to emphasize long-termism, actual practices continue to reflect short-termism in many cases. This dichotomy is reinforced through multiple channels: the media, how performance is measured, how incentive compensation is structured, and through the presence of multiple intermediary agents (e.g., consultants, money managers). There is no natural alignment between the financial interests of these agents and those of trust beneficiaries. In such an increasingly complex world, fiduciaries are seriously challenged to articulate the best short- and long-term interests of current and future beneficiaries, and to demonstrate they are actually serving these interests in a balanced manner through their investment policies.

3. **Over-Reliance on Simplistic Investment Theories:** While investment theories such as the Efficient Markets Hypothesis (EMH) are elegant,

the assumptions behind them are far from reflecting reality. For example, in the case of the EMH, material information about individual investments is not always known by all investors all the time; further, information that is generally known is not always interpreted identically by all investors, and is not always accurately reflected in asset prices. Also, investors are not always rational, and risk tolerances are not always stable. Investment returns are not independently and identically distributed. As a result, while events like the Global Financial Crisis (GFC) cannot happen in an EMH world, they do happen in the real world. The point is that attempting to exercise the fiduciary duties of prudence, loyalty, and impartiality by taking the assumptions and implications of the EMH as reality is not defensible conduct today. The board of trustees has an obligation to understand the world as it is, and not as it is posited in order to create elegant investment theory.

4. **Recent Legal Responses to Financial System Dysfunction:** The four legal experts in the two RIJPM articles point to a number of recent legal opinions and actions that bear on the evolving meaning of "fiduciary duty" in the 21st century. In a pensions dispute, the U.S. Supreme Court ruled that fiduciary duty requires "trustees to take impartial account of all beneficiaries...both present and future." The Dutch Pension Act requires fiduciaries to take into account the interests of all plan stakeholders in setting policy and making decisions. The GFC prompted a number of actions against financial institutions and individuals working in these institutions for fiduciary misbehavior. In contrast, the Supreme Court of Canada recently ruled against a class action initiated by a corporation's bondholders against its board of directors, ruling that the board had made reasonable decisions reflecting not only the interests of the corporation's creditors and shareholders, but also the corporation's broader obligations "as a good corporate citizen." Emerging out of these opinions and judgments is a new "reasonable expectations" standard for the exercise of fiduciary duty. This emerging view contrasts sharply with the historical view that attention to fiduciary duty could be demonstrated by engaging in a standard box-checking exercise drawn up by legal counsel.

There is a fifth "why now" argument I would add to the four offered by the cited legal experts:

5. **Passive Acceptance of Unsustainable Pension Designs:** Prior chapters have expressed my discomfort with the traditional defined-benefit (DB) and defined-contribution (DC) pension designs. Neither design fully acknowledges the differing needs of the young and the old today, as well as the financial interests of the young and the old of tomorrow.

As a result, these traditional designs are problematic in a number of ways (e.g., the one-size-fits-all problem, the fuzzy property rights problem, the fuzzy risk definition and allocation problem). If the duty of impartiality requires pension fiduciaries to consider and balance the divergent interests of various classes of beneficiaries and other risk-bearing stakeholders (including the intergenerational implications of their decisions), then it is reasonable to expect that these fiduciaries also have a duty to test the pension design of the plan they are governing for its long-term sustainability and for fairness regarding all plan stakeholder groups, present and future.

After the "why now" question comes the "what now" question. How should pension organizations individually, and collectively at the national and global pension community levels, respond to these five catalysts for action? Here are some responses to these questions.

RESPONSES AT THE PENSION ORGANIZATION LEVEL

Nothing much will happen at the organizational level unless its board of trustees (led by the board chair) is prepared to own the fiduciary duties file. If that is the case, the following six-point checklist will be helpful:

1. **Pension Design:** Do we have a fair, sustainable, understandable pension formula? How can we best address this question? What would we do if our formula doesn't pass a reasonable fair/sustainable/understandable test?
2. **Stakeholder Communications:** Are we clear about who our stakeholders are? Do we communicate with them effectively about pension design? About the value the pension organization is creating for them? How do we know our communication strategies are effective?
3. **Organization Design:** Do we have a cost-effective organization that produces value for risk and value for money as its key functions? How can we best address this question? What would we do if our organization doesn't benchmark well in its key functions, using credible metrics?
4. **Board Effectiveness:** How effective are we as a board? Do we have the right mix of skills and experience? Are we seen as trustworthy by our plan stakeholders? Are we public-minded? Do we measure our own effectiveness and improve our own performance?
5. **Risk Management:** What risks do we need to measure and manage? Do we have the people, protocols, and technology to do this well? If not, what are we going to do about it?

6. **Investment Beliefs and Policies:** Do we have an investment program geared to generate plan member wealth through long-horizon return compounding? Is it working well? How do we know? Do we have an investment program geared to meeting the payment obligations to retirees? Is it working well? How do we know?

While living by this six-point checklist would undoubtedly produce a good score on the organizational fiduciary duties scale, there is another fiduciary duty dimension that also needs attention.

COLLECTIVE RESPONSES AT THE NATIONAL AND GLOBAL LEVELS

In their 2014 "Reconnecting the Financial Sector to the Real Economy" article, Waitzer and Sarro propose four specific initiatives that financial institutions such as pension organizations, as well as lawmakers and regulators, could collectively undertake to strengthen the expectations and responsibilities attached to the fulfilling of their fiduciary duties:

1. **Foster Win–Win Collaborations:** There is a trust dilemma in situations where there is no clear short-term net (i.e., after-cost) benefit for a single organization to become a first mover on an issue that may be of great long-term collective benefit. The way out of such a dilemma is for multiple parties to agree on the importance of the issue, and to share the cost of addressing it. Examples of such collaborations already exist (e.g., ICGN, PRI, WEF, CII, CCGG, Eumedion, NAPF, ASFA, ACSI, and ICPM).[2] The recent FCLT (Focusing Capital on the Long-Term) initiative opens up the prospect of direct investor/investee collaboration on such issues as fostering a long-term perspective in investing and the measurement of organization success.[3]
2. **Create Legal Mechanisms to Protect Future Generations:** A possible measure to fight short-termism in political decision-making is to establish a commissioner or ombudsman to represent the rights of future generations. Such mechanisms already exist in the environmental and human rights spheres. More day-to-day decision-making could be delegated to nonpartisan, independent agencies or to senior administrators with guaranteed term lengths.
3. **Rethink Legislation:** Much post-GFC financial legislation and regulation has spawned complicated rules breeding complicated systems, which in turn feed a box-checking "is it legal?" mentality. A far-better approach would be to specify far-fewer broad, coherent, concise, enforceable rules

that focus on core expectations. Courts can also play a constructive role here through emphasizing the reasonable expectations principle.

4. **Reassert the Social Utility of the Financial Sector:** The GFC and the events that followed it greatly exacerbated the lack of public trust and understanding of the financial system writ large. Many years of hard work will be required to regain that public trust, and to enhance public understanding of the vital role the financial sector in general, and the pensions sector in particular, play in mobilizing capital and in pricing and allocating financial risks in a well-functioning economy. The CFA Institute's "Future of Finance" initiative is an example of the work already underway to address this challenge.

In the exercise of their fiduciary duties, pension boards of trustees need to be aware of these collective national and global initiatives, and they need to understand the roles their organizations are playing (or should be playing) in moving one or more of these four initiatives toward successful implementation.

DOING THE RIGHT THING

In conclusion, Waitzer and Sarro argue that too much of board governance in the financial sector has focused, and continues to focus, on doing things right, that is, on technical compliance with whatever rules exist at the time a decision needs to be made. They argue a fundamental mind shift is required. Instead of focusing on doing things right, boards must begin to focus on doing the right thing. In their view, this will be the basis on which their decisions and actions will increasingly be judged, both in courts of law and in the court of public opinion.

So doing the right thing, based on balancing the financial interests of all relevant stakeholder groups, is the new 21st-century standard for testing the proper fulfillment of fiduciary duty. It is all a board of trustees can reasonably be expected to do. Is your board meeting this standard?

CHAPTER 12

Pension Organizations and Integrated Reporting

Improving Stakeholder Communications

"Australia's largest super funds have thrown their support behind a new reporting system .... The Integrated Reporting Pension Funds Network is being taken around the world ...."
—*The Australian*, July 15, 2014

THE <IR> INITIATIVE

The International Integrated Reporting Council (IIRC) formed the Integrated Reporting <IR> framework initiative in 2010 to build a globally accepted framework to produce clear, comparable information about how business organizations create value over time.[1] Remarkably, <IR> has come to be supported by leaders across the international corporate, investment, accounting, regulatory, and academic communities. In just a few years, the <IR> initiative has produced a discussion paper on integrated reporting (2011), a prototype framework for integrative reporting (2012), a pilot program made up of a business network and an investor network (2012), and a detailed consultation draft on the proposed <IR> framework in early 2013. All this led to the issuance of the International <IR> framework in December 2013.

The leadership of the international pension management community should support this initiative. Not just because it will lead to more useful investor information about how investee corporations are creating value over the short, medium, and longer term, but also because the <IR>

framework is a useful tool for pension organizations themselves. Many pension organizations could do a better job of informing their own stakeholder groups (i.e., pensioners, workers, employers, investors, regulators, governments) on what they are doing to create value. As their decisions impact future stakeholder groups, too, relevant information about these impacts should be conveyed as well.

The Australian indicates pension organizations have indeed begun to embrace the <IR> message.[2] Under the umbrellas of AIST (Australian Institute of Superannuation Trustees) and ACSI (Australian Council of Superannuation Investors), a new <IR> Pension Fund Network has been formed by five Australian funds with a vision to become a multinational body. The two key focus points for the new network are: first, integrated report preparation for pension organizations themselves; and second, interacting with the international <IR> initiative and other relevant bodies (e.g., regulators) in the development and use of integrated reports.

This chapter summarizes the key features of the new international <IR> framework. It also assesses the Integrated Annual Report prepared by the South African Sentinel Mining Industry Retirement Fund in the context of the new framework. While this integrated report clearly demonstrates the power of the new initiative, I point to three areas where future versions could be improved.

The New International <IR> Framework—Guiding Principles

The framework sets out seven guiding principles in the creation of an integrated report:

1. **Strategic Focus and Future Orientation:** Explain how organizational strategies will create stakeholder value in the shorter and long terms and the related use of capital resources.
2. **Connectivity of Information:** Paint holistic picture of how various factors integrate to create value over time.
3. **Stakeholder Relationships:** Describe nature of stakeholders, their relationships to the organization, and the organization's accountability to them.
4. **Materiality:** Provide information on matters impacting the organization's ability to create value over time.
5. **Conciseness:** Use no more words than necessary.
6. **Reliability and Completeness:** Include all material matters with balance and accuracy.
7. **Consistency and Comparability:** Present information to enhance comparability over time, and to other organizations to extent possible.

These seven Guiding Principles naturally lead to eight content elements.

The New International <IR> Framework—Content Elements

Integrated reports should cover the following linked (i.e., not mutually exclusive) elements:

1. **Organizational Overview and External Environment:** What does the organization do, and what are its context and circumstances?
2. **Governance:** How does the organization's governance structure support value creation?
3. **Business Model:** How does the organization create stakeholder value over time?
4. **Risks and Opportunities:** What are the key risks and opportunities, and how are they addressed by the organization?
5. **Strategy and Resource Allocation:** Where does the organization want to go, and how is it going to get there?
6. **Performance:** What did the organization achieve over the period in the context of its strategic objectives, and what were the impacts on capital resources?
7. **Outlook:** What challenges does the organization face in achieving its strategic objectives? What are the implications for its business model and future performance?
8. **Basis of Presentation:** What is the determination process for deciding which matters to include in the integrated report?

How could these guiding principles and content elements translate into an integrated report for a pension organization? A South African pension plan is leading the way.

SOUTH AFRICA'S SENTINEL MINING INDUSTRY RETIREMENT FUND

Sentinel is a multi-employer pension plan in South Africa that completed a major merger on July 1, 2013. It now involves 102 employers and covers about 90,000 workers and pensioners. It is a hybrid plan in the sense that plan contributions are deposited into worker retirement accounts, and accumulated retirement savings are converted into annuities at retirement. The integrated annual report for the fiscal year ending June 30, 2013, is Sentinel's second one. In its introduction the organization acknowledges: "...this integrated reporting process is a journey, and this is a further step towards providing a balanced, accurate, and clear account of our performance relative to our strategy."[3]

The Sentinel report has six major sections in the following chronological order:

1. **Mission:** A short statement of why the organization exists and the purpose of the Integrated Annual Report[4]
2. **Key Organization Performance Highlights and Milestones:** Key events/accomplishments in FY 2012/13 and key organizational milestones going back to inception in 1946, mainly graphs and photos[5]
3. **Who We Are and What We Do:** Fund history; plan design; investment structure; stakeholder communications; organization design; board of trustees composition; and the meeting attendance records of its members[6]
4. **Board Chair and CEO Reviews:** Award-winning investment and pension operations outcomes despite difficult economic and financial markets conditions; successful completion of major merger; growth opportunities beyond the SA mining sector; unique basket of investment and pension product offerings; in-house member advisory service; strong product quality and risk controls; strong governance principles and practices; concerns about evolving government social security policies[7]
5. **Board of Trustees Report:** A matrix of Sentinel's six major stakeholder groups, their key issues, the organization's response/engagement strategy and outcomes, statements of four organizational objectives, the strategies through which they will be achieved, and key performance indicators to measure success; strategic performance review; a matrix of eight areas in which risks will be defined, monitored, and mitigated; four possibilities where risks might be converted into opportunities[8]
6. **Statutory Financial, Actuarial, and Administrative Reports:** Report of the independent auditor; financial statements and notes to the financial statements; report of the independent actuary; administrative information on contacts, addresses, and external service providers[9]

So how does Sentinel's Integrated Annual Report for 2013 stack up against the new <IR> framework of guiding principles and content elements? That is the question addressed next.

PRACTICE VS. THEORY

A first observation is that there are many similarities between Sentinel's Integrated Annual Report and any good "regular" annual report of a pension organization. So what is different? It is how the Board of Trustees integrated information about who Sentinel's key stakeholder groups are with the organizational objectives, strategies, outcomes, and with how risks were defined, monitored, and mitigated. The use of matrixes was especially effective in integrating information.

So, for example, the stakeholder matrix has five integrative elements:

1. **Stakeholder:** Seven stakeholder groups were identified (workers, pensioners, employers, organized labor, government, service suppliers, regulator).
2. **Key Issues/Concerns:** These were identified for each of the six stakeholder groups (e.g., for pensioners: "a sustainable pension that keeps track with inflation").
3. **Response:** Solutions were targeted to the key issue/concern (e.g., for employers wishing for benefits that meet employee needs: "a flexible benefit product with participation flexibility").
4. **Engagement Strategy:** Methods were devised through which the chosen responses were going to be delivered (e.g., website, newsletters, special studies, face-to-face meetings).
5. **Outcome:** Successful outcomes were envisioned (e.g., increased member satisfaction, enhanced reputation, stronger working relationships, and better government policies).

Similarly, the risk management matrix has two integrative elements:

1. **Risk to Be Managed:** The matrix describes eight risks to be managed (e.g., "longevity risk" is the possibility that actual average pensioner longevity exceeds expectations, leading to underfunding in the pensioner portfolio).
2. **Control:** The matrix describes how each of the eight risks is going to be managed (e.g., "We will manage 'liquidity risk' through ALM and cash-flow analyses and maintaining an adequate liquidity pool").

These two matrix examples show how integrated reporting forces integrative thinking about organizational objectives and strategies that should result in better outcomes. The Sentinel organization is to be congratulated for their impressive progress in what they called their integrative reporting journey.

THREE POSSIBLE NEXT STEPS IN THE JOURNEY

Sentinel noted that the 2013 Report was "...a further step towards providing a balanced, accurate, and clear account of our performance relative to our strategy." This chapter ends with the three ideas that could be considered as future steps on the integrative reporting journey.

1. **Actual Income Replacement Outcomes:** Given the purpose of the organization, there is one outcome that should stand above all others: maintaining workers' standard of living after they stop working. The report sets this target out as an income replacement rate of 75 percent of salary with 80 percent post-work inflation indexation. However, we could not find any information in the report as to whether this goal actually has been, is being, or will be achieved over time.

2. **Pensioner Annuity Balance Sheet:** While the report clearly states that at retirement "a monthly pension benefit (annuity) is purchased from the fund," there is no pensioner annuity balance sheet to be found in the report. Instead, there is an asset-only pensioner portfolio and a one-page actuarial report that simply states: "The pensioners have a separate pool of assets .... This pool was 113.9% funded as at 30 June 2013 ...." We were unable to find any support for this statement anywhere in the report. Given its materiality to the sustainability of the Sentinel enterprise, we would have expected significant support for this assertion in the report (e.g., the basis for the projected future pension benefits, the discount rate employed to estimate the accrued liability, the mortality table employed, and the target funded ratio to be achieved).

3. **Integration of Investment Strategies and Outcomes:** The report has separate sections on achieved fund returns versus benchmarks, and on its Responsible Investment (RI)/SRI activities. For example, it reports one-, three-, and five-year returns for its four major investment options versus CPI and market index benchmarks. It also reports in considerable detail on its RI/SRI program in the form of active proxy voting and corporate engagement activities and its outcomes. What we could not find in the report were any explicit linkages between the investment strategies of Sentinel's team of external investment managers and the organization's aspiration to be a leader in the RI/SRI space. For example, what kind of investments do its managers favor? Are they high-conviction investors? How have they interacted with investee organizations? Maybe most tellingly, what were their portfolio turnover rates? We could not find answers to these questions in the report.

Again, *Sentinel*'s 2013 Integrated Annual Report is an impressive document. However, steps could be taken to make an even more impressive one in the years ahead. Meanwhile, a number of thought-leading funds have already committed to join *Sentinel* on its integrative reporting journey. Peter Drucker once observed that "information is data endowed with relevance and purpose."[10] Integrated information makes it even more so.

Measuring Value-for-Money in Pension Organizations

A New Look

"What gets measured gets managed."
—Peter Drucker

DEFINING SUCCESS

A speaking invitation from the Australian Superannuation Funds Association (ASFA) offered an opportunity to address the fundamental question: How should pension organizations define, measure, and report success? There are two contexts in which the question can be addressed:

1. Pension organizations should measure and report the actual financial outcomes vs. targets for the members they are serving.
2. Pension organizations should measure and report value for money outcomes in the delivery of member services such as investing and benefit administration. They should also identify and report on the drivers of these value-creation processes.

An important framing for these two contexts is the Integrated Reporting (<IR>) initiative described in Chapter 12. The chapter noted that an international <IR> Pension Fund Network is being created to adapt the framework to a pensions context, and that the framework offers a case study on the application of the <IR> model to the pensions sector. Chapters 7, 8, and

9 have already expanded on the first of the two contexts just listed. This chapter does so on the second one.

MEASURING VALUE-FOR-MONEY

A functional "value-for-money" measurement framework has three key elements:

1. An unambiguous definition of what constitutes value and an ability to measure it
2. An unambiguous definition of cost and an ability to measure it
3. A database that permits the evaluation of value-for-money outcomes in the context of a peer group of organizations delivering the same service

Previous chapters noted that the CEM Benchmarking organization has been applying this three-element framework in international pensions space since 1991.

On the investing side, CEM defines value in two ways:

Measure #1: The difference between actual fund return net of costs, and the return on a passive investible portfolio with similar risk characteristics.

Measure #2: The difference between actual fund return net of cost, and the return on a passive investible low-risk liability portfolio that approximates the pension organization's future payment obligations. It defines costs as the total cost (both internal and outsourced) of operating the organization's investment function, expressed in basis points relative to fund assets. In the second value definition, risk is defined as the return volatility between the actual fund net return and the return on the liability portfolio.

On the member services/benefit administration side, CEM defines value as:

A "service score," which is an index between 0 and 100. It captures composite member services/benefit administration quality based on performance in such functions as speed and accuracy of member transactions, the quality of member communications, and disaster recovery capability. Cost is defined as the total cost (both internal and outsourced) of operating the member services/benefit administration function, expressed on a per-member basis.

Some examples will make these definitions tangible.

Ten-Year Value-for-Money Investment Results

Figure 13.1 displays the value-for-money investment results for all 125 pension funds in the CEM database with continuous data for the 2004–2013 period. As defined earlier, net value-added (NVA) on the vertical axis is the difference between a fund's actual return net of cost, and the return on a passive investible portfolio with similar risk characteristics. Excess investment cost is the difference between a fund's actual average 10-year investment operating cost and the 125 fund average. The average NVA for the 125 funds over the 2004–2013 period was 0.1 percent and the range was from −1.7 percent to 1.5 percent. The average operating cost was 0.5 percent of assets, and the range 0.1 to 1.4 percent.

If you were a board member of one of these pension organizations, what kinds of questions would Figure 13.1 prompt? Here are three that come to mind:

1. Is there any correlation between NVA and excess investment cost in Figure 13.1? (The answer is no.)
2. If you can achieve the same long-term net investment results with high or low cost structures, what would be the rationale for choosing to operate with a high cost structure?

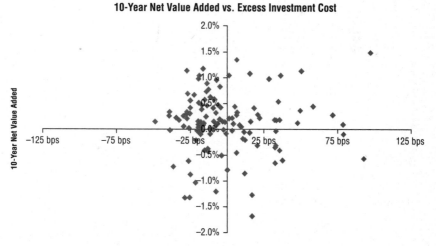

10-Year Net Value Added vs. Excess Investment Cost

10-Year Average Investment Costs/Holdings (less Average)

FIGURE 13.1 10-Year Net Value Added versus Excess Investment Cost
Source: CEM Benchmarking Inc.

3. Other than operating with relatively low cost structures, what do the funds in the upper-left quadrant (i.e., the positive 10-year NVA genera- tors with relatively low investment cost structures) have in common?

These questions would make good agenda items for the next board meeting.

Ten-Year Value-for-Risk Investment Results

Figure 13.2 displays the 10-year value-for-risk investment results for the 75 pension organizations that also provided CEM with a liability-based benchmark portfolio. As defined before, the value metric now is the differ- ence between the actual fund return net of cost, and the return on a passive investible low-risk liability portfolio approximating the pension organiza- tion's future payment obligations. The risk metric is the return volatility between the actual fund net return, and the return on the liability portfolio. The average net risk premium (i.e., net fund return – liability return) earned over the 2004–2013 period by these funds was 2.2 percent, and the range was from 0.1 to 4.4 percent. The average asset–liability (A-L) mismatch risk was 12.5 percent, and the range was from 8.1 to 16.0 percent.

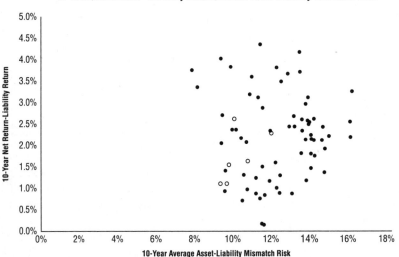

FIGURE 13.2   10-Year {Net Return–Liability Return} versus Asset-Liability Mismatch Risk
Source: CEM Benchmarking Inc.

If you were a board member of one of these pension organizations, what kinds of questions would Figure 13.2 prompt? Here are three that come to mind:

1. Is there any correlation between the net risk premiums earned and the A–L mismatch risk metrics in Figure 13.2? (The answer is no).
2. How do the 2004–2013 net risk premium realizations compare with much longer-term historical realizations? (The answer is that they are more modest.)
3. What is our current A–L mismatch risk exposure? Should we raise or lower it? Why? Why not?

The chapters in the Pension Design section of this book (Part II) addressed an even broader question: Should all plan members have the same mismatch risk exposure? This requires thinking through the respective preferences of young workers just entering the pension plan, and retirees dependent on a safe monthly pension income. Logically, young workers should prefer a long-term wealth-creating strategy, while retirees should want payment safety. This leads to the conclusion that serving both needs requires separate wealth-creation and payment-safety instruments. In terms of performance measurement, the wealth-creating strategy should be benchmarked vs. a passive strategy with similar risk characteristics, the payment-safety strategy vs. a liability portfolio that approximates the accrued payment obligations. These obligations could have legal stature in a defined-benefit (DB) context, or be simply aspirational in a defined-ambition (DA) or target-benefit (TB) context.

Measuring Value-for-Money in Member Services/Benefit Administration

Figure 13.3 displays the 2013 value-for-money member services/benefit administration results for the 51 pension organizations that provided CEM with the requisite information. The value metric now is a service score, an index between 0 and 100, which captures composite member services/benefit administration quality based on performance in such functions as member transactions, member communications, and disaster recovery capability. Cost is the total cost (both internal and outsourced) of operating the member services/benefit administration function, expressed on a per-member basis, all converted to U.S. dollars. The average service score attained in 2013 was 75, and the range was 51 to 92. The average cost per member was $133, and the range was from $37 to $380 (three cost experiences are not shown in Figure 13.3 as they exceeded an excess cost per member of $150).

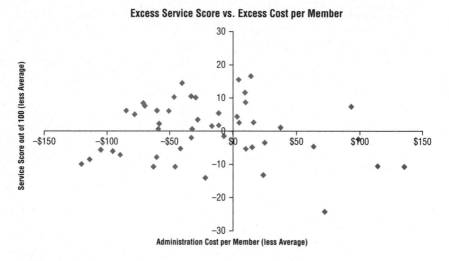

FIGURE 13.3 Excess Service Score versus Excess Cost per Member
Source: CEM Benchmarking Inc.

If you were a board member of one of these pension organizations, what kinds of questions would Figure 13.3 prompt? Here are three that come to mind:

1. Is there any correlation between the service scores and excess cost per member in Figure 13.3? (The answer is no.)
2. If you can effectively achieve the same service scores with low or high cost structures, what would be the rationale for choosing to operate with a high cost structure? Or is the high cost structure due to location or a lack of scale?
3. Other than operating with relatively low cost structures, what do the funds in the upper-left quadrant (i.e., the high service score/low cost generators) have in common?

Again, these questions would make good agenda items for the next board meeting.

Measuring Value for Money and Risk in Pensions

This chapter commenced by asserting that pension organizations should measure and report value for money and risk outcomes in the delivery of investment and benefit administration services to members. This in turn requires three things:

1. An unambiguous definition of what constitutes value and an ability to measure it
2. An unambiguous definition of cost and an ability to measure it
3. A database that permits the evaluation of value-for-money outcomes in the context of a peer group of organizations delivering the same service

Figures 13.1, 13.2, and 13.3 demonstrated the value of the resulting benchmarking processes. They put pension boards in a position to ask the really tough questions about the amount of value the organization is producing, and about the cost and risks being incurred along the way.

CHAPTER 14

Measuring Value for Money in Private Markets Investing

Why Investors Need a Standard Protocol

"Partnership agreements outlining private equity firms' practices are as closely guarded as the recipe for Coca-Cola..."
—Gretchen Morgenson, *New York Times*, May 4, 2015

A WAKEUP CALL FOR PENSION FUNDS

Gretchen Morgenson's article, "Hidden Fees Take a Big Bite Out of Pension Savings," continues to reverberate throughout the global pension investment industry.[1] The article effectively accuses many pension funds of channeling complex concoctions of fees into various forms of private markets investment schemes without being fully aware of the total costs being incurred.

This is a fiduciary no-no. A fundamental duty of pension fund boards is to ensure that all fund expenditures pass a reasonable value for money test. Stating the obvious, if the total amount of money being spent to produce value for beneficiaries in private markets investing is not known, conducting a reasonable value for money test becomes an impossibility. Arguably, such a situation constitutes a breach of fiduciary duty.

If measuring the total amount of money being spent isn't enough of a challenge, measuring the value that the resulting investment is producing is no cakewalk, either. Without markets that value investments on a daily basis, protocols must be devised to assign reasonable values to private investments over time. It is well known that there can be significant gaps between these reasonably calculated values and what the investment's market value might be if it traded in a public market. While these valuation gaps are unavoidable realities in private markets investing, care must be taken to eradicate systematic biases in how private markets investments are valued, and how returns are calculated over time.

The goal of this chapter is to identify concrete steps that can be taken to close the gap between current private markets value for money measurement practices in the pensions investment industry today, and those that would meet a reasonable fiduciary duty standards test.

MEASURING VALUE FOR MONEY IN PRIVATE MARKETS INVESTING: A RETROSPECTIVE

A study by Phalippou and Gottschalg (2009) provides both a practical value for money measurement framework for private markets investing, as well as estimates of historical private equity investment results using that framework.[2] They report that by their estimates, total fees on private equity investments may have averaged as high as 7 percent per year of capital invested. In a more recent private study, Phalippou offers a "back of the envelope" calculation to make the historical 7 percent average cost experience more concrete.

The average leveraged buyout (LBO) fund generated some 18 percent per annum before any fees in the cited study, which reduces to a net 11 percent after the 7 percent of capital invested fees. Disaggregating the 7 percent total fee, base management fees are usually 2 percent of capital committed payable in advance for the first five years, and then 2 percent of capital invested.

The capital is called linearly over the first five years, meaning that half of the capital committed is invested at any point in time during these five years. This implies management fees are 4 percent of capital invested during five years and then 2 percent of capital invested for the next five years. Assume the fund keeps all the investments until year ten. Management fees would then be 3 percent per annum. Next comes carried interest, which might be 20 percent of 18 − 3 percent (i.e., an additional 3 percent per annum). On top of that, additional fees such as portfolio company fees and the unreimbursed portion of fund-level transaction and operating costs add a further 1 percent per annum. Finally, there are also internal costs for the pension fund investor (e.g., for such functions as due diligence, accounting, etc.).

This is how the 18 percent gross of fees historical private equity return becomes 11 percent net of fees. Historically, this 11 percent is not far from the average experience of publicly traded small-cap equity return over most decades in most regions of the developed world. So it seems that, on average, private equity investing has historically produced materially higher gross returns than investing in public equities. However, on average, the excess returns have wholly accrued to the general partners of the private equity pools in the form of a complex mix of fees, leaving the limited partners (i.e., pension funds) with no better returns than they could have earned in the public equity markets.

MEASURING VALUE FOR MONEY: FROM RETROSPECTIVE TO PROSPECTIVE

Apologists might respond to the Phalippou–Gottschalg study findings by observing that, on average, private equity net returns were no worse than those in public equity markets. However, that was only because both markets produced extraordinarily high historical returns. Looking ahead, Chapter 20 shows that 7 percent is a reasonable long-term return expectation for public equity markets today. Prospectively, how much higher will the average expected gross return on private equity be today? Can we assume the same historical spread of 7 percent, leading to an expected gross return on private equity of 14 percent today? (i.e., 7 + 7). It seems to us that it is more realistic to assume the same historical proportional outperformance (i.e., by a factor of 18/11 = 1.6). In the latter case, the expected gross return on private equity becomes 11 percent today (i.e., 7 × 1.6), taking the historical 7 percent gross return spread down to a prospective 4 percent.

Now let's attach Phalippou's "back of the envelope" private equity fee formula to these new expected gross return expectations. The 3 percent base fee stays the same. The 1 percent in additional fees stays the same. The new carried interest calculation is 20 percent of 11 − 3 percent, which amounts to about 2 percent. All this takes the total general partner fee "take" down to 6 percent of capital invested from the historical 7 percent (i.e., 3 + 1 + 2). However, with the new 11 percent gross return expectation, a 6 percent fee takes the net return expectation to 5 percent, well below our calculated 7 percent for the public equity markets.

The key point here is that fully understanding the fee structures of private markets is critical to the future success prospects of pension funds investing in these markets. The calculations suggest that these success prospects appear to be dim today without a major restructuring of the historical private markets fee structures.

THE CEM STANDARDIZED MEASUREMENT INITIATIVE

CEM Benchmarking Inc. recently launched an initiative to create a standardized protocol for capturing the total costs associated with private markets

TABLE 14.1 Average Net Private Equity Returns in the CEM Database (1996–2012)

	Internal	Direct LP	Fund of Funds
Annualized Net Return	12.2%	9.6%	7.2%
Annualized Benchmark Return	8.7%	9.4%	8.8%
Annualized Net Value Added	3.5%	0.2%	−1.6%

Source: CEM Benchmarking Inc.

investing.[3] In its position paper, CEM reports three sets of net private equity return averages for its participating funds over the 1996–2012 period. They are displayed in Table 14.1. The distinction between the three return sets is implementation style: (1) internally managed (low cost), (2) outsourced/direct LP (higher cost), and (3) outsourced/fund of funds (highest cost). Note the direct link between realized net returns and implementation style: As costs rise, net returns fall. Also note the consistency between the Phalippou–Gottschalg findings and the CEM findings: On average, due to the high fee levels, the two outsourcing strategies produced no (or even negative) net value for fund beneficiaries over the long term.[4]

The CEM position paper proposes the allocation of the costs associated with private equity investing into four categories: management fees, carry/performance fees, other fees, and internal costs (e.g., for insourced management, monitoring, etc.). Historically, CEM has only been able to capture the management fee and internal cost components from its clients. However, the Dutch regulator DNB has begun to require Dutch pension funds to provide full cost information in the four categories. Table 14.2 sets out the preliminary results for 2012/2013.

The CEM paper notes that the reported Dutch management fees of 1.9 percent are very much in line with the average private equity

TABLE 14.2 Average Dutch Private Equity Cost Experience Applied to a $3B Portfolio (2012–2013)

Cost Type	Average Rate	Average Amount
Management Fees	1.9%	$57M
Carry/Performance Fees	1.5%	$45M
Other Fees	0.4%	$12M
Internal Costs	0.1%	$3M
Total Costs	3.9%	$117M

Source: CEM Benchmarking Inc.

management fee experience for the entire CEM database of 1.8 percent. However, as foreshadowed in the Phalippou–Gottschalg paper, the reported management fees represent less than half of the total costs of the typical private equity investment program. So in the $3B portfolio example, the total annual cost of the program is not the $57M typically reported, but $117M in total. In the cases where fund-of-fund implementation is used, total annual cost experience increases by 1.2 percent of assets to $153M.[5]

WHERE TO GO FROM HERE?

All this gets us to the question of where to go from here. This question prompts three further ones:

1. First, are the considerable efforts required to capture the full costs of private markets investing worth the trouble? After all, these costs do eventually show up indirectly in the calculation of the net returns these investments are earning. It seems to us that Table 14.1 provides a clear *yes* to this question. It tells us that costs are a material factor in net return outcomes in private markets investing. On average, the higher the long-term cost structure, the lower the long-term net return will be. This in turn tells us it is a fiduciary requirement for pension organizations to understand these cost structures, both "ex ante" (i.e., on a before-the-fact expected basis), and "ex post" (i.e., on an after-the-fact realization basis).[6]
2. This conclusion gets us to the next question: Is there value in reaching broad agreement on a standardized cost calculation protocol? This question, too, should receive a clear *yes*. It makes no sense to end up with a multiple number of non-comparable cost calculation protocols. The four cost categories defined in Table 14.2 would seem to offer a good starting point for discussion.
3. And finally, who are the key stakeholder groups who should take part in the development of a standardized cost (and return) calculation protocol? There is a clear, growing interest in this question around the world. At the governmental/regulatory level, the Dutch regulator DNB, as well as its counterparts in Denmark and Switzerland, have taken clear leadership positions on private markets costs disclosure in Europe. In the United State, the Government Accounting Standards Board (GASB) updated its disclosure requirements somewhat in 2012. However, in 2014 the SEC's Office of Compliance, Inspections, and Examinations uncovered cases of hidden fees and insufficient fee disclosure in a number of private markets arrangements in the United State. At the institutional level, the global Institutional Limited Partners Association (ILPA)

is doing good work to develop a voluntary standardized reporting protocol. However, to date, such a protocol has not been generally adopted. In contrast, the Federation of Dutch Pension Funds has worked closely with the DNB in the adoption of a mandatory protocol in the Netherlands. Finally, the global CFA Institute has also shown recent interest in playing a constructive role in this area.

In closing, it would appear that the topics of full private markets investing cost disclosure in particular, and a standardized approach to value for money disclosure in general, have reached an important inflection point. A window of opportunity has opened. Carpe diem!

CHAPTER 15

How Pension Funds Pay Their Own Investment People

"The most direct indicator of the quality of governance in a pension or other long-horizon investment fund may be how it pays its people...."
—From the "Lead Editorial," *Rotman International Journal of Pension Management*, Spring 2011.

A UNIQUE STUDY OF PENSION INVESTMENT PAY PRACTICES

This chapter reports on the pay practices in the investment functions of 37 pension funds from three continents with aggregate assets under management of $2.2 trillion. The study on which this chapter is based came about because one of those 37 funds persuaded me that KPA Advisory Services was uniquely positioned to design and conduct such a study at a global level.[1]

In summary, the key study findings and conclusions are:

- The 37 funds employ a surprisingly broad array of approaches toward such strategic issues as active vs. passive management, investing in public vs. private markets, and insourcing vs. outsourcing investment mandates.
- Average total compensation levels in the 37-fund sample can be judged high or low, depending on the reference points used. There is considerable variance in total comp levels within the sample.
- Many funds take a middle-of-the-road 50–50 approach to splitting total pay into its base and variable components, and also to splitting the variable pay component into organizational/personal and investment

performance–related components. However, once again, some funds diverge considerably from these general tendencies.

- Regarding the benchmarking of investment performance, there is a strong emphasis in the sample toward using market-relative yardsticks. However, absolute return targets and peer-relative performance also play an important benchmarking role in a number of funds.
- The most important two high-pay drivers in the sample turned out to be the total headcount of employees directly or indirectly involved in the investment function, and a Canadian location. On average, the higher the headcount, the higher average pay both at the total organization (ex–top five) and at the top five (in terms of total pay) levels. We tie this finding to the strategic decision by a number of funds in the sample to insource their private markets investment activities. Such a decision significantly increases the internal headcount of highly paid people. This strategy is currently most prevalent in Canada.
- The study indicates that the pension fund management sector must address three challenges in the sphere of compensation. The first is to eliminate the artificial pay ceilings that continue to be imposed on some funds; the second is to develop a more explicit rationale for how the investment benchmarking question should be addressed; and the third is to develop and integrate a more explicit risk-adjustment protocol into how investment-related pay for performance is calculated.

A STUDY IN FOUR PARTS

The study gathered data in four parts:

Part 1: Fund Characteristics ascertained the fund's legal structure/ sponsorship, location, and size by assets under management (AUM) and full-time equivalent employees (FTEs). These FTEs were confined to investment-related staff including all relevant support functions in the case of integrated pension organizations and fiduciary managers.

Part 2: Asset Allocation established fund asset allocations and management structures at the end of 2010 in six categories.

Part 3: Compensation Principles, Constraints, and Practices captured compensation philosophies, any constraints imposed by external authorities, target and actual compensation paid, and compensation design.

Part 4: Performance Benchmarking captured the organization's approach to benchmarking investment performance.

The detailed survey findings for each of these four parts follow.

Fund Characteristics

Responding funds were categorized as being (a) a stand-alone investment agency, (b) an integrated pension organization, or (c) a fiduciary manager. In terms of stakeholder sponsorship/affiliation, the categories were (a) public sector, (b) industry sector, and (c) corporate sector. The sample consists of 14 stand-alone investment agencies, 19 integrated pension organizations, and 4 fiduciary managers. In terms of sponsorship/affiliation, 23 were public sector–related, 9 industry sector–related, and 5 corporate sector–related.

Table 15.1 indicates that in total, the survey covered 5,162 FTEs who were paid total compensation of US$929 million over the course of their organizations' most recent fiscal year. Total compensation includes base salary, all forms of variable comp, and benefits. Compensation data was provided in local currencies, and converted to U.S. dollars at year-end 2010 exchange rates. In order to be able to analyze compensation principles and practices by region, we divided responding funds into the four geographical categories shown in Table 15.1. Note that the four sub-samples are of approximately equal size, ranging between eight and ten participating funds.

Finally, Figure 15.1 captures the size of the responding organizations by both AUM and FTEs. It indicates quite wide distributions in both the AUM (from under $10B to over $200B) and FTEs (from under 10 to over 800) dimensions. Note there is a positive, but not overly strong statistical relationship between AUM and number of FTEs. While many funds with low

TABLE 15.1 Characteristics of Responding Funds

	# of Funds	FTEs	AUM as at Dec 2010 (billions of USD)	Total Annual Compensation (millions of USD)
AUS/NZ	9	956	$315	$203
USA	10	1,463	902	187
Canada	10	2,164	631	448
Northern Europe/UK	8	579	399	91
	37	5,162	$2,247	$929

Source: KPA Advisory Services Ltd.

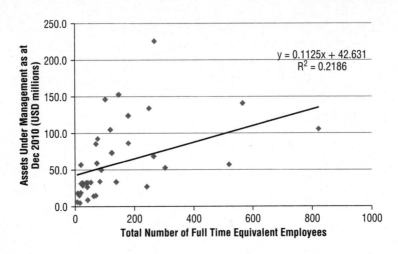

FIGURE 15.1 Size of Responding Funds by FTEs and AUM
Source: KPA Advisory Services Ltd.

FTE counts are also at the low end of the AUM scale, some are not. Similarly, while many funds with high FTE counts are also at the high end of the AUM scale, some are not. This constitutes evidence of significant differences in organizational structures and implementation strategies in the 37 funds.

Asset Allocations and Organizational Structures

The survey asked for assets under management at the end of 2010 to be allocated into six categories:

1. Public markets—internal-active
2. Public markets—internal-passive
3. Public markets—outsourced-active
4. Public markets—outsourced-passive
5. Private markets—internal
6. Private markets—outsourced

Figure 15.2 displays the distributions of these allocations, and indicates quite a wide variety of allocation/structure choices among the 37 funds. Note, for example, the differences in approaches to active management in public markets: Many funds continue to be overwhelmingly active in public markets investing, while some have chosen to have significant passive components. Similarly, many funds continue to largely outsource the investment management function, while some have chosen to manage

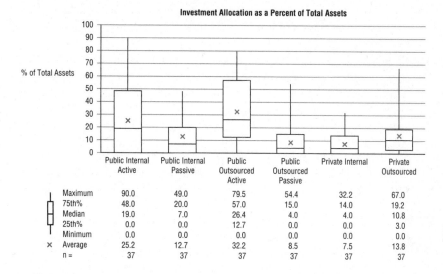

Investment Allocation as a Percent of Total Assets

	Public Internal Active	Public Internal Passive	Public Outsourced Active	Public Outsourced Passive	Private Internal	Private Outsourced
Maximum	90.0	49.0	79.5	54.4	32.2	67.0
75th%	48.0	20.0	57.0	15.0	14.0	19.2
Median	19.0	7.0	26.4	4.0	4.0	10.8
25th%	0.0	0.0	12.7	0.0	0.0	3.0
Minimum	0.0	0.0	0.0	0.0	0.0	0.0
× Average	25.2	12.7	32.2	8.5	7.5	13.8
n =	37	37	37	37	37	37

FIGURE 15.2 Asset Allocations and Organizational Structures
Source: KPA Advisory Services Ltd.

the bulk of the assets internally. Finally, many funds continue to invest largely through public securities markets, while some have large exposures to private markets investments.

Compensation Principles and Constraints

The survey asked an open-ended question about the relationship between organization mission, the organization's HR principles and practices, and its compensation structure. It also asked if there were any externally imposed constraints on compensation structures and ceilings. The intent here is to develop an understanding about how closely funds link their mission, their strategic plan to achieve it, and their HR principles and practices, including compensation; and also to understand what kind of constraints may lie in the way.

An assessment of the responses to the open-ended question led to the broad conclusion that most responses had a "by rote" element to them, logically linking organization mission to the requisite HR requirements, to the need to attract and retain the right people, and finally, to the recognition that this requires a competitive pay for performance scheme. However, there were notable exceptions to this broad finding:

- Some of the corporate funds defined performance in part by the pension plan's impact on corporate HR objectives and profitability.

- Funds that are part of integrated pension plans were more likely to consider plan member and balance sheet–related outcomes versus targets in their pay schemes.
- Some funds provided considerable detail on how their mission devolved into personal and organizational goals (both financial and nonfinancial), which in turn were assessed through a balanced scorecard discipline. Other funds directly emphasized investment performance as the organization's primary success driver.
- Funds with a commercial element in their mission (e.g., most Australian super funds) were more likely to use peer-relative performance metrics.
- Some funds gave consideration to both market-relative and absolute return benchmarks, but with a clear bias toward market-relative benchmarks.
- Where the ability to compensate is constrained by an outside authority, funds emphasized the nonfinancial attractions of working for the organization (e.g., intellectual stimulation, public service, etc.).

The incidence of this kind of outside authority constraint is set out in Table 15.2. Note that for 30 funds the board was the final arbiter of fund compensation, while the remaining 7 were subject to some kind of externally imposed compensation restrictions. These restrictions do appear to have

TABLE 15.2 Ultimate Accountability for Design of Compensation Structure

	Public Sector	Industry	Corporate	Grand Total
Board of Directors/Supervisory Board				
# of Plans	17	9	4	30
Average Compensation per Person Including Top 5 (USD)	163,766	222,172	190,818	184,894
External Authority				
# of Plans	2			2
Average Compensation per Person Including Top 5 (USD)	147,005			147,005
Some combination of the two				
# of Plans	4		1	5
Average Compensation per Person Including Top 5 (USD)	128,785		297,800	162,588

Source: KPA Advisory Services Ltd.

a restraining impact on organizational compensation in the public sector funds. We will revisit this question later in the context of top five compensation.

Compensation Practices Figure 15.3 sets out, for the most recently completed fiscal year, the average total compensation for the investment and related functions in each of the responding funds, both for the total organization excluding the top five, and for the top five. Median total organization (ex–top five) total comp experience is $130K, with a middle 50 percent range of $98K to $168K. Median top five total pay experience is $461K, with a wider middle 50 percent range of $362K to $669K. The chart indicates significant upside dispersion in a number of top five pay cases.

Figure 15.4 displays the ratio of average top five total pay to that for the total organization (ex–top five). Median experience is 3.8×, with a middle 50 percent range of 2.8× to 6.4×. Figure 15.5 compares average top five total compensation actually paid in the most recent fiscal year versus what would have been paid if both organizational/personal performance and investment performance had been at target. Note that some top fives

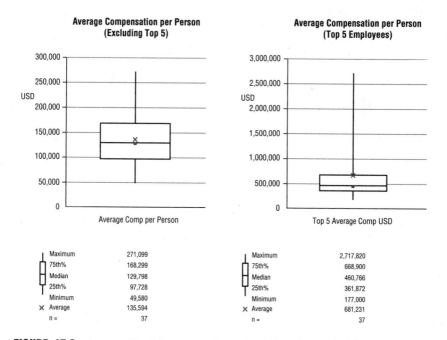

FIGURE 15.3 Average Total Compensation – Total Fund (ex–Top Five) and Top Five
Source: KPA Advisory Services Ltd.

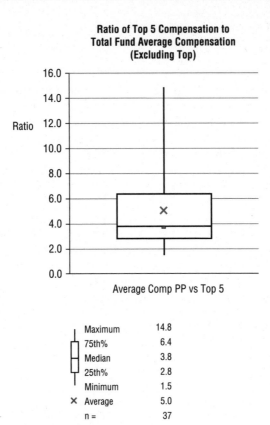

FIGURE 15.4 Ratio of Top Five Compensation to Total Fund Average Compensation (Excluding Top Five)
Source: KPA Advisory Services Ltd.

were paid well in excess of their target total compensation in the last fiscal year. The median ratio for the 37 funds was 94 percent, and the middle 50 percent range 83% to 101%. The implication is that three-quarters of the top fives received actual total compensation below target in their most recent fiscal year.

Figure 15.6 shows the distribution of base/variable comp splits at target performance for the positions of CEO, CIO, SH (Section Head), and SIP (Senior Investment Professional) within the responding fund organizations. The average and median splits were close to 60–40. However, Figure 15.6 also indicates quite a wide variance in practice at the individual fund level.

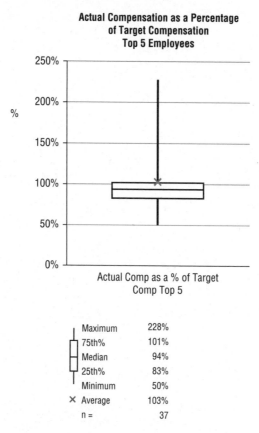

FIGURE 15.5 Top Five Employees' Actual Compensation as a Percentage of Target Compensation
Source: KPA Advisory Services Ltd.

Clearly, some funds are taking the pay for performance concept much further than others by structuring comp schemes with relatively low base amounts and high variable components. At the other extreme, a few funds have no variable comp component at all.

Figure 15.7 displays the splits in variable comp between organizational/personal performance and investment performance. Note that the median CEO split is 50–50, while the median splits for the three investment professional positions are more like 25–75. However, also note the lack of consensus in the sample on this issue. There is considerable variance in actual practices here.

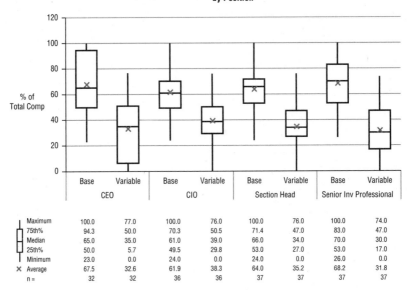

Base and Variable Compensation as a Percent of Total Compensation by Position

	Base	Variable	Base	Variable	Base	Variable	Base	Variable
	CEO	CEO	CIO	CIO	Section Head	Section Head	Senior Inv Professional	Senior Inv Professional
Maximum	100.0	77.0	100.0	76.0	100.0	76.0	100.0	74.0
75th%	94.3	50.0	70.3	50.5	71.4	47.0	83.0	47.0
Median	65.0	35.0	61.0	39.0	66.0	34.0	70.0	30.0
25th%	50.0	5.7	49.5	29.8	53.0	27.0	53.0	17.0
Minimum	23.0	0.0	24.0	0.0	24.0	0.0	26.0	0.0
✕ Average	67.5	32.6	61.9	38.3	64.0	35.2	68.2	31.8
n =	32	32	36	36	37	37	37	37

FIGURE 15.6 Base/Variable Compensation Splits at Target Performance
Source: KPA Advisory Services Ltd.

Table 15.3 shows the distribution of ceilings on variable pay related to organizational/personal goals expressed as a multiple of target variable pay at target performance. Similarly, Table 15.4 shows the distribution of ceilings on variable comp related to investment goals expressed as a multiple of target variable comp at target performance. For the funds that responded to these questions, the tables indicate that for some, target variable pay was also the maximum (i.e., maximum variable pay equals 1× target), while for others, higher than target pay is achievable, especially for the variable component related to investment performance (i.e., maximum variable pay equals 2× target or more).

The distribution of the number of years used to calculate investment performance and investment performance–based variable compensation is set out in Table 15.5.

Median experience is three years. Time periods are averaged if multiple periods are used in the compensation calculation. Many funds in fact do use multiple time periods. The majority of responding funds do have a proactive strategy to communicate their compensation philosophy and outcomes to their stakeholders (27 out of 37 funds).

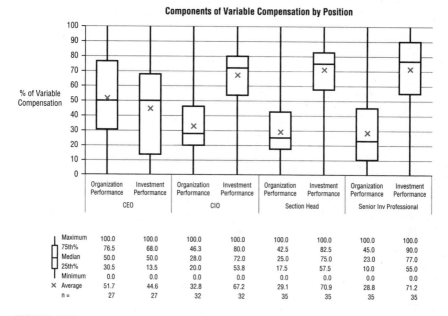

	Maximum	100.0	100.0	100.0	100.0	100.0	100.0	100.0	100.0
	75th%	76.5	68.0	46.3	80.0	42.5	82.5	45.0	90.0
	Median	50.0	50.0	28.0	72.0	25.0	75.0	23.0	77.0
	25th%	30.5	13.5	20.0	53.8	17.5	57.5	10.0	55.0
	Minimum	0.0	0.0	0.0	0.0	0.0	0.0	0.0	0.0
×	Average	51.7	44.6	32.8	67.2	29.1	70.9	28.8	71.2
	n =	27	27	32	32	35	35	35	35

FIGURE 15.7 Org + Pers/Investment Variable Compensation Splits at Target Performance
Source: KPA Advisory Services Ltd.

TABLE 15.3 Variable Compensation Ceilings for Organizational and Personal Performance

Multiples	CEO	CIO	SH	SIP
1×	7	10	10	10
Between 1 and 2×	15	19	19	19
>2×	1	2	2	2

Source: KPA Advisory Services Ltd.

Investment Performance Benchmarking Practices

Survey participants were asked how they benchmarked investment performance. They were asked to allocate the weightings used in their organization between three approaches: performance versus an investible market-based portfolio; a target absolute return; or a pre-defined peer group. In order to differentiate between organizational positions, the benchmarking question was asked separately for the CEO, CIO, SH, and SIP positions. The responses are set out in Tables 15.6, 15.7, and 15.8.

TABLE 15.4 Variable Compensation Ceilings for Investment Performance

Multiples	CEO	CIO	SH	SIP
1×				
Between 1 and 2×				
>2×	2	5	5	5

Source: KPA Advisory Services Ltd.

TABLE 15.5 Years to Calculate Variable Compensation

Number of Years	Number of Funds
1	2
2	6
3	15
4	8
5	3

Source: KPA Advisory Services Ltd.

TABLE 15.6 Investment Performance Benchmark—Market-Based

Investment Performance Benchmark—Market Relative Performance				
Number of Funds	CEO	CIO	SH	SIP
Between 81 and 100 percent	11	16	17	17
Between 61 and 80 percent	3	4	4	4
Between 41 and 60 percent	2	3	5	5
Between 21 and 40 percent	0	0	0	0
Between 0 and 20 percent	6	3	4	4

Source: KPA Advisory Services Ltd.

For those funds that responded to this question, the preferred approach was to place a heavy weighting on the investible market-based portfolio option. However, there were significant minorities where the target absolute return and peer-relative return options received considerable weight.

Survey participants were asked if they calculated investment performance net of costs and net of some kind of risk-adjustment process. The vast majority of funds (32 out of 37) do indeed calculate performance net

TABLE 15.7 Investment Performance Benchmark—Absolute Target

Number of Funds	CEO	CIO	SH	SIP
Between 81 and 100 percent	4	3	3	3
Between 61 and 80 percent	0	0	1	1
Between 41 and 60 percent	3	4	5	5
Between 21 and 40 percent	2	4	4	4
Between 0 and 20 percent	11	14	13	13

Source: KPA Advisory Services Ltd.

TABLE 15.8 Investment Performance Benchmark—Peer Relative

Number of Funds	CEO	CIO	SH	SIP
Between 81 and 100 percent	3	3	2	2
Between 61 and 80 percent	0	0	0	0
Between 41 and 60 percent	1	2	3	3
Between 21 and 40 percent	1	1	2	2
Between 0 and 20 percent	9	12	12	12

Source: KPA Advisory Services Ltd.

of costs (further questions could of course be asked related to what costs are included). However, that is not the case for adjusting investment results for any kind of risk exposure, which only 8 funds out of 37 indicated they did adjust for risk (29 did not).

FOUR INSIGHTS FROM THE SURVEY FINDINGS

So what is to be made of these survey findings? Four things stood out:

1. **Survey Participation:** I was pleasantly surprised at the mainly positive responses to our requests to participate in the survey. Thirty-seven funds managing a collective $2.2 trillion in assets constitute a very impressive database. The positive response implies that competitive compensation is seen as an increasingly important tool in the strategic toolkit of thought-leading pension funds around the world.
2. **Investment Allocations and Structures:** The survey indicates responding funds are employing a wide variety of investment allocations and structures (e.g., public vs. private markets, active vs. passive, and insourcing

vs. outsourcing) to achieve their missions. These choices in turn impact the size of the organization (i.e., from just a handful of FTEs to over 800). This variety raises some important questions. Are these differences being driven by history and culture? By specific externally imposed constraints? Or by the application of rational business model? Or some combination of all of the above?

3. **Compensation Levels and Structures**: Perhaps not surprisingly, the wide variety of investment allocations and structures is accompanied by an equally wide variety in the compensation levels and structures, both at the total organization and top five levels. However, there is also a sense in which the compensation levels and structures of the 37 funds are more similar than different. We estimate that the median top five average compensation in the pension fund sample ($461K) is roughly 10 percent of the top five average compensation for major commercial financial institutions. For example, that figure was $6.1 million for one of Canada's largest commercial financial institutions with assets of $726 billion and 72,000 employees. Similarly, while the median top five base/variable ratio split in the pension fund survey was about 60/40, it was 10/90 for the top five of the same commercial financial institution. Finally, the median top five/total org (ex–top five compensation ratio in the survey was a quite flat 3.8× versus about 50×.

4. **Benchmarking**: On the investment performance measurement side, survey respondents showed a clear preference for using market-based benchmarks. This reflects a widely held position that a low-cost reference portfolio, which reflects the risk tolerance of the risk-bearers, offers the clearest reference benchmark for assessing the value-added the investment function is delivering over long-horizon periods. Many respondents stated that, ideally, measurement periods are 10–20 years in length, but that practically, it is difficult to stretch these periods beyond 3–4 years. Having said this, a significant minority of respondents believes that absolute target returns also have a benchmarking role to play, if the long-term achievement of such a return is important to the asset base's risk underwriters. This potential duality of investment objectives raises important questions about how an investment organization should define, measure, and manage investment risk. It is telling that only 8 organizations out of 37 currently make an effort to risk-adjust returns in their investment performance calculations.

A final important question remains: What are the drivers of the considerable differences in total comp levels that the study uncovered? Recall that one has already been identified: this existence of externally imposed constraints on maximum total compensation. Can we identify others?

SEARCHING FOR HIGH-COMPENSATION DRIVERS

Previous research findings offer clues where to look. For example, the cited study by Professors Dyck and Pomorski, titled "Is Bigger Better? Size and Performance in Pension Plan Management," discovered that a statistically significant source of excess total fund return was the large-scale implementation of private markets investment strategies by specialized in-house pension fund investment teams.[2] The major success driver was a material reduction in investment costs (i.e., not having to pay high external management fees). However, the specialized nature of these private markets strategies also implies that attracting and retaining the requisite management and professional talent inside the fund itself requires relatively high compensation levels. The implication is that funds with high investment-related FTE counts likely also have higher average total compensation levels inside the pension fund organization.

Figures 15.8 and 15.9 indicate that the size of the organization measured by number of FTEs is indeed an important compensation driver, especially for the top five. For example, the median average total compensation (ex–top five) for the 25 percent of the funds with the most FTEs was $159K

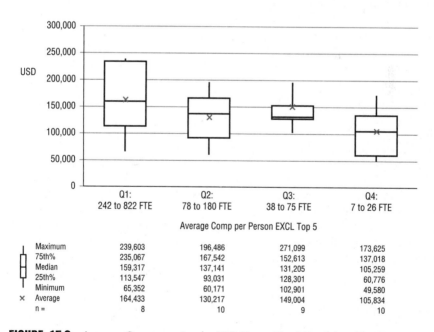

	Q1: 242 to 822 FTE	Q2: 78 to 180 FTE	Q3: 38 to 75 FTE	Q4: 7 to 26 FTE
Maximum	239,603	196,486	271,099	173,625
75th%	235,067	167,542	152,613	137,018
Median	159,317	137,141	131,205	105,259
25th%	113,547	93,031	128,301	60,776
Minimum	65,352	60,171	102,901	49,580
× Average	164,433	130,217	149,004	105,834
n =	8	10	9	10

FIGURE 15.8 Average Compensation by FTE Size – Total Fund (ex–Top Five)
Source: KPA Advisory Services.

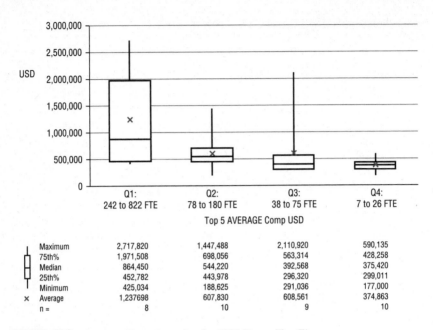

	Q1: 242 to 822 FTE	Q2: 78 to 180 FTE	Q3: 38 to 75 FTE	Q4: 7 to 26 FTE
Maximum	2,717,820	1,447,488	2,110,920	590,135
75th%	1,971,508	698,056	563,314	428,258
Median	864,450	544,220	392,568	375,420
25th%	452,782	443,978	296,320	299,011
Minimum	425,034	188,625	291,036	177,000
× Average	1,237698	607,830	608,561	374,863
n =	8	10	9	10

FIGURE 15.9   Average Compensation by FTE Size – Top Five
Source: KPA Advisory Services.

vs. $105K for the 25 percent of the funds with the fewest FTEs. Similarly, median top five compensation for the 25 percent of funds with the most FTEs was $864K versus $375K for the 25 percent of funds with the fewest FTEs. This is consistent with the observation that high-FTE funds have insourced significant parts of their asset management functions, especially in the private markets arena, and that people with management and operating experience and skills in these areas command high compensation levels.

It is well -known that large-scaled Canadian funds have taken this private markets internalization strategy the furthest. So we should expect to see this reflected in the distribution of compensation levels organized into the four geographical areas. Figures 15.10 and 15.11 show that this is in fact the case, especially at the upper end of the total compensation ranges. The 75th percentile break for average total compensation (ex–top five) for the Canadian funds is the highest of the four regions at $185K, as is the 75th percentile top five break at $1.95M.

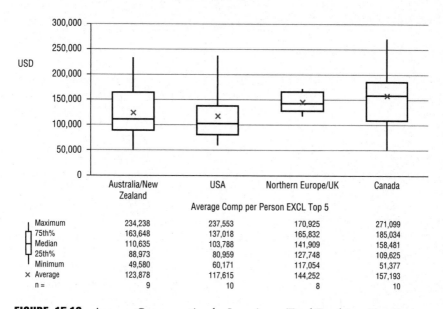

	Average Comp per Person EXCL Top 5			
	Australia/New Zealand	USA	Northern Europe/UK	Canada
Maximum	234,238	237,553	170,925	271,099
75th%	163,648	137,018	165,832	185,034
Median	110,635	103,788	141,909	158,481
25th%	88,973	80,959	127,748	109,625
Minimum	49,580	60,171	117,054	51,377
× Average	123,878	117,615	144,252	157,193
n =	9	10	8	10

FIGURE 15.10 Average Compensation by Location – Total Fund (ex–Top Five)
Source: KPA Advisory Services.

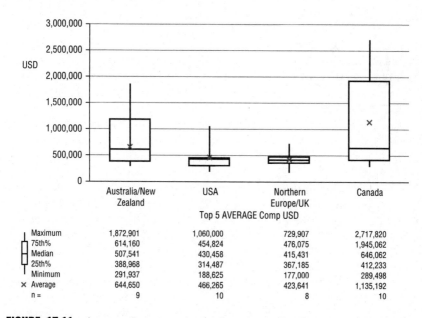

	Top 5 AVERAGE Comp USD			
	Australia/New Zealand	USA	Northern Europe/UK	Canada
Maximum	1,872,901	1,060,000	729,907	2,717,820
75th%	614,160	454,824	476,075	1,945,062
Median	507,541	430,458	415,431	646,062
25th%	388,968	314,487	367,185	412,233
Minimum	291,937	188,625	177,000	289,498
× Average	644,650	466,265	423,641	1,135,192
n =	9	10	8	10

FIGURE 15.11 Average Compensation by Location – Top Five
Source: KPA Advisory Services.

FIVE CONCLUDING OBSERVATIONS

Five concluding observations follow:

1. **Investment Allocation/Structure:** This is an important compensation driver in the 37-fund sample. Significant insourcing of investment activities (especially in private markets) drives up the FTE count with highly compensated people. The high-compensation "Canada effect" found in the survey is largely due to this phenomenon. The paper by Dyck and Pomorski, which examines the economics of this allocation/structure choice, finds it net value-adding, largely because of significant cost savings in external fees. This is a strategic issue the senior managements and boards of all large-scaled funds should address.

2. **Compensation Levels:** Senior management and investment professionals in pension funds around the world are well compensated relative to general wage levels, but with the noted exceptions, less so when measured against compensation levels for similar positions in the commercial financial services industry. In some cases, this is due to externally imposed constraints on fund compensation. The wisdom of placing such constraints should be carefully examined. On the other hand, it is not clear that pension funds need to compete directly with the commercial financial services industry for talent on a total compensation basis. Pension funds can, and should, be interesting, exciting places to work. There is also a public service element that will appeal to a subset of talented people working to invest retirement savings in a productive manner.

3. **Compensation Structure:** The base/variable compensation splits of many funds in the 50/50 area and the further relatively balanced splits of variable comp between organization/personal and investment performance seem sensible. Setting and achieving the right key performance indicators (KPIs) related to the right organizational and personal goals will always be key drivers of long-term organization performance, and should be recognized as such.

4. **Investment Benchmarks:** The survey indicated that most funds orient their benchmarking heavily toward market-relative investment policy proxies rather than absolute return targets. The obvious benefit of this approach is that excess return generation continues to be rewarded even when financial markets are going through low-return phases. The counterpoint made by some outside observers is that fund managers should not be paid potentially handsome bonuses while the average citizen or plan participant is going through difficult economic times. In our view, both perspectives are legitimate. As a result, the question is not whether to choose one benchmarking approach or the other. Instead, the question is one of relative weightings. As a practical matter, there is a strong

case for weighting the market-relative approach more heavily. However, we also believe that attaching some non-zero weighting to whether or not the fund is generating a return in excess of some pre-established target return sends out a strong and positive "solidarity" message to the fund's stakeholders.

5. **Compensation and Risk Management:** The global financial crisis triggered a re-examination of the relationship between incentive compensation and risk-taking in financial institutions across the world. In a number of cases, including in the pensions sector, this has led to a restructuring of the risk management function and to ensuring that the structure of incentive compensation does not lead to excessive risk-taking. This in turn requires the development of a risk-adjustment protocol, which a relatively small number of the survey-responding funds are doing. As always, the design challenge is to separate skill-driven outcomes from risk-driven outcomes. The survey findings confirm that this continues to be an underexplored area in the pension fund management industry. A major industry effort is required to develop and implement risk-adjustment protocols that help separate the skill/risk mix in realized returns and in performance-based compensation.

In short, compensation policy for the investment function and its implementation continue to be a work-in-progress in the pensions world.

CHAPTER 16

Investment Beliefs and Organization Design

Are They Aligned in Your Organization?

"The medium is the message."
—Marshall McLuhan

A RECENT BOARD CONVERSATION

The question posed in the title of this chapter was a recent topic of conversation with board members of a large European pension organization. The resulting dialogue was broad and rich enough to warrant a chapter in this book.

The conversation started with the end in mind: delivering adequate post-work financial security to plan participants. From there, we addressed the challenge of articulating and framing investment beliefs in an operationally useful manner: in other words, in a way that forges logical connections between the beliefs, investment goals, investment policies, and the structure of the investment organization. From there, we moved on to the people part of the puzzle. What are the respective responsibilities of the board and the organization's executive and professional functions? What kinds of people are needed to move from design to its effective implementation? And what kinds of incentive structures are needed to attract and retain these people? All these questions were addressed in turn.

INVESTMENT BELIEFS

Should the boards of pension organizations have clearly stated investment beliefs? Of course they should. Board members cannot meet their fiduciary duties and act in the best interest of the beneficiaries unless their decisions are guided by a well-grounded, clearly stated set of investment beliefs. So where to start the search?

I proposed the following three starting points to frame the discussion:

1. **Keynes' "Beauty Contest" Analogy:** In Chapter 12 of *The General Theory* Keynes sets out his investment beliefs, distinguishing between the short-horizon trading games played by the majority of institutional investors and the long-horizon, wealth-creating efforts in which the minority of institutional investors engage.[1] The question for us today is: How much has really changed in the last 75 years? And if the answer is "not much," why is that?
2. **Tinbergen's "Two Goals–Two Instruments" Principle:** He was awarded the Nobel Prize in Economics in 1969 for demonstrating that the number of economic goals to be achieved must be matched by the number of instruments designed to achieve them.[2] So, for example, two investment goals (e.g., return-seeking and liability hedging) require two separate instruments to achieve them (more on this later).
3. **Tobin/Sharpe's Separation Theorem:** James Tobin and Bill Sharpe are Nobel Prize recipients (1981 and 1990) for their work in investment theory, including the separation theorem and the related capital market line.[3] This work makes a clear asset mix distinction between return-seeking and liability-hedging portfolios, and the determination of optimal weightings between the two.

If a Board buys into the beliefs embedded in the insights offered by Keynes, Tinbergen, Tobin, and Sharpe, what are the action implications? What do they imply for the articulation of a pension organization's investment goals, investment policies, and for the design of its investment organization? That is where the conversation turned next.

TWO GOALS . . . TWO INSTRUMENTS

Rational return-seeking investors buy cash flows at prices where expected returns offer a requisite risk premium over risk-free alternatives. Following Keynes, if the investment goal is long-horizon wealth creation/maintenance, what matters most is the initial yield of the investment (i.e., the initial income-to-price ratio) and the expected growth (real plus inflation) and sustainability of that income flow over time. The longer the investment horizon, the less changes in how the market prices that cash flow at any point in time matter. Stated differently, only beauty contest investors care about short-term changes in security market prices. Long-horizon investors have a very different goal: to secure claims on the real economy (e.g., to finance their post-work years) 15, 25, 35, and 45 years from now. Short-term capital gains or losses no longer matter. Sustainable long-term cash flow generation potential net of expenses does.

Does that mean the short-term doesn't matter at all? Of course not. Today's pensioners want to be paid their pension at the end of this month, next month, and the months after that. So a very different investment goal for a pension fund is to ensure that those monthly claims can be met. So pension funds should not only have a long-horizon return-seeking goal, but a short-horizon payment certainty goal as well.

This raises an interesting question: What should the respective sizes of the return-seeking and payment-certainty portfolios be at any point in time? The right answer depends on two things:

1. The respective demands within any client/plan member group for (a) securing claims in the real economy 15, 25, 35, 45 years from now, and (b) requiring payment safety over the next, say, 10 to 20 years. These two types of demands are not mutually exclusive. Many individual client/plan members might want some of each.
2. The respective pricing of return-seeking and payment-certainty investments. For example, simple calculations showed that in the year 2000 the prices of return-seeking investments were generally very high in relation to payment-safety investments (e.g., a 1 percent dividend yield on the S&P 500 vs. a 4 percent yield on inflation-indexed bonds). The respective pricing of these two types of instruments is much more balanced today (e.g., a 2 percent dividend yield plus another 2 percent in net share repurchases on the S&P 500 vs. a 0.5 percent yield on inflation-indexed bonds).

There is another important question here. What legal claims do individual client/plan members have on the return-seeking and payment-certainty portfolios? In broad terms, individual client/plan members participate in the return-seeking portfolio by owning units. Logically, there are no payment guarantees here. In contrast, the payment-safety portfolio could offer payment guarantees. However, those guarantees would reflect market prices at the time they were purchased. So, for example, a dollar, pound, or euro bought a higher future guaranteed payment when interest rates were high than they do now, when interest rates are low.

MANAGING THE RETURN-SEEKING PORTFOLIO

So with the two goals and two instruments matter settled, how should boards think about monitoring and overseeing strategy implementation for each of the two investment instruments? Let's start with the return-seeking portfolio. A simple investment return identity will facilitate a good discussion on the important implementation questions:

$$\text{Investment Return} = Y + G + \Delta CAP - E$$

In words, any investment return can be decomposed into four components: a starting income yield of Y, plus an income growth rate of G, plus a positive or negative change (Δ) in the income capitalization rate (CAP), minus all investment expenses (E). Long-horizon investors will be mainly interested in Y, G, and E: What is my starting income in relation to my purchase price (Y)? What are the growth prospects for the income stream over time (G)? What will it cost me to manage the investment (E)? Stating the obvious, in a prospective context, Y and E are "knowns" while G is at best a credible, well-documented projection, or at worst (hopefully!) an educated shot in the dark.

The investment return equation is a great conversation catalyst between boards and the organization's senior management and investment professionals on the construction and oversight of return-seeking portfolio strategies. For example:

- It bridges the conversation across public and private market investment opportunities (i.e., the same return components matter in both types of markets, as do the associated investment expenses).
- It prompts discussions on the meaning of active management in both the public and private market spaces (e.g., does active management in public markets mean beauty contest investing? Or does it mean investors actively engaging corporate boards and management on such matters as corporate strategy, executive compensation, and dividend policy?).
- It draws attention to the importance of managing investment expenses (e.g., potentially higher returns in private markets don't mean much if they are accompanied by equally higher fees and carries).
- It focuses risk management discussions on the right questions (e.g., to what degree are the Ys and Gs we are acquiring in the return-seeking portfolio correlated?).
- It integrates traditional financial and ESG considerations into the same conversation (e.g., longer-term income stream sustainability must obviously include environmental, social, and governance quality considerations).

Boards and management must develop a similar conversation framework to address payment-safety portfolio questions.

MANAGING THE PAYMENT-SAFETY PORTFOLIO

The discussion framework now reverts from assessing long-horizon return prospects to ensuring there are sufficient financial resources in place to meet accrued and accruing defined payment obligations falling due over the course of the next 10 to 20 years. (Formal risk-free payment hedging strategies becomes increasingly unrealistic beyond 20 years, especially in real terms.) The following design issues should be addressed:

- The target of the post-work income stream (e.g., to replace, together with the pillar one pension, 60 percent of final earnings), and also the shape of that income stream (e.g., nominal or inflation-indexed, and/or first increasing and then declining with age)
- The length of the post-work income stream (e.g., at what target age does it start, and how is longevity insurance provided?)
- The process of converting units in return-seeking portfolio into claims on the payment-safety pool (e.g., when, and at what rate, do still-working plan members cash in their units, and begin to purchase claims on the payment-safety balance sheet?)
- If the best (i.e., evidence-based) answers to these questions help define the pension plan's default options, how does plan design best accommodate the "opt-out" wishes of plan participants who want to personalize the financing of their retirement with their own answers?
- How might the default option settings respond to changes in the bond yield curve and expected risk premiums? (e.g., pricing in 2000 versus pricing today?)
- How best to communicate with plan members about where they are in their financial life journeys as they progress from young workers, to older workers, to retirees?

The essential task of the team managing the payment-safety pool is to maintain balance sheet solvency and payment liquidity through time. So they must know their way around the globe's bond and derivatives markets. An intriguing question is the potential scope for a modest measure of risk-taking. For example, should the asset side of the balance sheet all be sovereign debt rated AAA? Or should there be room for picking up yield though the application of expert credit analysis? This question should receive careful consideration.

ORGANIZATIONAL IMPLICATIONS

Now the conversation with the board moved to the organizational implications of all this: Some implications are obvious, others less so. Possibly the most obvious implication is that pension organizations should have two investment functions, with one focusing on the long-horizon return-seeking goal, and the other on the payment-safety goal. Less obvious is whether these functions should be insourced or outsourced. The answer *would* be obvious if it were purely a matter of economics and cost-effectiveness. There are two logical reasons for this:

1. There are material scale economies to be harvested in building an investment function. So generally speaking, large asset pools provide opportunities to benefit from scale economies that small asset pools cannot provide.
2. However, scale opportunities will be wasted if a large asset pool organization cannot attract and retain the talent it needs to expertly execute the two investment functions in-house. Generally speaking, the requisite expertise is far more expensive to access outside, compared to inside. On top of that, outsourcing requires the management of an additional layer of agency issues.

Unfortunately, many pension organizations have a problem in this regard. They cannot directly access the labor pools necessary for the organization to be a top-tier pension services provider along the lines set out above. People with high levels of skill and experience in specialized investment markets are expensive, too expensive in many cases to be put directly on the pension organization payroll.

A BOARD DILEMMA

All this leaves the boards of large pension organizations with a dilemma. Aligning investment beliefs and organization design is an important fiduciary duty. But on the one hand, big compensation packages inside the organization leave boards open to the perception that they are breaching their fiduciary duty by paying too much, especially in times when fund returns are low, or even negative. On the other hand, if they knowingly incur unnecessary costs by outsourcing rather than insourcing, they are arguably *actually* breaching their fiduciary duty.

This is an interesting agenda item for the next board meeting.

CHAPTER 17

Norway versus Yale— or versus Canada?

A Comparison of Investment Models

"Both the Norwegian Government Pension Fund Global and Yale University's endowment, run by the popular David Swensen, have emerged as industry pillars in asset management, and a new paper compares and scrutinizes their reputations."

—*aiCIO* magazine

CANADA CALLING

This chapter's epigraph comes from an article in the e-magazine *aiCIO* titled "The Norway vs. Yale Models: Who Wins?"[1] It references a paper, "The Norway Model," by David Chambers, Elroy Dimson, and Antii Ilmanen (October 2011).[2] This paper describes the investment model of the Norwegian Government Pension Fund Global (GPFG) in considerable detail, and uses the Yale University endowment model as a standard against which to evaluate its effectiveness. The authors conclude that the Norway model "has become an exemplar for investors around the world ... and a coherent and compelling alternative to the Yale model ...."

This chapter offers a quite different and contrasting perspective. It argues that the Yale model is of at best marginal value as a benchmark against which to assess the effectiveness of the Norway model. A far more relevant benchmark is the Canada investment model in use by such globally admired organizations as the Canada Pension Plan Investment Board

(CPPIB) and Ontario Teachers' Pension Plan (OTPP), as well as by other major Canadian pension funds and the investment arms of such Canadian provinces as Alberta, British Columbia, and Quebec.

Knowledgeable observers of the global institutional investment scene have become well aware of the Canada model in recent years. It is also receiving increasing media attention.[3] Is the Norway model as coherent and compelling an alternative to the Canada model as it is to the Yale model? That is the far more relevant question this chapter addresses.

A More Relevant Comparator

Why is the Canada model a more relevant comparator? For two reasons:

1. **Scale:** Collectively, the Canada model is being applied to a similar size asset pool as the Norway model ($1 trillion); in contrast, at $25 billion, the size of the Yale Endowment Fund is less than 3 percent of each of these two pools.
2. **Intellectual Foundation:** The Canada model derives its intellectual foundation from an investment framework set out by John Maynard Keynes and an organization design model set out by Peter Drucker. Arguably, the Yale model starts in the same intellectual place, but its small scale hampers its implementation options, and its dependency on David Swensen, Yale's chief investment officer, hampers its replicability. In contrast, the Norway model derives its intellectual foundation from the modern asset pricing models initially set out in the 1960/70s by Markowitz, Sharpe, Lintner, Tobin, Fama, et al. On the organization design side, it is driven by "epistemic proceduralism" (i.e., the need by the organization to demonstrate transparent procedures in order to establish legitimacy, despite the fact that the resulting oversight and decision-making structures may be suboptimal).[4]

The implications of the intellectual foundation differences between the Norway and Canada models follow.

COMPETING INVESTMENT MODELS

This book has already noted the framing of investment model choices by John Maynard Keynes. He makes a key distinction between beauty contest investing and real investing. In the beauty contest model, investment professionals engage in a continuous zero-sum game (actually, a negative-sum game after transaction and management costs) of guessing which investments the market will deem most beautiful six months hence. In contrast, real investing is the physical process of turning savings into productive capital. This is the hard work of projecting uncertain cash flows into near-term and distant futures, and judging whether or not they meet or surpass some pre-established hurdle rate of return.

If this is how a professional investment organization frames its world, it has three investment style choices: It can join the beauty contest game; it can choose not to play and become a free-riding passive investor; or it can choose to acquire the requisite skills to become a "turn savings into productive capital" investor. The Canada model does see the world this way. It explicitly rejects the first two choices and embraces the third.

The modern investment theory spawned in the 1960s/70s is a special case in this general Keynesian investment framework. In this special case, all investors have the same information, use the same investment models, and hence have the same return expectations at any point in time. These expectations only change when new information hits the marketplace. Investments are priced based on their perceived beta exposure to the market portfolio. Special efforts should be taken to minimize portfolio exposure to non-market risks, as these exposures will not be rewarded. Historically at least, the Norway model has largely embraced the view of the investment world, although some wiggle room has been granted it to engage in a marginal amount of active management.

COMPETING ORGANIZATIONAL MODELS

On the organizational structure side, Chapter 1 set out my interpretation of Peter Drucker's formula for building high-performance pension investment organizations. There are five critical elements:

1. Mission clarity and organizational autonomy
2. Good governance
3. Sensible investment beliefs
4. Right scale
5. Right people

The Canada model embraces all five of these success elements. Organizational missions are clearly spelled out, and legal structures are built to strike a balance between organizational accountability and autonomy. Blue-ribbon nominating committees are struck to ensure governing boards have the requisite skill/experience sets, as well as a strong sense of public duty. Care is taken to ensure the organization's investment beliefs are grounded in the messy real world, rather than in elegant modern investment theory. Adequate scale is converted into strong insourcing strategies, especially in the expensive private markets spaces (e.g., real estate, infrastructure, private equity). Finally, Canadian funds are increasingly populated by people with hands-on experience in turning savings into productive capital in these private markets spaces, and in financing and governance of publicly–traded corporations.

The Norway model does not score as well on this five-point success formula. For example, while its fund has a clear mission, Norway is still struggling with achieving the right balance among organizational accountability, autonomy, and good governance. It requires the Clark and Monk concept of epistemic proceduralism to explain an organization design/decision chain that runs from the Norwegian Parliament, to the Ministry of Finance, to Norges Bank, to NB Investment Management, and finally to a web of outside investment agents and advisors. To be clear, I accept that this procedural chain may well be necessary in Norway for its fund to be sustainable in a political sense. However, the chain should also be recognized as a potential material barrier to innovative wealth-creation.

The Norway Fund's procedural governance construct also raises important questions about the investment beliefs, scale, and people elements of the five-point success formula. For example, to what degree are the Fund's investment beliefs shaped by its procedural constraints rather than seeing the world the way it really is? Is it using its large scale and projected positive cash flow for many years to come to maximum advantage? Is it hiring people with hands-on experience in turning savings into productive capital? Each of these questions deserve a hard, close look.

WHICH FUND MODEL "WINS"?

Deductive logic suggests that if you believe in the combined wisdom and insights of Keynes and Drucker, and if you believe these insights can be effectively implemented in the real world, then you should believe that the Canada model will produce higher net risk-adjusted returns. On the other hand, if you believe modern investment theory captures the essential realities of institutional investing today, you should bet on the Norway model. Is there any confirming evidence in support of one model vs. the other? Yes, there is.

Ontario Teachers' is the logical comparator to the Norway Fund. Prior chapters noted that before its rebirth as the first fund to adopt the Canada model in 1990, it was a government agency that only invested in non-marketable Government of Ontario bonds. In the mid-1980s, the government commissioned a study on how Ontario Teachers' (and other provincial agencies) could become more effective, value-producing organizations. The study set out the Canada model, and recommended its adoption by the Ontario Government and the Ontario Teachers' Federation.[5] The recommendation was accepted and OTPP was born. A high-quality board of directors was appointed. The board attracted a high-quality management team and gave it a broad mandate to produce measurable value for the fund's stakeholders. The mandate and the model to implement it have now been in place for 25 years.

Table 17.1 displays the performances of OTPP and the GPFG since the latter's inception in 1998. In calculating performance, we remove the effects of differing investment goals, risk tolerances, and currency regimes. These differences are largely captured in the two reference portfolios. This leaves us with the excess returns relative to passively implemented reference portfolios that capture those policy differences. Next, the average management costs are deducted, leading to the net excess return calculations. These net excess returns offer a fair basis to examine the ability of each of the two models to generate value for its stakeholders over and above what passive market exposures provided over the 16-year measurement period.[6]

What about the risk side of the equation? Did OTPP undertake materially riskier strategies to earn its additional 1.6 percent/year? A statistical way to address this question is to see how much additional return volatility its active investment program added to its balance sheet mismatch risk relative to the mismatch risk generated by the passive reference portfolio. Table 17.1 indicates an estimate of 0.6 percent of additional return volatility. This implies an active management reward/risk ratio of 2.7 for OTPP (i.e., 1.60/0.60). The Norway Fund does not have an explicit liability it is investing against. However, the fund does measure how much "tracking error" return volatility its active management program generates versus the

TABLE 17.1   Investment Results—OTPP vs. Norway Fund

Investment Results—OTPP vs. Norway Fund from 1998 to 2014

	OTPP	Norway Fund
Return of Fund	8.76%	5.81%
Return of Reference Portfolio	6.94%	5.56%
EXCESS RETURN	**1.82%**	**0.25%**
Average Management Cost	0.22%	0.09%
NET EXCESS RETURN	**1.60%**	**0.16%**
Mismatch/Tracking Error Risk	0.60%	0.40%
Reward/Risk Ratio	**2.7**	**0.4**

Sources: OTPP and GPFG Annual Reports and KPA Advisory Services Ltd.

return of the reference portfolio: 0.4 percent tracking error volatility for the 1998–2014 period. This implies an active management reward/risk ratio of 0.4 for Norway (i.e., 0.16%/0.40%).

The results in Table 17.1 indicate that both funds have successfully achieved their objectives over the 1998–2014 period. However, due to the materially different investment and organization models employed, success means different things to OTPP, to the GPFG, and to their respective stakeholders. In the OTPP case it means generating a material level of additional wealth over an extended period of time, while taking only a modest amount of additional risk. In the GPFG case it means eking out a very modest amount of additional wealth for taking on a modest amount of additional risk. Specifically, the respective reward/risk ratios indicate Ontario Teachers' produced almost seven times more additional wealth per unit of risk over the 1998–2014 period.

THE BEST WAY FORWARD FOR THE NORWAY FUND

To their credit, the Norwegians have not been afraid to ask for advice on the best way forward for the Fund. They employ a standing four-person strategy council of experts (two of the authors of the cited "The Norway Model" paper are council members). They also commission occasional special studies by outside experts to bolster the work of the council. Real estate has already been approved as a new asset class, and an investment program has commenced. What other kinds of things are these bodies recommending? The cited paper offers a list, including the following five:

1. **Consider additional risk factors** (in addition to just asset class exposures) in building the fund and monitoring and managing its risk exposures. However, questions about how these factors are priced continue to be debated. Possible exceptions are the quite persistent undervaluation of value stocks and existence of illiquidity premiums.
2. **Become more active in top-down factor allocation** rather than being only active in bottom-up security selection.
3. **Simplify and concentrate the fixed-income portfolios** based on stronger macroeconomic, emerging markets, and credit research and analysis.
4. **Exploit the fund's advantages of size and horizon,** suggesting that more contrarian investment approaches should be explored and acted on. Also, consider writing various forms of insurance (e.g., selling equity volatility and tail-risk insurance, buying positive carry).
5. **Keep up with the growing data, systems, and IT needs** as the organization grows larger and more complex.

On the whole, these are sensible recommendations for the Norwegians to consider. But it is important to recognize they are largely extensions of an investment model based on the modern investment theory that evolved out of the 1960s/70s and an organization model driven by epistemic proceduralism rather than organizational effectiveness.

SHOULD NORWAY GO CANADIAN?

Should Norway consider moving to the Canada model? Given its compelling logic and performance record, the Canada model would seem to warrant serious consideration. "Pro" arguments include the following four:

1. **The GPFG becomes an exemplar Keynesian investor,** turning nonrenewable oil wealth into sustainable, wealth-producing capital. Adherence to the UN Principles of Responsibility ensures the conversion process takes place within explicit environment, social, and good governance norms.
2. **Its multipronged investment implementation strategies** permit it to become a proactive, innovative, value-adding first mover investor, operating at the front of multiple wealth-creation chains, rather than at the rear.
3. **The fund becomes a magnet for global investment talent** that wants to build institutional capitalism into a measurable force of good rather than greed.
4. **At the same time, it is adding to the wealth of current and future generations of Norwegians** at a significantly higher potential rate than the current Norway model.

Conversely, I can think of two "con" arguments:

1. **Going Canadian implies moving NB Investment Management out of Norges Bank** and setting it up as an arm's-length Crown Corporation (e.g., Norway Investment Management Corporation or NIMC). Many barriers stand in the way of making such a significant organizational change.
2. **NIMC might fail** for any one of a number of faulty implementation reasons. Saying is one thing; doing is quite another.

This is something for Norwegians to ponder.

CHAPTER 18

Does Culture Matter in Pension Organizations?

"Culture is a system of shared values that define what is important... and norms that define appropriate attitudes and behaviors for members of the organization."

—O'Reilly and Chatman

"Culture is a pattern of shared assumptions that has been learned by a group... that has worked well enough to be considered valid... and therefore to be taught to new members as the correct way to perceive, think, and feel about matters of importance to the organization ...."

—Edgar H. Schein

ADDRESSING THE CULTURE QUESTION

Given the two definitions above,[1] is culture something worth considering in the design, governance, and management of pension organizations? Pension consultant Roger Urwin and MIT academic Andy Lo certainly think so. Urwin has been addressing the culture question recently on the conference circuit. Lo has just published a 38-page paper on the topic, titled "The Gordon Gekko Effect: The Role of Culture in the Financial Industry."[2]

Looking back to previous chapter topics, this book, too, has touched on the organizational culture question in such contexts as defining and measuring the value pension organizations should be producing for their stakeholders, setting out the meaning and implications of fiduciary duty, communicating clearly with stakeholders, and designing and implementing effective compensation structures. This chapter will address the culture question head-on. Following the structure of Lo's paper, it explores the meaning of culture, why it is important, and how to foster a good culture in your organization.

BAD CULTURES, BAD OUTCOMES

Lo opens his paper by recalling the famous Gordon Gekko speech in the 1987 movie, *Wall Street*, which leads off with the declaration that "Greed is good." Lo tells us the Gekko character (played by Michael Douglas) is not entirely fictitious. Before he was convicted of insider trading, Ivan Boesky actually gave a speech with that theme at University of California–Berkeley in 1986. Lo tips his hat to Michael Lewis, who captured the spirit of those times in his 1989 book, *Liar's Poker*.[3]

Later in the paper, Lo reviews some of the financial industry's more spectacular post-1980s failures, pointing to the role the organization's culture played in those failures:

- **Long-Term Capital Management (LTCM):** LTCM was founded by three individuals (John Meriwether, Robert Merton, and Myron Scholes), each supremely confident in his own special skills and capabilities (e.g., market savvy, high intelligence, and superior risk management mathematics). As importantly, LTCM's lenders believed that these special LTCM skills and capabilities created a unique "no risk" opportunity for everybody to make money. In fact, LTCM was effectively a high-risk, experimental financial engineering firm that would go where no other firm had ever gone before in the use of leverage. All this led to LTCM's demise and a major Wall Street bailout in the 1998 financial crisis triggered by Russia's default on its GKO bonds.
- **American International Group (AIG):** For a long time AIG was managed in a "feudalist" style by CEO Hank Greenberg. He demanded lifetime loyalty from his executives and personally kept his finger on AIG's key risk exposures as an insurance underwriter. Fearing headline risk, AIG's board of directors replaced Greenberg in 2005 with Martin Sullivan, who had risen steadily through the AIG ranks after starting as an office assistant decades earlier. However, Sullivan was no Greenberg. He assumed that AIG's risk management system could operate without Greenberg-like tight oversight. It could not, with the Financial Products Group going rogue through the massive issuance of credit default swaps (CDSs, default insurance) on toxic collateralized debt obligations (CDOs, packages of high-risk mortgages). All this led to Sullivan's dismissal and yet another massive bailout during the 2008–9 global financial crisis.

- **Lehman Brothers:** This company offers another example of a feudalist culture led by "the gorilla of Wall Street," Dick Fuld. However, unlike Greenberg, Fuld was no risk management hawk. A key element in Lehman's downfall was Fuld's alleged willingness to conceal its true financial condition and its degree of leverage through accounting tricks to the tune of $50B. While outside law and accounting firms played facilitating roles, these tricks were never disclosed to Lehman's board of directors or to the SEC. Lehman filed for bankruptcy protection in September 2008. To this day, Fuld continues to claim he did nothing wrong.

- **Societe Generale (SG):** At its peak, low-level trader Jerome Kerviel had managed to accumulate an unauthorized long position in index futures of €49B against the bank's total risk capital of €26B. By the time his positions were unwound, he had lost SG €6.4B. An internal investigation found that his first supervisor had turned a blind eye to Kerviel's small (but above his limit) intra-day trades. This supervisor quit, leaving Kerviel unsupervised for three months. His next supervisor did not use required risk monitoring programs. However, Kerviel's trades were making money, creating a permissive environment up the chain of executive command. Finally, it was SG's accounting/regulatory division that blew the whistle on Kerviel's unauthorized, unsupervised, and now-extreme trading activities. How could this happen? Apparently, because an elitist SG senior executive group thought the prop trading group to be a cash-generating backwater, deserving little senior management attention.

- **Securities and Exchange Commission (SEC):** Fraudster Bernie Madoff was turned in by his own sons in December 2008, and pleaded guilty to running a massive Ponzi scheme in March 2009. Prior to these two events, the SEC had eight opportunities to go after Madoff, starting in 1992. These opportunities came in the form of client complaints, expert analyses on the statistical impossibility of Madoff's investment performance, and media articles questioning the legitimacy of his business operations. None of these opportunities was seriously pursued by the SEC. The U.S. Government Accountability Office (GAO) was assigned the task to find out why. Lo reports that the GAO uncovered a dysfunctional SEC culture plagued by issues such as "lack of mission commitment," "low morale," "lack of internal communication," and "high risk aversion to external criticism." Apparently, GAO's seven recommendations to address these issues are now having a positive effect at the SEC.

If bad cultures produce bad outcomes, do good cultures produce good outcomes?

GOOD CULTURES, GOOD OUTCOMES

Lo mentions one good culture/good outcome case in his paper: the U.S. National Transportation Safety Board. Recalling Michael Lewis' 2014 book, *Flash Boys*, I add the Royal Bank of Canada to the good culture/good outcome list. Here is the way Lewis himself put the *Flash Boys* story: "One of these people ... a Canadian of all things ... was willing to throw open a window on the American financial world. ... It still takes my breath away."[4] In short:

- **National Transportation Safety Board (NTSB):** The NTSB is a government agency with no regulatory authority. Its mission is to investigate transportation accidents, conduct careful research into their causes, and make recommendations as to how they can be avoided in the future. It and other agencies like it elsewhere in the world have established a remarkable transportation safety record, saving many lives over the course of many decades. In sharp contrast to what the GAO reported in its SEC investigation, the NTSB's culture descriptors include "clear shared-purpose and accountabilities," "strong prestige and morale," "definitive expertise," and "cohesive, effective teamwork."
- **Royal Bank of Canada (RBC):** While Brad Katsuyama is the hero in Lewis' *Flash Boys* story (he takes on Wall Street's front-running high-frequency trading culture), RBC was the institution that stood behind him. When Katsuyama and his team developed Thor, an electronic counter-weapon with which to fight the high-frequency trading (HFT) crowd, RBC was faced with a choice. Should it use Thor for its own financial benefit, or as a tool to create a fairer, more transparent marketplace? To its credit, "RBC nice" (reflecting its perceived corporate culture) chose the latter route. This decision did not go unnoticed by an appreciative institutional investment community. RBC's quality ranking for institutional equity trading as surveyed by Greenwich Associates shot up from #19 in 2009 to #1 in 2010. Who says nice guys (and nice institutions) have to finish last?

What should we make of these stories where bad cultures produce bad outcomes and vice versa? What are the drivers of organizational culture?

A BIOLOGY FRAMEWORK

Lo argues that we have to go beyond economics and its "rational actors" assumptions to understand organizational culture. A biology framework is more useful: What are the transmission mechanisms that create good or bad cultures? He suggests three: leadership, group composition, and environment.

1. **Leadership:** Charismatic leaders such as Hank Greenberg or Dick Fuld drive organizational culture for good or bad by sheer force of personality. However, charisma is not the only possible culture transmitter. Factors such as mission, tradition, hubris, and greed can also play important roles. For example, saving lives was a powerful organizational motivator in the NTSB good culture case. Arguably, the tradition factor played important, but very different roles in the SG and RBC cases. In the SG case, the elitist tradition was to consider trading a low-grade function not worthy of senior management's time. In the RBC case, the "RBC nice" tradition was to be customer-friendly, and to not exploit the informational advantages of the organization vis-a-vis its clients. Finally, the technical hubris factor nicely explains the downfall of LTCM, with greed explaining the downfall of its lenders.

2. **Group Composition:** Organizational hiring processes are an important culture driver. For example, Michael Lewis contrasts Wall Street's "best and the brightest" hiring practices from famous Ivy League universities with how Brad Katsuyama came to join RBC. He was a talented, but low-key hire from a good, but small, non-famous Canadian university. Lewis notes that RBC has an unwritten "no assholes" rule. In less colorful language, people who are loud, brash, and think they walk on water will not fit into the "RBC nice" culture, and hence need not apply.

3. **Environment:** The Madoff story indicates that the SEC's unwritten rule seems to have been to avoid headlines and external criticism at all costs. This cultural trait cost Madoff's victims billions of dollars over decades of time. On a broader scale, Hyman Minsky's Financial Instability Hypothesis suggests that all of us become more risk-tolerant in environments when easy money is made without (apparently) taking a great deal of risk. Investment horizons shrink in such environments, as does the capacity of some organizations to see danger lurking behind the easy money. And when the easy money music stops, many of these organizations get trampled running for the exits at the same time.

What happens when we apply this biological framework to exploring culture issues in pension organizations?

CULTURE ISSUES IN PENSION ORGANIZATIONS

While there have been outright misdemeanors in pension organizations, they have been few and far between. Using Lo's framework, the reasons for this can be attributed to all three sources of organizational culture transmission. Pension organizations exist to help members maintain their standard of living after they retire. So logically, pension organizations seek people attracted to that kind of organizational mission. And on paper at least, pension organizations claim to lift their eyes above the short-term ups and downs of financial markets, and to focus on the long-term sustainability of the pension arrangement they manage, and of the economies that these arrangements are part of.

Having said that, there are a number of culture issues worth exploring:

- **Legal Structure:** Is the pension organization a stand-alone arm's-length organization, or an appendage of some larger parent organization such as a government, a labor union, or a corporation? Arm's-length pension organizations have choices in how they intend to achieve their mission. They can choose to be bold and creative or conservative and conventional. Appendage pension organizations don't have that option. They have to adopt the cultural stance of their parent. An arm's-length example is the bold and creative stance chosen by Ontario Teachers' Pension Plan at its inception in 1990. In contrast, the previous chapter noted that Norway's Government Pension Fund Global exemplifies the constraining consequence of being at the end of a control chain that runs from Parliament, to the Ministry of Finance, to Norges Bank, and only then to the division that actually manages the GPFG.

- **Tone at the Top:** In addition to legal structure, a pension organization's board of trustees (and how it is selected/elected) is another important determinant of its culture. A recent study by Andonov, Bauer, and Cremers confirms that boards selected through sound merit-based processes are more likely to exhibit independence of thought and action than Boards elected through political processes. Politics-driven governance processes are associated with more risk-taking and lower returns.[5]

- **Investment Beliefs:** Lo makes an important distinction between the mechanistic Efficient Markets Hypothesis view of financial markets and his more realistic Adaptive Markets Hypothesis. A mechanistic view of how financial markets work leads to mechanistic rules of how to invest. An adaptive view offers scope for creative, contrarian thinking about how to generate excess returns. This book's chapters on investment beliefs and long-term investing reflect this adaptive stance. Adopting it requires a creative, entrepreneurial culture.

- **Organizational Structure and Compensation:** Scale creates opportunities to insource rather than outsource investment mandates. However, insourcing also creates reputational risks. Large organizations require more governance and senior management resources than do small ones.

Also, insourcing private markets investing means competing for talent in highly paid labor markets. This can easily lead to public criticism despite the fact that, overall, insourced private markets program can run at as low as 10 percent of the cost of outsourcing such programs. So once again, significant insourcing of the investment function requires a creative, entrepreneurial culture.

In conclusion, does culture matter in pension organizations? Yes it does. Just like in other fields of endeavor, pension organizations with good cultures are far more likely to produce good outcomes for their members/clients than organizations with bad cultures. How good is your organizational culture?

Pension Investing

"Investing: Expend money with the expectation of achieving a profit or material result by putting it into financial schemes, shares, or property, or by using it to develop a commercial venture."

Oxford Dictionaries online

CHAPTER 19

Are Investment Returns Predictable?

"Theories of Rational Expectations and Efficient Markets demonstrate that it is impossible to outperform the market on any systematic basis.... Nonetheless, while many investors do not outperform the market on a long-term basis, some do, and they have achieved enviable, well-documented track records."

—Woody Brock

RECONCILING INVESTMENT THEORY AND PRACTICE

The cost of buying payment safety through a liability-matching bond portfolio is expensive today. While that high cost is not material to investors requiring payment safety tomorrow, it is very material to long-horizon investors seeking to maintain their post-work standard of living 20 to 30 years from now at an affordable price. For these latter investors, buying a diversified stream of dividends with reasonable inflation protection and modest real growth prospects seems a far better proposition today. For example, $100 invested in a 2 percent bond compounds to only $150 in 20 years. In contrast, investing the $100 in a portfolio of blue-chip equities yielding 4 percent and with a dividend growth rate of 3 percent generates a return of 7 percent per annum, compounding the $100 to materially higher $400 in 20 years. (This assumes stocks continue to be priced on a 4 percent yield basis 20 years from now.)

Are these two calculations just illustrations? Or are they credible 20-year return predictions? And if they *are* return predictions, how accurate are they likely to be? And, how do we bring risk and uncertainty into the conversation? Finally, is investment theory helpful in addressing any of these questions? Stated differently, how do we ensure there is consistency between how we believe financial markets work, how we make return predictions, and how those predictions translate into actual investment decisions? These challenging questions are the topic of this chapter.

THE PREDICTABLE RETURNS THESIS

Some time ago, Woody Brock published a paper that offered fresh perspectives on some of the questions addressed in this chapter, including the quote above.[1] Through a deductive, step-by-step reasoning process, he arrives at a series of important conclusions:

- While the twin theories of rational expectations and efficient markets produce elegant results (e.g., it is impossible for any investor to outperform the market on any systematic basis), its underlying assumptions do not square well with reality.
- For starters, economic and capital markets structures are dynamic rather than static. Structural changes do occur in spheres such as politics, demography, technology, productivity, and climate change. A superior understanding of these dynamics and their implications should lead to a comparative investment advantage.
- Next, while modern technologies do indeed make new public information widely and instantaneously available to investors around the world, it is *not* interpreted uniformly and identically by all investors. Just as there will be correct interpretations, so will there be wrong ones.
- Further, mistakes occasionally become highly correlated and persistent, exacerbating mispricing problems in financial markets. These correlated mistakes created, for example, the dot-com bubble of the late 1990s, and the housing/leverage/securitization bubble in the global financial crisis less than 10 years later.
- While economic and capital markets structures are dynamic, they *do* operate within some ultimate logical and statistical averages and boundaries. Examples are P/E ratios and dividend yields vs. interest rates, GDP growth vs. interest rates, labor vs. capital income shares of GDP.
- All this creates investment opportunities for investors whose investment beliefs fit these realities, and who have developed the requisite discipline to act on them. Ergo, it is indeed logically possible to outperform the market.

So in terms of the starting questions in this chapter, Brock's paper suggests that making return predictions that may be at odds with history and the twin theories of rational expectations and efficient markets can be a rational, legitimate activity. The caveat is that making such predictions should be based on an explicit framework that is consistent from both logical (deductive) and factual (inductive) perspectives.

LO'S ADAPTIVE MARKETS HYPOTHESIS

MIT's Andrew Lo sketched out such a framework in his 2004 *Journal of Portfolio Management* (JPM) article, "The Adaptive Markets Hypothesis." He starts by contrasting the different perspectives of economists and psychologists. The latter build theories inductively (i.e., through observation and experimentation). Economists tend to go the other way: from abstract theories to empirical confirmation. Lo argues that it is the resulting obsessive requirement for internal consistency that created the theoretical economists' love affair with the rational expectations and efficient markets theories. As a result, he gently suggests, these theories have lost much of their operational usefulness.

If we are going to develop operationally useful asset pricing theory, he argues, we are going to have to bring the theoretically messy field of sociology into the mix. This means understanding human behavior, which in turn means accepting that people are less "rational utility maximizers" and more "bounded rationality satisficers." In short, there is a great deal of trial and error in how people develop investment beliefs and make financial decisions. Thus, Lo proposes the adaptive markets hypothesis (AMH) as a more operationally useful alternative to the efficient markets hypothesis (EMH). Not surprisingly, the AMH leads to many of the same conclusions set out in Brock's paper:

- Risk/reward relationships will be unstable. For example, the equity risk premium will vary predictably, based on the relative sizes and preferences of various market participant groups.
- Arbitrage opportunities will exist. Searching for and understanding complex opportunities will have positive payoff potential.
- The popularity of various investment strategies will wax and wane.
- Research and innovation have positive payoffs.

Neither Brock nor Lo explicitly bring institutional structure into their analytical frameworks. Yet, arguably, this, too, is an important piece of the puzzle of constructing an operationally useful theory of goal-based investing.

KEYNES' "BEAUTY CONTEST" INVESTORS

John Maynard Keynes would have liked Lo's AMH, but would have extended it to include the incentives and behaviors of institutional investors. In his famous Chapter 12 of *The General Theory of Employment, Interest, and Money* (1936) he observed that most professional investors seemed perfectly happy engaging in a zero-sum "beauty contest" game with each other. The objective of the game is to guess which stocks the market would deem most beautiful some short period of time (e.g., six months) from now. By acquiring these soon-to-be-deemed beautiful stocks early, successful investors would earn higher returns. Keynes noted that this game could be played by professionals as long as their clients were willing to pay them the fees necessary to stay in business.

Keynes contrasted this majority investment style with that of a much smaller contrarian investor group, which attempted to turn savings into productive capital. This is much harder work, requiring investors to actually understand the businesses they were investing in, and assess the quality of the people managing these businesses. Yet, Keynes observed, this much harder, far more productive work was seldom appreciated by the market. As he famously observed, "It is the long-term investor promoting the public interest who will in practice come in for the most criticism...if in the short-run he is unsuccessful...he will not receive much mercy. Worldly wisdom teaches that it is far better for reputation to fail conventionally than to succeed unconventionally."

AKERLOF'S "LEMONS" THESIS

Notwithstanding his graphic description of the dysfunctional investment sociology of the 1930s, Keynes did not offer a direct explanation of why clients hired (and continue to this day to hire), professional "beauty contest" investors. It took until 1970 for Nobel Laureate George Akerlof to offer a plausible explanation in his famous "The Market for Lemons" article.[2] The cause, Akerlof argued, is informational asymmetry between buyers and sellers. If the latter know more about what they are selling than the former know about what they are buying, then buyers will pay too much for too little. Akerlof illustrated this principle at work in the market for used cars (hence the "lemons" reference). He could just as well have illustrated his principle at work in the market for investment management services.

If the buyers of beauty contest investment management services truly understood the zero-sum nature of the game, most would surely stop paying too much for too little. But realistically, left to their own devices, most buyers will never figure it out. In Keynes' words, most buyers continue to prefer failing conventionally to succeeding unconventionally. Thus we have a case of genuine market failure on our hands, which can only be remedied through the creation of expert fiduciary investment institutions legally required to act in the sole best interest of their clients. Fortunately, such organizations now exist and are growing in numbers.

DRUCKER'S FIDUCIARY INVESTMENT INSTITUTIONS

We have already met Peter Drucker and his *Unseen Revolution* book. One of its key messages was that effective pension institutions are not exempt from the principles that define any effective organization: mission clarity, alignment of interests between principals and agents, informed oversight, strong executive function, right scale, and competitive in the requisite labor markets. Deductively, pension institutions with these attributes *should* be able to produce client/beneficiary value at a reasonable cost. Do they in practice?

Data limitations make this a difficult question to answer using traditional statistical methods. Fortunately, this situation is now changing. Prior chapters recounted my personal involvement with building Drucker pension institutions started in the mid-1980s, leading to the eventual creation of the globally respected Ontario Teachers' Pension Plan (OTPP) and its long-term record of outstanding investment performance over a 25-year period. A growing number of pension institutions have been and are being built on the same Drucker principles.

At the same time, data limitations for research purposes are diminishing. So, as an example, research studies such as the cited one titled "Is Bigger Better? Size and Performance in Pension Fund Management" by Dyck and Pomorski are throwing new, important light on the drivers of institutional investment performance.[3] The study documented increasing net excess returns as pension fund asset values increase. An important performance driver is increased insourcing of private markets investing as asset size increases, thus materially reducing asset management costs without reducing gross returns. OTPP was an early successful adopter of these insourcing strategies.

AMBACHTSHEER'S RETURN PREDICTION JOURNEY

My personal quest to find answers to the return prediction questions posed in the chapter introduction started in 1969. Sun Life wanted to measure the predictive accuracy of its security analysts' stock rankings, and to see if they were good enough to be used as return predictors in the organization's portfolio management processes. This micro-measurement work would extend over the course of the 1970s to many organizations and methodologies. It culminated with the 1979 article (with Jim Farrell), "Can Active Management Add Value?"[4] The answer was: "Yes, it can add value at the margin, if the investment organization can deal with processing many hundreds of low-information-content alpha predictions in a systematic manner."

I also developed a longer-horizon macro return prediction process in the 1970s.[5] This scenario-based approach has since evolved into the "Seven

Coherent Investment Eras in the Last 100 Years" narrative that I have been updating ever since. Has this adaptive, story telling approach to divining future return prospects been useful? It certainly has been for me personally, and for my long-time clients who have been willing, in Keynes' words, "to succeed unconventionally." The next chapter offers the most recent update of this narrative.

BACK TO THE STARTING QUESTIONS

So are the equity and bond return calculations at the start of the chapter credible 20-year return predictions? I believe they are. They are grounded in the market pricing realities set out by Brock and Lo. But that is only half the story. It is equally important to ask how such return predictions should be linked to producing client/beneficiary value at a reasonable cost. Addressing this institutional design and governance challenge requires the insights of Keynes, Akerlof, and Drucker. While credible return predictions are a necessary condition for producing client/beneficiary value, they are not enough. Those predictions must also be translated into investment decisions that truly serve client/beneficiary needs. And that is where the Drucker pension organizations come in (see Chapters 12, 13, and 17).

CHAPTER 20

Investment Returns in the 21st Century

"Piketty sees the 60-year WWI–1970s period as an anomaly...
which is now well behind us.... Future annual real returns on
capital will likely fall below the 5 percent experience of the 18th
and 19th centuries ...."

—Keith Ambachtsheer[1]

RETHINKING INVESTMENT BELIEFS

The previous chapter noted that investment theories continue to evolve. Just as Thomas Piketty saw the 60-year period from World War 1 to the 1970s as a socioeconomic anomaly in the grander sweep of things (Chapter 4), the efficient markets hypothesis (EMH) is increasingly seen as an interesting anomaly in an investment context. The EMH cannot be invoked as a substitute for thinking about how investment markets *really* work, and for thinking about how the resulting investment beliefs should lead us to invest the financial wealth of other people.

Chapter 19 notes that Andrew Lo has offered a plausible alternative to the EMH: the adaptive markets hypothesis, or AMH for short. He explains it as taking a biological/evolutionary approach to understanding investment markets and the people in them, rather than a robotic "physics" approach. It is fear and greed that drives these markets more than sober, rational calculation. In a similar vein, Washington University's Hyman Minsky posited the financial instability hypothesis (FIH), arguing that financial stability in developed economies would naturally become a source of future instability through speculative risk-taking. His work was largely ignored until people acknowledged that the global financial crisis offered a textbook example (a "Minsky moment") of the FIH in action.[2]

TELLING THE CAPITAL MARKETS STORY

The previous chapter also noted that, in the tradition of Lo's AMH and Minsky's FIH, I have been writing and updating my own capital markets narrative since the late 1970s, based on the history captured in Table 20.1. This framing continues to be a powerful tool for three reasons:

1. The table reflects the FIH by reminding us that financial markets have mindsets that swing from extended periods of growing optimism to extended periods of growing pessimism.
2. It also reflects the AMH because these mindset swings impact pricing in the capital markets in predictable ways. Growing optimism leads to rising prices for risk assets, generous risk premium realizations, and hence falling prospective risk premiums. Conversely, growing pessimism leads to falling prices for risk assets, negative risk premium realizations, and hence rising prospective risk premiums.
3. The table facilitates focused conversations about past investment eras, about the current one we are living through, and about periods during which one era transitions into another.

For example, I set out my belief a few years ago that the "double-bubble blues" era had ended around 2010–11, and that we have been transitioning into a new "mature capitalism" era. The challenge now is to visualize how this new era might play out. A clue from Table 20.1 is that we should give it an optimistic spin, contrary to the prevailing mood of pessimism.

TABLE 20.1 Entering the Eighth Capital Markets Era Since WWI

Investment Era	Investor Mindset	Approximate Time Span	Dividend Yield Change	Realized ERP*
The WWI Decade	Pessimistic	10 years	5% → 7%	−5%
Roaring Twenties	Optimistic	10 years	7% → 4%	+12%
Dirty Thirties/Fateful Forties	Pessimistic	20 years	4% → 7%	0%
Pax Americana I	Optimistic	20 years	7% → 3%	+8%
Scary Seventies	Pessimistic	10 years	3% → 6%	−3%
Pax Americana II	Optimistic	20 years	6% → 1%	+9%
Double-Bubble Blues	Pessimistic	10 years	1% → 2%	−6%
Mature Capitalism?	Optimistic?	20 years?	2% → ?%	?%

*Stock returns come from *Triumph of the Optimists* by Dimson, Marsh, and Staunton. Bond returns are based on a hypothetical CPI-linked bond with a real yield of 2.5 percent. If the actual LT TIPS return had been used for the "double-bubble blues" era, the realized ERP (Equity Risk Premium) would have been −10 percent.

Conventional Narratives about Mature Capitalism

Today's dreary prognostications about the unfolding future have four defining elements:

- **Demographics:** As populations age and worker/retiree ratios fall from 4:1 to 2:1 in the developed world, consumption, capital formation, and productivity will weaken, and hence, economic growth will also weaken.
- **Fiscal Deficits:** Both families and governments are borrowing to make ends meet. This cannot go on forever. Eventually, a day of reckoning will come. This, too, will dampen future economic demand, and hence growth prospects.
- **Geopolitical Risks:** These seem to always be with us, with an assertive China, a belligerent Russia, and an unsettled Middle East making current headlines.
- **Environmental Risks:** These are also in play in the form of global warming and changing weather patterns, which in turn cause widespread floods and droughts. The concomitant financial risk relates to assets becoming "stranded" as the full costs of production are internalized (e.g., for carbon emission and water pollution). More on this in Chapter 27.

If these four elements fully defined the now-unfolding mature capitalism era, one would think they would be reflected in how markets are pricing long-horizon financial assets such as equities. Yet, the earnings yield of the S&P500 is about 5 percent today, versus a long-term average somewhere between 6 percent and 7 percent. In short, the pessimism embedded in the demographics, debt, geopolitical conflict, and climate change narratives don't seem to be embedded in the pricing of risky USA-based assets. European and emerging markets equities appear to be somewhat more conservatively priced at earnings yields of 6 percent and 7 percent, respectively.[3] Why are equity prices not deep in the dumps? An article by William Bernstein, "The Paradox of Wealth," offers a plausible explanation.[4]

The Paradox of Wealth   Bernstein offers four reasons for why mature capitalism might turn out better than most people expect:

1. **Scientific Rationalism:** It is unduly pessimistic to assert that all things worth discovering or inventing have already been discovered and invented. New discoveries and inventions will continue to accumulate and add to societal wealth in this century.
2. **Property Rights Buttressed by the Rule of Law:** The evidence in support of this prosperity factor is overwhelming. Wealthy developed economies

already have this property rights/rule of law attribute. Poorer developing economies would benefit greatly from acquiring it.

3. **Well-functioning Capital Markets:** Despite the realities of the AMH and FIH, well-functioning capital markets are essential to transforming savings into wealth-producing capital on a large scale. Institutional investors can and should play a critical role in making capital markets more functional.

4. **Modern Communication and Transportation Technologies:** It is not sufficient to simply produce the goods and services consumers want. They also need to know about them and be able to easily access them. To this end, communication and transportation technologies continue their march toward greater effectiveness and lower costs.

Now for Bernstein's paradox: Increasing societal wealth in a developed economy does not logically mean increasing returns on capital. In fact, quite the opposite: Increasing wealth logically leads to lower returns on capital. Why? Because increasing capital productivity decreases demand for new capital. At the same time, the decreasing urgency of spending income on immediate consumption increases the supply of capital.

Piketty comes to the same "lower future returns on capital" conclusion in *Capital in the 21st Century*. He calculates a steady 5 percent return on productive capital (including real estate) in 18th- and 19th-century France and the UK. He then observes an extended period of capital destruction through WWI, the Great Depression, and WWII, followed by an extended, post-WWII high-growth reconstruction/Baby Boom period accompanied by high returns on capital (i.e., the Pax Americana I and II eras in Table 20.1). That period is now behind us. With high-return opportunities declining, and a potentially increasing savings rate as societal wealth and income continue to concentrate, he foresees a decline in the return on productive capital from 5 percent to 4 percent as a logical consequence.

THE S&P 500 ENTRAILS: A CLOSER LOOK

A quick look back at Table 20.1 confirms Bernstein's and Piketty's "lower returns on capital" assessment. Note the S&P 500 divided yield was 7 percent at the start of Pax Americana I (i.e., 1950s). Fifty years later, by the end of Pax Americana II (i.e., 2000s), it had dropped to 1%. Table 20.2 offers a closer look at the S&P 500 entrails in the double-bubble blues era (approximately 2000–2010), and the first four years of the mature capitalism era.

To read the table, some definitions are required:

- **Dividend Yield:** Dividends paid in the year divided by average index value.

TABLE 20.2 S&P 500 Fundamentals in Transition from Double-Bubble Blues to Mature Capitalism

Year	Dividend Yield	Net Buyback Yield	Payout Yield	Plowback Yield	Earnings Yield	LT TIPS Yield	Implied ERP	Index Value	Trailing Earnings
2000	1.20%	0.70%	1.90%	1.70%	3.60%	3.70%	−0.10%	1320	$50
2001	1.30%	0.80%	2.10%	0.00%	2.10%	3.50%	−1.40%	1148	$25
2002	1.60%	0.80%	2.40%	0.60%	3.00%	2.70%	0.30%	880	$28
2003	1.80%	1.10%	2.90%	2.10%	5.00%	2.30%	2.70%	1112	$49
2004	1.70%	1.50%	3.20%	1.80%	5.00%	1.90%	3.10%	1212	$59
2005	1.80%	1.70%	3.50%	2.50%	6.00%	2.00%	4.00%	1248	$70
2006	1.90%	2.20%	4.10%	2.00%	6.10%	2.80%	3.30%	1418	$82
2007	1.90%	4.10%	6.00%	−1.50%	4.50%	2.50%	2.00%	1468	$66
2008	2.60%	2.40%	5.00%	−3.60%	1.40%	2.40%	−1.00%	903	$15
2009	2.50%	0.90%	3.40%	2.30%	5.70%	2.00%	3.70%	1115	$51
2010	2.00%	2.10%	4.10%	2.70%	6.80%	1.80%	5.00%	1258	$77
Mean	1.80%	1.70%	3.50%	1.00%	4.50%	2.50%	2.00%		
2011	2.10%	3.10%	5.20%	1.80%	7.00%	0.80%	6.20%	1258	$87
2012	2.30%	2.60%	4.90%	1.40%	6.30%	0.40%	5.90%	1426	$87
2013	2.10%	2.40%	4.50%	1.60%	6.10%	1.60%	4.50%	1848	$100
2014	2.10%	2.60%	4.70%	0.70%	5.40%	0.80%	4.60%	2059	$103
Mean	2.10%	2.70%	4.80%	1.40%	6.20%	0.90%	5.30%		

Sources: Bloomberg, Standard & Poor's, Garland, Lazonick.

- **Net Buyback Yield:** Net share repurchases in the year divided by average index value. While gross repurchases data is generally available, new share issuance is not. Based on some rough calculations, we assumed a relatively low rate of new share issuance at 0.5 percent of share value per year.
- **Payout Yield:** Sum of dividend yield and net buy-back yield.
- **Plowback Yield:** Difference between earnings yield and payout yield. These are the earnings retained by S&P 500 companies after paying out dividends and net share repurchases divided by average index value.
- **Earnings Yield:** Net earnings for the year divided by average index value.
- **LT TIPS Yield:** Year-end 30-year TIPS yield.
- **Implied ERP:** Difference between earnings yield and LT TIPS yield. The calculation implicitly assumes zero real earnings growth, and hence is arguably a conservative long-term estimate.
- **Index Value:** Year-end index value.
- **Trailing Earnings:** Net earnings for the year.

Table 20.2 makes it clear why the double-bubble blues era was as painful as this analytical framework predicted it would be in 2000: The implied equity risk premium at that time was negative. It took until 2010 for the implied ERP to reach a comfortable 5.0 percent. Note that even recently, with the S&P 500 up 800 points since 2010, the ERP still stands at 4.6 percent.

Should investors still be comfortable? Certainly 'yes', relative to the 2000 situation. And plausibly yes if (a) U.S. stocks in the index can maintain or grow their real earnings from here; and if (b) there is no permanent material spike in the LT TIPS yield from current levels. Further, recall the earlier observation that European and emerging markets equities are priced more cheaply than U.S. equities.

Table 20.2 points to another unfolding trend: an apparent secular rise in net share buybacks from under 1 percent of the S&P 500 index value in the early 2000s to figures approaching 3 percent recently, compared to a dividend yield of 2 percent.[5] So corporations are now using more of their earning to buy back stock than they are to pay dividends. Further, when you add the two yields together (i.e., the payout yield), the sum of the two almost approaches the earnings yield. The implication is that corporations are now returning most of their earnings to shareholders in the form of dividends and share buy backs, and retaining little for capital reinvestment. This is yet another indication of the arrival of mature capitalism.

REASONABLE PRICING

So where does all this lead? The most important conclusion is that, despite the strong rise in the S&P 500 in the first four years of the mature capitalism era, its valuation is not in bubble territory. Pricing is consistent with a lower return-on-capital, lower growth, and lower long-term interest rate environment. In such an environment, an equity risk premium in the 4 percent area does not seem out of line.

CHAPTER 21

Long-Termism as the Dominant Investment Paradigm

Not There Yet

" . . . I am becoming more optimistic that a movement towards long-termism is afoot, one that is pulling in corporations and institutional investors and that has the potential to get enough traction to change behavior . . . ."

—Theresa Whitmarsh

MOVEMENT TOWARD LONG-TERMISM?

This chapter's epigraph is from the Guest Editorial in the Fall 2014 edition of the *Rotman International Journal of Pension Management* (RIJPM). Theresa Whitmarsh, executive director of the Washington State Investment Board, offers three reasons for her optimism that a movement toward long-termism is afoot:

1. The widely recognized need to restore trust in the modern business economy, especially in its financial sector
2. The growing recognition that capitalism must be inclusive to be sustainable (i.e., must benefit the many, not just the few)
3. The growing recognition of the threat of carbon emission–induced climate change to sustainable wealth-creation in the 21st century

Further, she points out, there is increasing evidence that these concerns are leading to concrete initiatives to lengthen the time horizon in which investment decisions are made, and in which the success of these decisions are evaluated. These initiatives coalesce around three themes:

1. Movement by institutional investors toward disintermediation through direct ownership of private assets
2. Movement toward more concentrated portfolios of publicly traded equities by institutional investors, leading to greater influence over corporate behavior
3. More effective collaboration strategies between and among institutional investors and investee corporations with the goal to shift both investment and corporate decision-making into longer time frames

She pointed to the Focusing Capital on the Long Term (FCLT) initiative led by CPPIB's Mark Wiseman and McKinsey's Dominic Barton as an especially promising new development. The mission of this initiative is "to develop practical structures, metrics, and approaches for longer-term behaviors in the investment and business worlds." This is to be achieved through a mix of actions ranging from conducting research, to organizing discussion forums, to identifying and championing practical ideas to achieve the longer-term behaviors goal.

In support of the FCLT initiative, I agreed to do two things. The first was to make the case for long-termism in an article that would offer a new, compelling perspective on the topic. The second was to assess the current state of institutional long-horizon thinking and actions through surveying a large sample of major pension organizations around the world on these questions. This chapter reports on the outcomes of both of these efforts.

THE CASE FOR LONG-TERMISM

The resulting article titled "The Case for Long-Termism" followed the Whitmarsh editorial in the same RIJPM issue.[1] To make the case compelling, the article makes it twice: deductively and inductively. Following the *Oxford Dictionary* definitions, the article first uses "knowledge about things that are generally true in order to think about a particular situation and problem" and then reverses the sequence by "inferring a general law from a set of particular circumstances." Happily, both approaches lead to the same conclusions, expressed in the article as "The case for long-termism is strong in both logic and outcomes. Embracing it is both an opportunity and a responsibility."

Why such a strong, affirmative conclusion? Because the process of making the case for long-termism twice strengthened my own conviction of its power:

1. **The Deductive Case:** Without long-termism, we would still be subsistence societies of hunters and gatherers. It was wise foresight—that is, responsible long-termism—that led our forebears to save and to invest part of their meager incomes in seeds, tools, and shelter, so that their children could have a better tomorrow. Centuries later, those investments led to roads and ships to explore and trade in a wider world. Still centuries later, they produced trains, planes, and automobiles. Even today, centuries later again, there are still better tomorrows to be had. But now we live in far more complex societies that suffer from principal–agent problems in all three of its important functional dimensions: political, commercial, and financial. A rough estimate of the collective cost of these agency problems in terms of forgone long-term returns arrived at a number of 1.5 percent per annum. How to capture this missing wealth-creation potential? Institutional investors around the globe, led by the pension sector, are well placed to play a "lead wagon" fiduciary role in driving those agency costs down by focusing the capital at their disposal on the long-term. Qualitatively, such a stance will foster good citizenship; quantitatively, it could boost the return on that capital by as much as 1.5 percent per annum.

2. **The Inductive Case:** The second part of the article summarizes four investor stories with a common theme. Independently, separated in space and time, all four investors produced carefully documented, extraordinary excess returns over market benchmarks for periods of time exceeding two decades. What were the particular circumstances that produced these extraordinary investment results? It was that all four investment processes were guided by the steady application of a set of investment beliefs firmly grounded in the long-termism philosophy. Looking for the common threads in these four stories, I identified six. They are set out in Table 21.1. Have a close look: How well do these six common threads describe your organization? If the answer is "not very well," your organization is not equipped to be a serious long-horizon investor and generate extraordinary excess returns over multiple decades.

AN INSTITUTIONAL SURVEY

Table 21.1 lists effective governance as one of the six common threads in executing a successful long-horizon investment program. Prior chapters noted that effective governance has been a focus area for me for a long time, leading to participation in identical surveys assessing the state of pension

TABLE 21.1 Six Common Threads to the Four Extraordinary Investor Stories

Articulating a clear investment stance and living it
Having autonomy to act
Effective internal governance and management
Requisite human capital to be competitive
Investing in real businesses
Balancing conviction and humility

fund governance in 1997 and 2005. In support of the FCLT initiative, this same survey was conducted once again in 2014. As was the case in 1997 and 2005, survey participation was strong, with 81 completed responses from pension fund leaders managing a collective $5 trillion.[2]

Chapter 10 noted that, on the governance side, the survey requested pension fund CEO responses to 23 statements. A good news survey outcome was that, compared to an average governance score of 4.5 in 1997 and 4.7 in 2005, the average 2014 governance score was 4.8. So, on average, governance quality appears to be (slowly) heading in the right direction. The not-so-good news was that the same five governance statements received the lowest scores in 1997, 2005, and once again in 2014. The implication is that board selection and development processes continue to be problematical, with two important consequences: board meddling in operational matters (e.g., in manager selection) and human capital constraints (e.g., noncompetitive compensation policies).

In addition to effective governance and competitive compensation, Table 21.1 listed four other long-horizon investing success factors: articulating and living a clear stance, autonomy to act, investing in businesses (rather than trading pieces of paper), and a willingness to be occasionally wrong. The second part of the 2014 survey assessed the degree to which these success factors were present or absent in the responding organizations. To that end, 22 additional survey statements were crafted, and again, respondents were asked to score them on the same 6-to-1 scale used for the governance statements.

Survey Findings on Long-Horizon Investing

The average long-horizon investment score turned out to be 4.9 (recall the average governance score was 4.8). Both average scores reflect a natural tendency of survey respondents to bias their scores toward the higher end of the range. Hence, it is a comparison of the statements receiving the relatively highest and lowest scores that will provide the most information.

Table 21.2 offers this comparison, and leads to an important conclusion: There is currently a material aspiration/implementation gap in the

TABLE 21.2 The State of Long-Horizon Investing in the Global Pension Sector

	Long-Horizon Investing		
Highest Scores	**Mean Score 2014 Rank**	**Lowest Scores**	**Mean Score 2014 Rank**
We believe that the capability to invest for the long-term is a significant advantage in creating value.	1	We (or our managers on our behalf) have explicit policies for engaging corporations (or other organizations) we invest in when we think proactive engagement is warranted.	18
Our organization's statement of investment policy explicitly states that we invest for the long-term.	2	The mandates for each long-term component explicitly express long-term objectives and shorter-term downside tolerance.	19
Specific components of our fund are explicitly designated to focus on investing for the long-term.	3	Our approach to evaluating long-term fund components is meaningfully different from other components.	20
We have a specific overall allocation policy to implement a long-term orientation in our fund.	4	The investment manager compensation for the long-term fund components has been explicitly designed to reflect the long investment horizon.	21
We believe that our long-term investing protocols create significant value.	5	We (or our managers on our behalf) explicitly integrate environmental and social factors into deciding which corporations we invest in.	22

Source: Ambachtsheer and McLaughlin (2015), "How Effective Is Pension Fund Governance Today? and Do Pension Funds Invest for the Long-Term? Findings from a New Survey," KPA Advisory Services Ltd.

long-horizon investing space. On the left-hand side of Table 21.2, there is a surprising degree of agreement on the potential value of designing and implementing long-horizon investment programs. However, the right-hand side suggests that much needs to be done to realize that potential value. Mandates need to be better articulated. Performance measurement and compensation systems need to be redesigned. Effective corporate engagement strategies still need to be invented, as do the integration of environmental and social factors into investment decision processes.

As in the governance section of the survey, a few actual quotes from survey respondents add some color to these findings:

- "Despite agreement that we are LH investors...sensitivity to peer performance gets in the way..."
- "We are experiencing material regulatory constraints to be truly LH investors..."
- "High external fees are a problem...insourcing has become an important aspect of LH investing for us..."
- "We find that most external investment managers are not really aligned with our LH investing aspirations..."
- "While our organization is on board with LH investing conceptually, we are struggling to build a new monitoring and guidance framework...we need a new language...."

The good news in these survey findings is that embedding long-termism into pension investment programs is increasingly seen for what it is: good for society and good for investment returns. The not-so-good news is that there is still a material aspiration/implementation gap in the design and management of long-horizon investment programs.

CHAPTER 22

Investing for the Long Term I

From Saying to Doing

"In a recent study of public and private pension and sovereign wealth funds, respondents overwhelmingly agreed that while the ability to invest long-term is an advantage, they do not necessarily have an effective set of implementation strategies/tools to help them realize their aspirations...."

—Focusing Capital on the Long Term (FCLT) Initiative

THE FCLT INITIATIVE

The epigraph to this chapter comes from the 2015 "Long-Term Portfolio Guide," a major work-product of the Focusing Capital on the Long Term (FCLT) initiative. The reference in the quote is to the key findings of the Ambachtsheer-McLaughlin institutional investor survey set out in Chapter 10, and further in the previous chapter.[1] One of those key findings indeed was a serious aspiration/implementation gap in investing for the long term.

The FCLT initiative, launched in 2013, is now supported by a diverse group of influential international investment and corporate leaders. As its name indicates, FCLT's goal is to refocus investment decisions on the long term. It is worth repeating the initiative's motivation:

Too many investors continue to seek returns on their strategies as quickly as possible. Companies are missing out on profitable investments for fear of missing quarterly earnings guidance. Corporate management significantly undervalues and underinvests in long-term prospects. Savers are missing out on potential returns because stock markets are penalizing companies that make long-term investments. Society is missing out on long-term growth and innovation because of underinvestment.

FCLT identifies four action areas to change this rather depressing picture:

1. Reorienting the portfolio strategies and management of institutional investors
2. Unlocking value through engagement and active ownership
3. Improving the dialogue between investors and corporations
4. Shifting the board's focus to support long-term strategy and sustainable growth

The purpose of FCLT's *Long-Term Portfolio Guide* is to support action area #1 by offering practical advice to institutional investors on how to actually refocus investment decisions on the long term. This chapter summarizes the five key suggestions in the 54-page document, and adds my own observations and suggestions to them.[2]

REORIENTING PORTFOLIO STRATEGIES AND MANAGEMENT IN FIVE CORE AREAS

The introduction to the guide recognizes the contributions of 24 investment professionals from 10 different investment organizations based in Europe, United State, Canada, and Asia/Pacific Rim, managing a collective $6 trillion. Their stated goal in creating the guide was to offer a collection of practical ideas in five core areas to foster long-term investment value-creation. The five core areas are:

1. **Investment beliefs** provide a compass to determine sustained long-term investment strategies and navigate short-term turbulence.
2. **Risk appetite statement** forces the identification of key risks and uncertainties, relevant time horizons, and the asset owner's ability and willingness to bear these risks and uncertainties.
3. **Benchmarking processes** should measure long-term value-creation and distinguish between the contributions of strategy and its implementation.
4. **Evaluations and incentives** align financial interests between principals and agents with an emphasis on long-term outcomes.
5. **Investment mandates** should be used as mechanisms to align investment manager interests and priorities with those of the asset owner.[3]

A closer look at the practical ideas the 24 experts recommend in each of the five core areas follows.

Investment Beliefs

This section of the guide offers a blend of philosophy and practical case studies. Its heart is to address the *why?* question: Why is the clear articulation of investment beliefs so important to being a successful long-term investor? The guide offers six reasons:

1. **Consistency:** An agreed-upon set of investment beliefs leads to consistency in thinking about how financial markets work (e.g., price momentum in the short-term but mean-reversion in the longer term), and thus create a holistic, integrative context for strategy formation and execution.
2. **Relevance:** An agreed-upon set of investment beliefs should be tied to the investment organization's mission. For example, what is more important to the organization's beneficiaries/owners: long-term loss of capital or short-term capital value volatility?
3. **Long-Term Focus:** Two important investment strategy questions are: (1) What creates investment value over the long-term? and (2) How are investments priced today relative to an explicit valuation standard? An agreed-upon set of investment beliefs provides critical guidance to addressing these questions.
4. **Behavioral Biases:** There is a rich literature on the behavioral biases of investors, and institutional investors are not immune to them. An agreed-upon set of investment beliefs will help ward off our natural tendency toward short-termism when financial markets become volatile.
5. **Principal–Agent Problems:** Every investment process has a "value chain" attached to it, which has owner/beneficiaries at one end and investment professionals at the other. Clear investment beliefs help ensure that strategy determination and execution focus on the needs of the owner/beneficiaries, and not on those of the investment professionals.
6. **Communication:** An agreed-upon set of investment beliefs helps explain why a chosen investment strategy is appropriate, given the investment organization's mission. For example, if ESG factors are judged to be important drivers of long-term value-creation, they will naturally be integrated into investment strategy decisions and their implementation, rather than be dealt with as a separate topic.

The case studies in the guide provide tangible examples of how an agreed-upon set of investment beliefs helps address these six challenges, and they are worth reading. And of course, investment beliefs have been a central theme in the previous four of chapters in this book.

Risk Appetite Statement

The guide offers both philosophy and case studies on composing a risk appetite statement. The construction of an organizational risk identification matrix is a good starting point. The matrix organizes 10 types of risks into the categories of asset risks, organizational risks, and stakeholder/environmental risks. See Table 22.1.

Now comes the question of an organization's appetite for bearing each of these 10 types of risks. Answering it will be a healthy, enlightening exercise for the board and management of any investment organization. The guide offers a risk appetite matrix to help sort this out, reproduced in Table 22.2. Where would *you* position each of the 10 types of risks to be managed in the risk appetite matrix?

There is one risk dimension that did not emerge cleanly out of the two risk matrixes in the guide: a clear distinction between the risks facing the organization versus the risks facing the ultimate asset owners/beneficiaries/clients. While this distinction may not be material in some contexts, it is material in others. Take the pensions context, for example. Prior chapters have noted that young workers and pensioners face

TABLE 22.1   Risk Identification Matrix

Asset Risks	Organizational Risks	Stakeholder/Environment Risks
Impairment	Operational	Peer Comparisons
Valuation	Strategic/Fiduciary	Legal/Regulatory
Funding/Liquidity	Reputational	Clients/Beneficiaries/Sponsors
Counterparty/Collateral		

Source: Adapted from the *FCLT Long-Term Portfolio Guide.*

TABLE 22.2   Risk Appetite Matrix

		Willingness	
		Low	High
Ability	Low	Simple, conservative	Need to lower willingness and/or increase ability
	High	Complex, conservative	Complex, aggressive

Source: Adapted from the *FCLT Long-Term Portfolio Guide.*

very different risks. The #1 risk for young workers is that they miss the compounding magic of high long-term returns. The #1 risk for pensioners is that there are insufficient funds to make next month's pension payment. Risk appetite statements for pension organizations should address this distinction.

Benchmarking Processes

The guide provided a thorough treatment of benchmarking quite consistent with the approach set out in Chapter 13. A key guide message is to distinguish between benchmarking strategy and implementation decisions:

1. **Benchmarking Strategy:** Absolute return targets, risk-adjusted return targets, and simple reference portfolios that reflect the organization's (or its owners/beneficiaries/clients') tolerance for risk-taking all have possible roles in measuring investment strategy expectations versus outcomes.
2. **Benchmarking Implementation:** The emphasis here should be on creating more refined, low-cost, passive strategy implementation benchmarks that focus on long-term investing. As an example, the guide showed how to build an equities reference portfolio with selection criteria such as ROA, ROIC, and FCF margins, and nonfinancial considerations such as governance quality, social, and environmental considerations. More on this in the next chapter.

Chapter 13 noted that CEM Benchmarking Inc.'s "value for money and risk" benchmarking services reflect the distinction between benchmarking strategy and its implementation, and are widely used by asset owner organizations around the world. Its databases have become a valuable research tool for testing and innovating bench-marking processes. As an example, research studies have found that certain strategy implementation approaches are more cost-effective than others.[4]

Evaluations and Incentives

The Evaluation and Incentives section of the guide has two major themes which echo those set out in Chapter 15. The obvious one is the length of the evaluation period, and the message is to emphasize four- to five-year periods over one-year periods. So both in measuring performance and in designing compensation schemes, implementing long-term investment programs logically calls for four- to five-year time frames.

The other theme is that effective evaluation and incentive schemes have a strong qualitative dimension. At the portfolio level this means testing for the consistency between the organization's investment beliefs, its investment strategy, and how it is being implemented. So if the organization believes that corporations that achieve high sustainability ratings will be superior long-term investments, do its portfolios actually reflect this belief? At the individual level, if the organization believes that personal skills and behaviors such as communication, persuasion, and collaboration are important organization success dimensions, that should be reflected in how people are evaluated and compensated. There will be more on this in the next chapter.

Investment Mandates

This section of the guide pulls all the previous sections together, using a series of practical examples. It asserts that investment mandate construction should be guided by three principles:

1. Aligned investment beliefs and interests through the entire investment chain
2. Mitigation against behavioral biases that often get in the way of staying the course in long-term investment programs
3. Clear evaluation protocols (both quantitative and qualitative) to assess long-term investment success (or lack of it) through time

With these three principles in mind, an effective mandate addresses the investment goal(s) to be achieved, the underlying investment beliefs and risk appetite to guide the process, the actual investment process to be employed (e.g., selection criteria, engagement protocols, sell triggers), the guidelines to be followed (e.g., portfolio concentration, turnover), and the terms to be observed (e.g., benchmarks, time-horizon, fee/incentive structure).

FROM SAYING TO DOING

Chapter 27 will address climate change risk, raising the question of the continuing lack of urgency in many quarters to address this issue. Research suggests a strong "in my lifetime" bias when we prioritize the issues we face. Specifically, most of us use high discount rates for events not likely to occur in our lifetime. So we should not be surprised that in adult population surveys, there is a strong negative correlation between age and the perceived urgency of dealing with climate change issues.

A similar kind of inertia exists in many boardrooms of asset owner organizations on the challenge of moving investment mindsets from short-term beauty contest to long-term value-creation thinking. To their credit, the writers of the guide point to the work of legal expert Ed Waitzer and co-authors, which suggests the "trajectory of the law" has now reached a point where the exercise of fiduciary duty to consider intergenerational fairness is a "reasonable expectation."[5] Chapter 11 asserted that a direct implication is that boards now have a fiduciary duty to move investing for the long term from saying to doing.

Let's get on with it.

CHAPTER 23

Investing for the Long Term II

How Should We Measure Performance?

"What gets measured gets managed."
—Peter Drucker

LONG-TERM INVESTING: MEASURING RESULTS

The references in the previous two chapters to the Focusing Capital on the Long-Term (FCLT) initiative were not meant to suggest it is the sole initiative to that end. The United Nations (UN) wants more long-term investing, as does the OECD and the World Economic Forum. According to the survey results reported in Chapter 21, many pension organizations themselves want to shift in this direction.

This building momentum raises an important governance question. Paraphrasing Peter Drucker: "If we are going to manage a long-term investment program, how should we measure its performance?" A simplistic response would be "over long-horizon evaluation periods." It is simplistic because boards cannot wait 10–20 years to see how their organization's long-term investment program turned out. Boards should insist on sensible progress markers along journeys lasting 10–20 years. What might such markers look like? That is the question this chapter addresses.

SENSIBLE PROGRESS MARKERS

So what is it that we want to measure the performance of? What *is* long-term investing? Keynes described it as participating in a process that converts savings into wealth-producing capital, which in turn pays income back to investors. It is *not* trading securities in investment markets with the goal of producing capital gains at the expense of other traders (Keynes called this "beauty contest" investing). Yet, it is the success or failure of these beauty contest trading strategies that most current investment performance measurement systems are best designed to measure. And to invoke Drucker once again, what gets measured gets managed. If we measure the wrong things, we will manage the wrong things.

So how do we steer performance measurement away from its short-term trading focus, and toward measuring success (or failure) to create value for beneficiaries in a longer-term time frame? The answer must lie in focusing less on short-term total return outcomes, and more on the size, quality, and growth of the income streams the investments are producing, and on the governance and managerial effectiveness of the investee organizations actually producing these income streams. With this reorientation, it becomes reasonable for boards to ask for regular progress reports on the performance of these investment income streams, and on the health and effectiveness of the investee organizations generating them.

ASSESSING INVESTEE ORGANIZATION HEALTH AND EFFECTIVENESS

How can we monitor the health and effectiveness of the investee organizations generating investment income streams? Chapter 12 provided part of the answer by describing the Integrated Reporting (<IR>) initiative. The initiative has led to a fundamental redefinition of 'material' corporate information. The four key <IR> concepts are:

1. **From Mission/Vision to Business Model:** Develop a clear narrative that links the purpose of the organization to a description of how it converts inputs to outcomes. This conversion process involves assessing opportunities and risks, strategy and resource allocation decisions, and results evaluation, all overseen by a robust governance process.
2. **The Six Capitals:** Think carefully about the relevance and importance for organizational success of six forms of capital: financial, manufactured, intellectual, human, social, and natural. All are stores of value, and all are potentially important inputs into the organization's business model, and hence potential factors in assessing the organization's long-term sustainability and success.
3. **Outcomes:** Are the internal and external consequences (positive and negative) resulting from the organization's business activities and outputs? Internal examples could relate to employee morale or organizational

reputation. External examples could relate to customer satisfaction or environmental effects.

4. **Value Creation:** It goes beyond assessing the organization's financial performance (e.g., as might be measured by changes in the present value of future cash flows). A broader context includes an understanding that future cash flows and other conceptions of value are dependent on broader definitions of capital (e.g., competitive advantage), and an expanded range of time horizons.

An article by Roland Burgman and Mark Van Clieaf offers a more finance-oriented perspective on assessing the health and effectiveness of investee corporations.[1] They emphasize the importance of metrics such as economic profit (EP) and return on invested capital (ROIC). EP captures corporate profitability net of a capital charge. ROIC minus the weighted cost of capital captures a corporation's excess return on corporate capital employed. They note that management's job is to organize to maximize longer-term EP growth and excess ROIC on a sustainable basis through continuous innovation, using all forms of capital available to the organization. They also note that many executive compensation schemes in the corporate sector today are not driven by these financial and nonfinancial indicators of longer-term value creation.

Michael Mauboussin and Alfred Rappaport cover similar ground by asserting that corporate value-creation is about maximizing the present value of future risk-adjusted long-term cash flows.[2] As a practical matter, this means investors must monitor three things:

1. **The Governing Objective:** Is the corporation's governing objective clearly expressed?
2. **Supporting Policies:** Is the corporation actually doing the things needed to achieve its governing objective (e.g., in product quality, innovation, customer satisfaction, employee satisfaction, safety)?
3. **Disclosure:** Is the corporation using the <IR> framework to disclose what and how it is doing?

The point here is that engaged long-term investors know a lot about the organizations they invest in. They have clear expectations at the time the original investment is made. They have effective tools to assess actual unfolding investee organization behavior and results versus expectations, and they will engage the boards and managements of these corporations when deemed necessary. An article by Alex van der Velden and Otto van Buul demonstrates how this long-term investing approach can work in practice.[3] It is periodic information on these long-term investment and assessment processes that the boards of the investment organizations should be seeking as part of fulfilling their fiduciary duty.

INVESTMENT INCOME PRODUCTION AS PERFORMANCE

The production of a predictable investment income stream back to the investment organization is a critical success element in long-term investment programs. It follows that whether this is in fact happening (or not) should be a critical focus for performance measurement in these programs. Why? Because capital allocated to these programs should be patient capital, with only the investment income it generates available for pension or endowment payments, or for reinvestment. Shorter-term capital value dips should be of no consequence in this case unless they reflect an impairment of the investee organization's future ability to pay out investment income. As the investment horizon stretches out into the longer term, healthy, rising income streams will eventually produce rising capital values as well.

So what does a protocol that monitors investment income production look like? To the best of my knowledge, this question was first addressed by Robert (Tad) Jeffrey in a 1977 *Journal of Portfolio Management* article titled "Internal Portfolio Growth: The Better Measure," with the subtitle explanation, "Unless you're in a liquidating mode, what really matters is the growth in earnings and dividends, not the market value, of your portfolio." Jeffrey observed that investment income behavior is much more predictable than changes in capital values, and that presumably, investment managers monitor predicted investment income experience vs. actual experience closely over time. To his surprise, he found that "no managers who we contacted were able to answer this question satisfactorily."

A Harvard MBA by training, and the CEO of a manufacturing company by experience, Jeffrey designed a simple investment income monitoring protocol himself. As he had converted the manufacturing company into a family investment company by selling its business assets for cash, he had strong personal motivation to do so. Today, 40 years later, Jeffrey's protocol (improved and updated over time) continues to provide the board of directors of the family investment company with valuable investment income performance information critical to determining the dividend payout policy of the company. A simplified mockup of it is set out in Table 23.1.

With this investment income monitoring protocol as a guide, the company has been able to achieve its primary long horizon objective over the course of the last 40 years: to pay out a growing stream of inflation-adjusted dividends to family beneficiaries over time, while also maintaining the capability of corporate assets to continue to do so into the indefinite future. Since inception, both corporate assets and annual dividends paid out to beneficiaries have doubled in real terms. This remarkable result was due in

TABLE 23.1   A Simple Investment Income Monitoring Protocol

Performance Factor	Monitoring Criteria
Dividend Income	Is actual dividend income in line with expectations? If not, why not? Answering this question requires tracking dividend payout policies, actual dividend changes, currency impacts, asset mix changes, etc. Looking ahead, what should we expect from here?
Interest Income	Is actual interest income in line with expectations? If not, why not? Answering this question requires tracking the shape of the yield curve, bond portfolio duration, use of leverage, currency impacts, asset mix changes, etc. Looking ahead, what should we expect from here?
Other Income Sources	(e.g., security lending, option writing): Is actual income from other sources in line with expectations? If not, why not? Looking ahead, what should we expect from here?
Total Investment Income	Is actual total investment income in line with expectations? If not, deviations will be explainable based on analysis of the investment income components making up the total. Looking ahead, what should we expect from here? Are we on track to meet our longer term goals? If not, what are our decision options?
Distributions	How are we spending our investment income? Is it in line with our goals (e.g., payout vs. reinvestment)? What are the communication implications to beneficiaries? Looking ahead, are our projected distributions in line with our distribution goals? If not, what are our decision options?
Cash-Flow	Are we cash-flow positive, neutral, or negative? Is this in line with expectations? If not, why not? Looking ahead, what should we expect from here? If projections show we will go cash-flow negative, what are the action implications?

Source: KPA Advisory Services Ltd.

no small part to how the company defined and measured success over that 40-year period.[4]

TOTAL FUND RETURN STILL MATTERS

The primary message of this chapter is that long-term investors should care about and really understand the investment income performance of the funds they manage. This does not mean that they should ignore total fund return performance (i.e., returns that include capital value changes). Instead, the point is that long-term investors understand the importance of putting the horse (income generation) before the cart (capital values). They understand that ultimately, it is the quantity and quality of the investment income stream that drives capital values, and not the other way around. This understanding gives long-term investors a fundamental advantage over short horizon beauty contest investors. Even if long-term investors are only approximately right about the quantity, quality, and price of investment income streams they are buying and holding, they should be able to generate higher risk-adjusted net total returns over long periods of time (i.e., 10 years or longer) than most short-horizon investors playing trading games. A growing body of actual results is confirming this hypothesis.[5]

The chapter ends where it started. Long-term investing is moving from saying to doing. Thus we must think carefully about the performance measurement implications of this shift. This means separating the role of the income-generating horse from that of the capital cart. We must measure what we want to manage.

CHAPTER 24

Investing for the Long Term III

Does It Produce Better Outcomes?

"In this study, we explore the organizational and performance implications for organizations that integrate (sustainability into their) corporate policies. Our overarching thesis is that such organizations represent an alternative and distinct way of competing for the modern corporation, characterized by a governance structure that in addition to financial performance, accounts for the environmental and social impact of the company, a long-term approach to maximizing inter-temporal profits, an active stakeholder management process, and more developed measurement and reporting systems . . . ."
—Robert Eccles, Ioannis Ioannou, and George Serafeim

BETTER OUTCOMES?

Chapters 10 and 21 reported the results of a survey-based study on pension governance quality and long-term investing effectiveness. The survey results indicated that many of the 81 pension organizations in the survey have some way to go in devising effective organizational governance and long-term investing processes. A hopeful finding was a positive correlation between perceived governance quality and long-term investing effectiveness. While these findings are material, they beg an important question: Do effective long-term investing processes really produce better results over the long term? The stronger the evidence that this is actually the case, the stronger the investment case that pension organizations and their stakeholders should actively work to raise the quality of their long-term investing game. Indeed, they would have a clear fiduciary duty to do so.

A recent study titled "The Impact of Corporate Sustainability on Organizational Processes and Performance" by Robert Eccles, Ioannis Ioannou, and George Serafeim (called EIS in this chapter) provides the kind of evidence that, in my view, fits the "strong evidence" bill.[1] This chapter summarizes EIS's findings and sets out their implications for the governance and investment strategies of pension organizations. It closes with a brief case study on the Unilever Corporation.

THE DESIGN OF THE EIS STUDY

The essence of study design was to create a long-term database on the key characteristics of what EIS called high-sustainability (HS) and low-sustainability (LS) corporations. Through a series of statistical routines they created a matched sample of 90 HS and 90 LS corporations, with detailed data sets for each over the 1993–2010 measurement period. In selecting the 90 HS corporations, EIS determined that they had adopted a coherent set of sustainability policies by 1993. What made these policies coherent? It was the adoption of a broader long-term stakeholder value-creation model as distinct from the traditional, more narrowly based, shorter-term share price maximization model.[2] The basic idea behind the long-term stakeholder value-creation model is that corporations do not exist for the benefit of short-term beauty contest traders, but for the benefit of their long-term investors, and for their customers, workers, and the larger community as well.

EIS suggest this broader stakeholder value-creation model has five distinct features:

1. **Strong board of director involvement** in adopting the long-term stakeholder value-creation model and ensuring it is in fact implemented.
2. **Performance-based compensation schemes** reflect the sustainability imperative by including a series of nonfinancial key performance indicators (e.g., ESG-related).
3. **Stakeholder identification and engagement processes** receive high priority.
4. **Long-term orientation** permeates throughout the organization.
5. **Emphasis on measurement and disclosure** of material nonfinancial information.

Not surprisingly, they show that the 90 HS corporations achieve much higher scores by these five nonfinancial criteria than the 90 LS corporations.

And what about the respective financial performances of the two sets of corporations? What differential performance (if any) should be expected? EIS argue in favor of the HS corporations. Why? Because they believe that corporations will "do well by doing good." Why? Because they believe that moving to the long-term stakeholder value-creation model reduces agency costs to the benefit of *all* corporate stakeholders, including shareholders. At the same time, a broader value-creation model is more likely to spot longer-term organizational risks in the form of avoidable surprises.

Do the empirical results support their expectations? Yes they do, in two distinct ways:

1. **Accounting Performance:** The HS corporations outperformed the LS corporations by both return on assets and return on equity criteria over the 1993–2010 period. On average, on a value-weighted basis, the HS corporations turned $1 invested in their assets in 1993 into $7.10 in 2010 (vs. $4.40 for the LS corporations), and $1 invested in their equity into $31.70 (vs. $25.70 for the LS corporations).
2. **Market Performance:** A $1 invested in the shares of the value-weighted HS portfolio grew to $22.60 over the 18-year period (vs. $14.30 for the LS portfolio). This translates into an average return outperformance of 4.8 per year with 20 percent lower return volatility. Apparently, the market materially underestimated the ability of the HS corporations to generate greater value for their shareholders than the LS corporations did.[3]

The implications of these findings for pension organizations should not be underestimated. The three overarching ones are:

1. **Organizations can do well by doing good** is, in our view, an idea that is equally salient in the corporate and pensions sectors. Drucker described this as "doing the right things rather than doing things right." This was the central theme of Chapter 11 on fiduciary duty.
2. **Leadership from the organization's board of directors** is critical in choosing and implementing the broad-based stakeholder value-creation model. Again, this idea is equally salient in the corporate and the pensions sectors.
3. **Long-term investing is inherently value-creating** if it is properly executed. This provides direct impetus for the pensions sector to actually adopt and effectively implement long-horizon investment programs.[4]

We now turn to the specific case of the Unilever Corporation to drive these points home.

THE CASE OF UNILEVER

Unilever is a global consumer goods company with $56B in revenues and 174,000 employees worldwide. It ranks #1 on global corporate sustainability indexes produced by Tomorrow's Value Rating and Globe Scan, making it the ultimate HS corporation in the EIS study context. In line with the findings in the EIS study, Unilever's accounting return on assets and equity are 10 percent and 34 percent respectively. Its 15-year stock market return was 9.1 percent versus 5.0 percent for the S&P 500, with a relatively low beta of 0.73.

CEO Paul Polman was recently interviewed by the *Rotman Management* publication. Here are four highlights from the interview:

1. **On Global Reach and Perspective:** "We operate in 190 countries, with a supply chain that touches the two billion people who use our products every day . . . . These products are the main tools through which we engage on issues like food security, climate change, water scarcity, and social instability . . . ."
2. **On Unilever's Sustainable Business Blueprint:** "Our Sustainable Living Plan was launched in 2010 . . . it sets out three overarching goals: (1) to improve the health and well-being of the world's people, (2) to reduce our environmental impact by 50 percent, and (3) to enhance people's livelihoods globally. This leads to more specific commitments in areas like health and hygiene, nutrition, water use, waste and packaging, sustainable sourcing, fairness in the workplace, and opportunities for women."
3. **On the Greatest Remaining Hurdles:** "International leadership is one . . . many of these issues require transformations beyond what one company can achieve . . . governments have a hard time internalizing global challenges . . . businesses may be better equipped to create global, long-term frameworks. Another key challenge is accounting . . . in addition to financial results, we need to account for environmental and social factors. A third thing that slows us down is the continued pressure for short-term performance . . . that's why we put an end to quarterly reporting."
4. **On Which Unilever Program Best Personifies the Potential for Business to Make Positive Change in the World:** "I would point to our total model. To my knowledge, no company our size has ever made the integrated set of commitments we have. They touch on every aspect of our business model."[5]

Paul Polman is also chair of the World Business Council for Sustainable Development, and a board member of both the UN Global Compact and the Global Consumer Foods Forum.

LESSONS FOR PENSION ORGANIZATIONS

For me, the biggest lesson from the EIS study and the Unilever case is for boards of pension organizations to consciously *adopt the broader, more inclusive stakeholder value-creation model* to guide their investment programs, as well as their own organizational goals and strategies. Such a choice would signal the explicit rejection of narrower business models that would focus on the specific interests of special groups, whether they be beauty contest investors in a corporate context, or pensioners, older workers, younger workers, future workers, or their employer equivalents in a pensions context. Given its superior organizational performance, explicit adoption of the long-term stakeholder value-creation model is consistent with the "reasonable expectations" doctrine of fiduciary duty set out in Chapter 11.

The adoption of the long-term stakeholder value-creation model by pension organizations also has a number of more specific implications. Five come to mind:

1. **Pension Plan Design:** This topic was covered in some detail in Chapters 7, 8, and 9. Any design should be consistent with the principles of simplicity, fairness, sustainability, and efficiency. The old "DB vs. DC" debate needs to be permanently buried as dysfunctional.

2. **Stakeholder Communications:** A good place to start here is to ask, "Who *are* our stakeholders?" Another good question is, "Are we aiming for one-way or two-way communications?" A third question is, "What do we want to communicate and receive feedback on?"

3. **Board Effectiveness:** The survey-based research set out in Chapter 10 continues to point to a pensions sector challenge here, specifically, the processes through which board members are selected. While it is true that representativeness creates an important sense of legitimacy, it is not enough. Boards must also embody the collective skills and experience sets required to be an effective oversight body. Specifically, they must "get" the importance of adopting the stakeholder value-creation model for the pension organization, and be able to oversee its implementation.

4. **Organization Design and Investment Beliefs:** Is the organization capable of generating value for money in its benefit administration function? And value for risk and money in its investment function? What are the organization's beliefs about these matters based on? Are they reasonable beliefs? For example, do they reflect the findings of the EIS study? Is there a clear link between our beliefs and our organization design? And is incentive compensation aligned with our goals?

5. **Collaboration Strategies:** Paul Polman noted that there are limits to what a single organization can do to create stakeholder value in a corporate context. Collective action strategies are sometimes required. In the

pensions space, that may mean collective action to change legislation and regulations if current versions hamper value-creation. Or it may require collective action to steer investee corporations toward adopting the stakeholder value-creation model. The implication is that not only should internal organization design be an important governance matter, but external multi-organization collaboration designs as well.

The EIS study findings suggest that these five steps will materially enhance the value-creation potential of your pension organization's investment program, and its benefit administration program as well. Is your board up to the challenge of taking them?

CHAPTER 25

Are Alphas and Betas Bunk?

"Only the smallest fraction of economic writings, theoretical and applied, has been concerned with the preconception that economic laws deduced from a priori assumptions possess rigor and validity independently of any human behavior. But only very few economists have gone as far as this. The majority would have been glad to enunciate meaningful theorems if any had occurred to them...."

—Paul Samuelson, Nobel Prize Laureate

OPERATIONALLY MEANINGFUL THEOREMS

Paul Samuelson's withering critique of the economics profession occasionally comes to mind while scanning through articles and papers on the "science" of investing. Apparently, we don't just have alphas and betas anymore. Investment scientists now believe that betas can be "smart," "exotic," "dynamic," and yes, even "scientific"! Presumably, this distinguishes these beta types from others that are dumb, plain, static, and faith-based. What are we to make of this scientific investing explosion? Is it resulting in operationally meaningful theorems and guides to crafting wiser investment policies? And to making smarter investment and risk management decisions? These are the questions this chapter addresses.

I start with a very brief recounting of my own experiences in the alpha-beta landscape of the 1970s, where I soon learned to appreciate the critical role of understanding human behavior at both the macro and micro levels in the construction and implementation of operationally meaningful theorems. From there this chapter transitions to my current understanding of what useful theorems look like in the construction and implementation of 21st-century retirement income systems. It concludes with an assessment of whether, and how, the current scientific investment paradigm can improve the chances that real people will actually achieve their post-work pension payment goals at affordable contribution rates.

MAKING PORTFOLIO THEORY USEFUL, AND MOVING ON

My first job in the investment industry in 1969 was to figure out whether, and how, portfolio theory could be made useful in the practice of portfolio management. Some ten years later, in two separate *Financial Analyst Journal* articles, I expressed the view that yes, it can indeed be done *if* careful attention is paid to the human behavior aspects of both macro capital markets pricing dynamics, and of micro security analysis and portfolio rebalancing processes.

At the macro level, the breakthrough was to encourage knowledgeable people to tell plausible prospective capital markets "stories" grounded in the sociopolitical-economic realities of the time. At the micro level, the breakthrough was to adjust raw excess-return (i.e., alpha) predictions for information content and transaction costs before feeding them into portfolio optimizers. Both articles were "exit" articles of sorts, as I shifted my professional interest to the design and management of pension systems in the 1980s.[1]

MAKING DRUCKER'S "UNSEEN REVOLUTION" VISIBLE

Reading Peter Drucker's 1976 book, *The Unseen Revolution*, was an important turning point. Previous chapters noted that he posed fundamental questions about the future shape of pension systems that did not yet have answers:

- In whose interest would the rapidly growing pool of retirement savings be managed?
- How and by whom would the inherent risks embedded in pension systems (e.g., investment, inflation, longevity) be borne?
- What kind of institutions would be best equipped to reliably turn retirement savings into future claims on goods and services? What would be the key success drivers for these pension institutions?

Today, 40 years later, this book documents the emerging answers to these questions:

- The financial interests of pension plan members are still not as foremost as they should, and could be. Agency costs of various kinds (e.g., poor governance, misdirected investment policies, high investment management fees) continue to extract their tolls. These agency costs are increasingly being understood and addressed.

■ The high investment returns of the 1980s and 1990s created the illusion that pre-funded pension systems with 60–40 equity–bond asset mixes were all-weather, low-risk/low-cost propositions.

■ The post-2000 period has been serving up a dramatically different experience, combining aging plan memberships, high return volatility, and low average returns. Incomplete and dysfunctional pension contracts have turned win–win formulas into win–lose ones, leading to the death of traditional DB and DC plans, and the birth of hybrid defined ambition/target benefit pension plans.

■ There is increasing recognition that sustainable defined ambition/target benefit plans offer separate return-seeking and payment-safety instruments, with plan members transitioning the bulk of their retirement savings from the former to the latter as they age.

■ The return-seeking and payment-safety instruments operate in fundamentally different time horizons, requiring fundamentally different definitions of risk and risk management. The dominant risk for younger workers is that the contribution rate they can afford is insufficient to allow them to maintain their standard of living when they stop working 30 or 40 years from now. Thus their primary risk is earning a too-low long-horizon return on their retirement savings. The dominant risk for retirees is that next month's pension check will not be in the mail. Thus, their primary risk is plan insolvency.

■ Institutions that are best equipped to manage defined ambition/target benefit pension arrangements without conflicts of interest are noncommercial, well-governed and managed, and have the requisite skills and scale to cost-effectively manage all the key components of defined ambition pension plans.

The consequences of these answers for the investment function of 21st-century pension institutions are worth exploring in greater detail.

KEY CHARACTERISTICS OF RETURN-SEEKING AND PAYMENT-SAFETY INVESTMENT PROGRAMS

Chapter 19 asserted that the essence of success in any long-horizon return-seeking investment program is to acquire a diversified portfolio of healthy (but not guaranteed) cash flows and to maintain and nurture those cash flows decade after decade. For example, with a steady 4 percent income yield, a 3 percent growth rate, and 100 percent income reinvestment, a

$100 pool yielding $4 today will compound to a $400 pool yielding $16 in 20 years. In contrast, a $100 bond of an AAA sovereign credit with a fixed 2 percent coupon will compound to only $150 yielding $3 in 20 years. The difference of course is that the principal and interest of the 2 percent bond is guaranteed, while the capital and income values of the risky growth investment yielding 4 percent are not.

Thus the essence of successful long-horizon, return-seeking investment programs is to understand the sources of the uncertain cash-flows, understand the risks that are attached to those cash-flows, and diversify those risks to the degree practically possible. As importantly, the spirit of the Heisenberg Uncertainty Principle applied to finance comes into play here: Long-horizon investors with wealth-creation mindsets can positively impact outcomes by effective engagement with the boards and managements of the investee organizations generating those cash flows. This positive win–win interplay lies at the heart of sustainable capitalism.

In contrast, effective payment-safety programs require professionals who can combine a strong knowledge of the globe's fixed income and derivatives markets with high-powered mathematics and complex ALM modeling techniques. Their focus is the solvency of the payment-safety balance sheet over time. Effective pension organizations also have a group managing plan participant exposures to the two investment instruments based on a mix of participant ages, preferences, and the changing relative risk/reward prospects of the two investment instruments over time. As importantly, this client service group has thought carefully about designing and communicating individual plan member success metrics, as well as separate collective success metrics for the return-seeking and payment-safety investment programs.

This is the essence of the 21st-century pension paradigm.

THE ESSENCE OF THE SCIENTIFIC INVESTMENT PARADIGM

So where does the scientific investment paradigm fit into this story? The most accessible, coherent description of it I have been able to find are the writings of AQR's Cliff Asness and Antti Ilmanen and their various co-authors.[2] Here is my understanding of it:

- At its best, the paradigm offers a dynamic quantitative footprint of the behaviors of financial markets participants over time, and of how these behaviors impact financial markets pricing.
- So it confirms, for example, the existence of a positive (but variable) equity risk premium through time, which logically compensates

risk-averse investors for material return variability, especially over shorter-term investment horizons.

- Additional positive (but also variable) return premiums seem to exist in equity markets related to corporations that exhibit value, size, and/or defensive characteristics. These premiums, too, have behavioral rationales if investors are systematically overoptimistic about the earnings prospects of large growth companies and are systematically averse to holding smaller, dull, boring ones.

- A different kind of return premium is available to investors willing to arbitrage term-related yield spreads in the debt and currency markets (i.e., borrow short, lend long). As term premiums are positive most of the time, "carry" investors will make money most of the time.

- A different again systematic return premium relates to price momentum persistence in financial markets. Such premiums will persist as long as investors generally underreact to new positive or negative information and exhibit trend-following herding instincts.

- Diversifying across these different return premium factors materially reduces risk if it is defined as short-term total return volatility. For example, Ilmanen shows an over-50 percent reduction in return volatility (from 11 percent to 5 percent) when shifting from a typical asset class diversification strategy to a factor diversification strategy. Why? Because the identified return premium factors seem to be largely uncorrelated with each other and with equity market direction.[3] These historical risk/reward relationships will persist as long as investors are skeptical they exist, are adverse to shorting and leverage, follow their herding instincts, and prefer, in Keynes' words, "to fail conventionally rather than succeed unconventionally."

How well (or poorly) does this scientific investment paradigm fit with the 21st-century pension paradigm sketched out earlier? It seems to me that some pieces can be logically fitted together, but others not.

FITS AND MISFITS

The scientific investment paradigm proceeds from the conventional investment theory premise that all participants in a risky investment pool define risk as short-term return volatility, and that all have the same degree of intolerance to it. The 21st-century pension paradigm questions the validity of that premise on a number of grounds. For example, short-term return volatility risk is effectively irrelevant to younger pension plan participants. Their primary risk is that the pension contributions they can afford to make now and tomorrow won't be sufficient to maintain a target post-work standard of living 30 or 40 years hence.

Hence their optimal investment strategy involves acquiring and nurturing a diversified portfolio of healthy, growing cash flows (e.g., dividends, rents, tolls). How the market capitalizes those cash flows week-to-week, month-to-month, or even year-to-year doesn't matter. On the other hand, actively ensuring those cash flows stay healthy over time matters a great deal (i.e., the spirit of the Heisenberg Uncertainty Principle applied to finance in action).

Similarly from the payment safety perspective of retirees, they are far more interested in receiving their monthly pension checks than they are in optimally trading off return expectations against return volatility. So in the dual goals/dual instruments framing of the pension paradigm, the relevance of the scientific investment paradigm is not obvious.

Having said that, opportunities to generate returns that are incremental to the basic bread-and-butter returns, associated with the pension organization's return-seeking and payment-safety investment programs, should not be ignored. The test is whether these incremental strategies would detract from or hinder the execution of the bread-and-butter investment programs in some material way. For example, tilting the return-seeking portfolio toward dividend-paying companies that may be attractively priced because they are not in exciting businesses, and/or have only modest growth prospects, seems like a logical marriage between the two paradigms. Using some risk capital on the payment-safety balance sheet to carry out attractive-looking carry strategies could be yet another way to earn additional returns in a risk-controlled way.

ARE ALPHAS AND BETAS BUNK?

Alphas and betas were exciting concepts in the 1970s. They were symbols of a new, more structured way of thinking about investing. But as times change, so do the investment paradigms that capture the essential issues and challenges of those times. In that spirit, Paul Samuelson was right to insist that we speak and write about operationally meaningful theorems in understandable ways. In the institutional investing world, today's essential issues revolve around delivering sustainable wealth creation and post-work income security for real people in an aging, slower-growth world. Alphas and betas are only useful concepts to the degree they help deliver these outcomes.

CHAPTER 26

Risk Management Revisited

"Few really believe that the Global Financial Crisis rewrote the book on Modern Portfolio Theory. But perhaps some editing is needed...."

—From Commonfund's "Forum 2011" Agenda

DOES MPT NEED EDITING...OR HOW WE APPLY IT?

There is nothing like an invitation to do some editing on modern portfolio theory (MPT) in front of 600 people to get the creative juices flowing. What started out as a few speaking notes in preparation for this event has morphed into this full-blown chapter. The more I thought about the topic, the stronger became the conviction that it is not so much modern portfolio theory that needs editing, but our interpretation and application of it. That is the theme developed here.

A brief review of MPT's basic insights is followed by the question whether these insights are still relevant today in light of the global financial crisis, and the lessons it taught us about risk and risk management. This examination uncovers my sense of a growing disconnect between MPT's strictures and the current practices of many leading pension and endowment funds. This disconnect is described here in some detail, and leads to the identification of three steps many pension and endowment funds should take to reconnect their practices with MPT's timeless principles.

MPT'S INSIGHTS

Harry Markowitz's 1952 article, "Portfolio Selection," kicked off a wave of ferment and innovation in investment and finance theory that continues to this day.[1] His fundamental insight was that if investors could specify their reward/risk expectations for an investment universe, as well as their tolerance for risk-taking, a unique 'optimal' portfolio could be identified. A key element of this radically new way of thinking about portfolio construction was the idea that how investments co-varied with each other determined their diversification power.

Other academic thought-leaders (e.g., Black, Merton, Sharpe, Scholes, Tobin, and Treynor) took Markowitz's basic idea, and expanded it in a number of important dimensions. One such expansion was "the separation theorem," which combined Markowitz's efficient frontier of risky assets with a risk-free asset. The investment opportunity set expands as a result, allowing aggressive investors to use leverage (i.e., borrow and invest the proceeds in the risky portfolio), and more risk-averse investors to split their wealth between the risky and safe investment alternatives. And so the all-important asset mix decision was placed into a structured reward/risk decision framework.

The next expansion followed from the question, "What if all investors do investment analysis the same way using the same information?" Now the optimal risky portfolio becomes the market portfolio, with all investors holding a piece of it, while they are short or long the risk-free asset, depending on their tolerance for investment risk. And so the efficient market hypothesis (EMH) was born, with its message that the vast majority of investors are best off passively holding some combination of the market portfolio and the risk-free asset. The commercial consequence is that index funds make most economic sense for most investors most of the time. Chapter 3 noted that price discovery can be left to a relatively small group of investments experts capable of balancing the marginal costs and benefits of investment information and its transformation into investment decisions.

The final major MPT thrust was a formal framework to apply the broad concept of "optionality" to investment and finance. The dictionary defines optionality as "the potential for making additional choices which are available only after an initial choice is made." In the investment and finance arena that potential translates most famously into defining and pricing various types of options. A good risk management example is a "collar option" that protects against adverse downside return outcomes at the cost of giving up upside potential. Clearly, such an option adds a powerful tool to the risk management toolkit.

FROM THEORY TO PRACTICE: HOW HELPFUL IS MPT?

How helpful are MPT's insights in the real world? Enormously so, as long as the insights are kept in perspective:

1. **Risk tolerance** is a critical element of the MPT edifice and in the real world. Our ongoing challenge is to translate the idea into something

meaningful and actionable in an institutional structure typically involving layers of internal and external agents. This is equally so in the pension and endowment worlds. It is easy for the fears and aspirations of the current and future beneficiaries in these arrangements to get lost in a complex world of contributors, boards, investment committees, CIOs, consultants, and multiple layers of investment managers.

2. **Reward/risk expectations** are another critical element of the MPT edifice and in the real world. While on the one hand, the "same expectations" assumption behind the EMH clearly does not hold in the real world, on the other, the question of what *is* predictable continues to be hotly debated. Ironically, while there is considerable evidence that longer-term reward/risk investment prospects are to some degree predictable for many pension and endowment funds, current convention continues to be that the past is the best predictor of the future. Chapter 19 showed that the pre-2000 dot-com bubble and the pre-2008 financial leverage bubble are just the most recent examples in a long line of such bubbles caused by decision-making based on rearview mirror–driven reward/risk expectations.

3. **Rational actors and decision-making** is a third critical element of the MPT edifice. Without this assumption, all the clear MPT insights become blurred, and are replaced by far fuzzier possibilities. For example, the periodic dynamic toward asset bubbles leads to undue optimism, and their bursting leads to knee-jerk panic reactions that, with the benefit of hindsight, turn out to be costly mistakes. Should we blame MPT for the fact that in the real-world actual investment decisions are often inconsistent with its "rational actors and decision-making" assumption? Of course not. If we fail to establish governance and decision-making processes that do not meet the rational actors and decision-making test, the blame lies with us, not MPT. This does not imply that real-world pension and endowment funds must apply MPT literally in all its complexity in making decisions. It *does* mean funds should take Einstein's admonition to "make things as simple as possible, but no simpler" very seriously.

But what does Einstein's admonition mean in practice?

AS SIMPLE AS POSSIBLE, BUT NO SIMPLER

Three important examples come to mind. The first relates to MPT's stricture to understand investor risk tolerance, and how to respect that understanding in the establishment of the fund's risk policies. Placing this in a pension or endowment context raises some very challenging questions, starting with "Who is at risk?" A series of equally challenging questions follow: about intergenerational fairness, about guarantees, about risk buffers, about property rights, about embedded options, about liquidity requirements, and so on. In my experience, many boards and investment committees have finessed these difficult questions by such mantras as "Our liabilities are long-term, so we invest for the long term, and don't have to worry about these kinds of questions." In my view, boards and investment committees with this attitude have crossed the line from "as simple as possible" into "too simple" territory.

The second example relates to risk management simplification in the real world. Obviously, we can't apply the Markowitz formula literally to universes of thousands of risky assets. So we restate the problem to something more manageable by creating asset classes (e.g., domestic equities, foreign equities, emerging market equities, private equity, real estate, high-yield bonds, hedge funds, etc.), and factors (e.g., size, value, growth, momentum, volatility, liquidity, etc.). Then we bound the possible solutions by setting upper and lower limits and handing out investment mandates to multiple managers to further enhance risk diversification. Again, the question arises if this abbreviated approach to risk management is an appropriate or inappropriate simplification of theory. And again, my view is that this approach places funds in potentially too-simple territory (see Chapter 24).

The third example relates to organizational competencies and design. Specifically, what kind of organizational competencies and design are required to be able to draw the line correctly between making things as simple as possible and stepping into too-simple territory? Many pension and endowment fund boards continue to underestimate the minimum internal skill/experience set required to manage such critical elements as mission, risk tolerance, investment beliefs, and dynamic implementation of investment policy through time. Once again, this problem leads to funds ending up in too-simple territory. Scale and smart in/outsourcing strategies are critical factors to getting fund organization right (see Chapters 16 and 17).

These three examples lead logically to action plans for fund boards that are prepared to face the reality that they may not be serving their beneficiaries as well as they could be. We address each in turn.

WHO IS AT RISK?

Many boards would do their institution a great service if they sat down and seriously addressed the "Who is at risk?" question. Previous chapters provided important insights that would come out of such a discussion. For example, if we are required to be evenhanded between the current and future generations, can we demonstrate that we are meeting that requirement? What does that requirement imply for our investment and payout policies? A simple thought-experiment demonstrates that these questions are not as easy as they are often made out to be. Consider the following facts.

A donor sets up a $1 million endowment fund in perpetuity with the intent of funding scholarships annually, starting one year from now. However, the scholarship has to be announced now, including its dollar value. Also, the donor insists that the endowment should be managed so that it is intergenerationally fair. There are two investment choices today: a risk-free investment that pays 2 percent each year in perpetuity, and a risky investment with an expected annual return of 4 percent and a return standard deviation of 10 percent. The questions are: (1) At what dollar value should the endowment fund trustees set the scholarship? (2) How should the $1 million be invested?

The simple answer is that the annual face value of the scholarship should be set at $20K, and the $1M should be invested in the risk-free investment. Why? Because setting the face value at $40K and investing the $1M in the risky strategy effectively involves a $20K wealth transfer from future scholarship recipients to the first recipient. Why is there a wealth transfer involved? Because the first recipient is effectively guaranteed a 4 percent return in a 2 percent risk-free world. But isn't there an even chance that the actual risky return will be less or greater than 4 percent? Yes, but the economic values of the up- and downsides are not equal. Specifically, the value of an at-the-money put to protect the downside in this example is $50K, while the value of an at-the-money call on the upside is $30K.

Is there a way of offering a $40K scholarship, investing the $1M in the risky strategy, and being intergenerationally fair at the same time? Yes, there is. A third-party risk underwriter is required. For example, the original donor could be asked to play this role. Or the institution could raise enough money in undesignated donations to play this role. Or the institution has an unallocated contingency reserve as a hedge against return shortfalls in the endowment fund. The point here is that setting mutually consistent payout and investment policies in endowment funds (or pension plans) should not be based on some simplistic heuristic. Such decisions should be based on clear understandings of how and by whom risk is being borne.

WHAT IS OUR RISK EXPOSURE?

It is one thing to decide on the maximum risk an investment fund should be exposed to; it is quite another to assess what the actual exposure is. MPT offers a guide to how the question can be simplified. In its original formulation, each risky investment was defined to have two types of risks: market (beta) risk and specific (alpha) risk. Most individual investments have lots of specific risk and a modest amount of market risk. The reverse is true for well-diversified portfolios. New empirical ground continues to be covered here. The market risk concept has flowered into multiple beta exposures to such factors as growth, value, size, duration, credit, liquidity, inflation, and currency. It is also taking on more of an integrated balance sheet perspective, rather than assets-only. These are all useful improvements at the margin.

The global finance crisis added an important new dimension to the risk management framework. Not only do the known risks need to be considered and managed, but also the less-known/unknown ones, especially if they have nasty tails. Understanding these risks and their economic consequences is part of the new normal for at least the larger, thought-leading pension and endowment funds. A related realization is that risk management must be a dynamic rather than a static process. Importantly, it includes understanding how and when to hedge not just against the normal risks, but against less-known/unknown tail risks as well.

SALIENT STRATEGIC ADVICE AND IMPLEMENTATION

I close by connecting this chapter back to the earlier chapters on organizational competencies and design. The reason so many pension and endowment funds continue to have trouble putting all the pieces together is that they continue to rely heavily on outside agents. Outside agents are not evil people, but most *do* have commercial interests of their own to pursue. This often results in a fund with an under-resourced inside and a too-expensive outside. An important message of this book is that funds that have both scale and good governance have a clear competitive advantage over those that have neither. Why? Because they have the internal capability to clearly understand their mission and what must be done to achieve it. While many continue to outsource some activities, they have also successfully insourced the critical ones, including risk management.[2]

Smaller funds don't have this option. They *do* have the option to engage fiduciary managers with scale offering an integrated package of strategic advice and implementation services. Likely, this will serve their beneficiaries better than continuing with the "under-resourced inside/too-expensive outside" model.

From an Unknown to a Known

Managing Climate Change Risk

" ...as we know, there are known knowns ...there are known
unknowns ...but there are also unknown unknowns ... "
—Donald Rumsfeld, Former U.S. Secretary of Defense

The pace of consumption, waste, and environmental change has
so stretched the planet's capacity that our unsustainable lifestyles
can only precipitate catastrophes ... "
—Pope Francis

CATEGORIZING RISKS

While the language may be a bit tortured, Donald Rumsfeld's 2002 observation about the possibility of WMDs (weapons of mass destruction) in Iraq makes an important point. Not all risks (or uncertainties) are the same. The really dangerous ones are in the unknown category, or what Nassim Taleb called "the black swans," with the 2008/09 global financial crisis a vivid example still fresh in our minds. This chapter raises the question of where climate change fits on the unknown/known risk scale. Pope Francis' recent pronouncements on the topic suggest it is rapidly moving from the unknown to the known end of the scale.

Psychoanalysts point out there is even a fourth risk category beyond the three Rumsfeld mentions: the "unknown known." It covers situations where we know about a reality, but pretend not to. This fourth category came to mind reading through the Mercer study, "Investing in a Time of Climate Change."[1] While the study will undoubtedly be useful to investors who currently treat climate change risk as a known unknown, it also has the potential to impact investors who continue to treat climate change risk as an unknown known (i.e., pretend it doesn't exist). In our view, the structure of the study, and the detailed analyses carried out within that structure, makes plausible deniability an increasingly untenable stance to maintain.

The goal of this chapter is to share my take on the action implications of the Mercer study from both unknown known and known unknown risk management perspectives.

RISK AND PENSION MANAGEMENT

The previous chapter conducted a post-GFC review of risk management. After a brief walk through portfolio and capital markets theory, the chapter made four key points:

1. **Be Clear about Whose Risks You Are Managing:** In a world of principals and agents, this is a critical question to address. In a pensions context, the focus must be plan stakeholder risks and not manager risks. Within stakeholder risks, intergenerational risk sharing is an especially challenging issue to address. Specifically, are the interests of future stakeholders fairly represented in the decisions made today?
2. **Make the "Ex Post"/"Ex Ante" Distinction Clear:** Assuming the past will always be a good guide to the future is a sign of intellectual laziness. While the future sometimes echoes the past, it does not repeat it. Visualizing possible futures is hard, but necessary work.
3. **Time-Horizon Matters:** How much short-term changes in portfolio value matter is a key question to address. Investors who can answer "they don't matter to us" have an important comparative advantage by being able to focus on the longer-term generation of growing cash flows and wealth.
4. **Good Governance Matters:** Effective pension organizations have clearly stated investment beliefs and live by them. This in turn requires strong governance processes that ensure this actually happens in practice.

Chapter 11 made these same key points from the perspective of fiduciary duty, as did Chapter 21 in the context of implementing a long-term investment program.

At the June 2015 Rotman ICPM Discussion Forum, Harvard Business School's Luis Viceira shared preliminary findings from his research on the impact of time-horizon on the benefits of portfolio diversification. His work is supporting the intuition that while short-horizon return correlations have indeed increased materially since the 2008/09 GFC period, long-horizon return correlations have not. Why? Because short-term return correlations are largely driven by the degree to which capital value changes are correlated, while long-term return correlations are largely driven by the degree to which investment cash flow changes are correlated (e.g., changes in coupon, dividend, and rent payments). There is no evidence the correlations of these cash flow changes have been rising.

THE MERCER CLIMATE CHANGE STUDY

This important distinction between short- and long-horizon risks is a good transition path to the Mercer climate change study. In essence, the study is about possible rates of conversion out of today's fossil fuels–driven economy into an economy with materially lower net carbon emissions, and the investment risks and opportunities arising from that conversion process. To address these questions, the study posits three possible 2015–2050 scenarios:

1. **Transformation:** Strong climate change mitigation puts us on a path to limiting global warming to 2°C above preindustrial-era temperatures this century.[2]
2. **Coordination:** Substantial climate change mitigation limits global warming to 3°C above preindustrial-era temperatures this century.
3. **Fragmentation:** Sees only limited climate-mitigation action and a lack of coordination, resulting in a 4°C or more rise. The study further splits this scenario into lower- and higher-economic-damages sub-scenarios.

With these scenarios in place, the study draws on a series of integrated assessment models to project plausible interactions between climate science, economics, costs, and mitigation/adaptation strategies. Through these processes, three investment risk factors are monitored:

1. **Technology:** The interplay between technology and the path to a low-carbon economy. Speed, scale, and success of low-carbon technologies, coupled with the extent of transformation/disruption of existing sectors, or the development of new sectors, are the key metrics for this factor.
2. **Resource Availability/Impacts:** Weather-driven impacts on the valuation of investments. These impacts can be chronic (e.g., driven by long-term changes in temperature or precipitation), or acute (e.g., driven by extreme or catastrophic events).

3. **Policy:** International, national, and local measures (e.g., laws, regulations, targets, mandates) intended to reduce climate change risk by increasing the cost of carbon and/or incentivizing the use of low-carbon alternatives.

This structure is then applied to assess the investment implications for asset classes and industry sectors over time on a scenario-by-scenario basis. These implications were found to be material- and scenario-dependent. Here is a summary of the key findings:

- On the whole, the climate impact on long-term public and private equity returns is projected to be marginally negative.
- Real estate, infrastructure, and emerging market equity are expected to benefit from the technology and policy factors.
- Agriculture and timber show the widest ranges of scenario-driven impacts (i.e., from positive in transformation to negative in fragmentation).
- The energy (especially coal and oil) and utilities (especially electric) industries have negative sensitivities to the policy factor, and also to the resource availability/impacts factor.
- The renewables and nuclear industries have positive sensitivities to the policy and technology factors.

In the following section, the study addresses the implications of these key findings.

So What? Now What?

The action implications come in five parts:

1. **Climate Risk Is Inevitable, but Being Prepared Can Improve Investment Outcomes:** Uncertainty about the future should not be a barrier to action. Good governance is important here. It starts with realistic investment beliefs that encompass climate change risk. The study clearly points to investment policy implications at the asset class and industry levels.
2. **Be Clear about Who Is Accountable for What in the Investment Decision-Making Process:** A clear accountability line from the board through the investment chain will have to be drawn. Implications for how risk budgets are allocated and how investment results will be benchmarked need to be decided.
3. **Certain Asset Classes Deserve Particular Attention:** The study pointed to real estate, infrastructure, emerging markets equity, renewables, nuclear, agriculture, timber, energy, and utilities as deserving special attention.

The three-scenario structure forces attention on judging their probabilities of occurrence, and feeding those judgments back into investment policy decisions.

4. **Achieving the Transformation Scenario Has Materially Positive Investment Implications Relative to the Fragmentation Scenario:** This means collaboration efforts toward achieving the transformation outcome have a potentially large payoff. Arguably, the study findings suggest such efforts amount to the required exercise of fiduciary duty.[3]

5. **Climate Risk Is More Complex and Longer Term than Most Other Investment Risks:** Traditional economic and financial risks related to inflation, the course of the business cycle, interest rates, etc., are typically analyzed in three- to five-year time frames. The longer-term risks associated with climate change (e.g., sea-level rise, water availability, carbon price developments) usually fall outside this time frame. Conscious effort will be needed to bridge the shorter- and longer-term time frames for risk management and mitigation of this diverse combination of investment risks.

The study concludes that all this adds up to an action catalyst for the people and organizations it calls "future makers," and a wakeup call for the people and organizations it calls "future takers."

RISK MANAGEMENT REVISITED

There are interesting and important parallels between the four key points made in the previous chapter about risk management, the new Mercer Study on climate change, and its implications for risk management. For example:

- **Be Clear about Whose Risks You Are Managing:** Specifically, the focus must be plan stakeholder risks and not manager risks. The Mercer study makes a convincing case that climate change risks translate directly into plan stakeholder risks. In a macro sense, the transformation scenario is an outcome well worth championing in collaboration with likeminded investors. In a more micro sense, a strategy of divesting from high-carbon emission investments doesn't require moral justification. There is a far simpler "high risk/low return prospects" justification.

- **Make the Ex Post/Ex Ante Distinction Clear:** My own work on developing investment return expectations over the last three decades has been based on the explicit premise that the past is not a good guide to the future, and that visualizing possible futures is hard, but necessary work.

The Mercer Study was clearly conducted with those realities in mind. A good deal of time and effort went into building the scenarios, the integrated assessment models, and identifying the relevant risk/return factors.

- **Time Horizon Matters:** Investors who can ignore short-term capital value fluctuations have an important comparative advantage by being able to focus on the longer-term generation of growing cash flows and wealth. This makes ESG (Environmental, Social, and Governance) considerations of primary importance to these investors. The Mercer Study throws new light on these considerations.

- **Good Governance Matters:** Effective pension organizations live by clear investment beliefs, and this in turn requires strong governance processes. The Mercer Study offers multiple examples of this reality. For example, the "So What/Now What?" section noted that the boards and senior managements of pension organizations have critically important roles to play in converting the findings of the study into organizational accountabilities and actions.

In conclusion, the Mercer Study adds considerably to investor knowledge about the risk-and-return implications of climate change. It need not be an unknown any longer. For climate change deniers, plausible deniability about the risks of climate change and its potential impact on future investment returns is becoming an increasingly untenable stance to maintain.

Conclusion

My 2007 *Pension Revolution* book ended with a "call to arms" to complete the pension revolution first set out by Peter Drucker in his visionary 1976 book, *The Unseen Revolution*. An underlying message of this new book is that the pension revolution will never be fully completed. The best we can realistically hope for is continuous movement in the right direction.

Continuous movement in the right direction requires two things. First, it requires sound ideas as to where we should be heading in pension design, governance, and investing. The goal of this book has been to update these ideas, reflecting the best current thinking and research findings in each of these three key areas. Second, it requires resolute leadership by the tens of thousands of men and women involved in the design, governance, and investing functions of the globe's pension systems. Paraphrasing George Bernard Shaw, this will require unreasonable doses of courage and determination.

All progress depends on it.

Notes

Chapter 1. Improved Pension Designs and Organizations

1. See William Bernstein's article, "The Paradox of Wealth," in the *Financial Analysts Journal* (Sept–Oct 2013) for greater detail on the evolution of capitalism.
2. Jensen and Meckling "solved" this problem theoretically in "Theory of the Firm: Managerial Behaviour, Agency Costs, and Ownership Structure," *Journal of Financial Economics* (July 1976). They predicted that the market system would naturally lead to monitoring and control activities carried out by institutions and individuals "who possess comparative advantages in these activities." Observation suggests such monitoring and control activities don't come about "naturally." They must consciously be put in place through deliberate collective action by investors.
3. Chapter 12 of Keynes' *The General Theory of Employment, Interest, and Money* (Macmillan, 1936) may still be the best-ever essay on sensible investment beliefs, their implications, and their consequences.
4. Full disclosure: I am a CEM Benchmarking Inc. co-founder and co-owner. Visit its website to access its research papers on the drivers of good investment and pension administration performance by using its extensive databases.
5. See "Effective Pension Governance: The Ontario Teachers' Story" by Claude Lamoureux in the *Rotman International Journal of Pension Management* (Fall 2008). There may be a dozen or so "5 success drivers" pension organizations in the world today. Another dozen or so have publicly declared their aspiration to join this elite club.

Chapter 2. Pension Plans for the Masses

1. Bradford (2014), "Harkin's Universal Retirement Plan Called Good Start Despite Some Hurdles," *Pensions & Investments*, Feb 3.
2. Ambachtsheer (2008), "The Canada Supplementary Pension Plan: Towards an Adequate, Affordable Pension for All Canadians," C.D. Howe Institute.
3. At this time of writing, some of the important specifics of the ORPP remain unresolved. For example, whether its design is to have a target benefit orientation, the role of guarantees, the income range to be covered by the plan, and what constitutes a "comparable" pension plan that exempts an employer from having to participate in the ORPP.

4. See Sandbrook and Gosling (2014), "Pension Reform in the United Kingdom," *Rotman International Journal of Pension Management*, Spring, for a full exposition of the UK pension reform story.
5. Reported by former NEST CEO Tim Jones to the author in a 2015 conversation.

Chapter 3. Does Institutional Investing Have a Future?

1. Akerlof's most famous article on the topic was "The Market for Lemons," *Quarterly Journal of Economics*, August 1970. See also the books by Akerlof and Shiller, *Animal Spirits*, Princeton University Press, 2010, and *"Phishing for Phools: The Economics of Manipulation and Deception,"* Princeton University Press, 2015.
2. French (2008), "The Cost of Active Investing," National Bureau of Economic Research.
3. Ambachtsheer (2005), "Beyond Portfolio Theory: The Next Frontier," *Financial Analysts Journal*, Jan–Feb.
4. See for example, Bauer and Kicken (2008), "The Pension Fund Advantage: Are Canadians Overpaying Their Mutual Funds?," *Rotman International Journal of Pension Management*, Fall.
5. See, for example, Ambachtsheer, Capelle, and Lum (2008), "The Pension Governance Deficit: Still with Us," *Rotman International Journal of Pension Management*, Fall.
6. Visit the CEM Benchmarking Inc. website for research supporting these findings.
7. Lamoureux (2008), "Effective Pension Governance: The Ontario Teachers' Story," *Rotman International Journal of Pension Management*, Fall.
8. Bertram and Zvan (2009), "Pension Funds and Incentive Compensation: A Story Based on OTPP Experience," *Rotman International Journal of Pension Management*, Spring.
9. Data obtained by the author from OTPP Annual Reports and from CEM Benchmarking Inc.

Chapter 4. Thomas Piketty's *Capital in the 21st Century*

1. Towers Watson (2015), "Global Pension Assets Study."
2. From Piketty (2014), *Capital in the 21st Century*, Belknap Harvard.
3. Drucker (1976), *The Unseen Revolution*, Harper & Row.

Chapter 5. Why We Need to Change the Conversation about Pension Reform

1. Ambachtsheer (2013), "The Third Rail: Teachers' Jim Leech and *The Globe*'s Jacquie McNish Make Pension Reform Simple," *Globe & Mail*, November 8, 2013.
2. Leech and McNish (2013), *The Third Rail: Confronting Our Pension Failures*, McClelland Stewart.

3. While TIAA-CREF doesn't match up perfectly against the "five features" test set out before, it comes close.

Chapter 6. On the Costing and Funding of Defined-Benefit Pensions

1. See Brock, "SED Client Memo" dated August 2013.
2. The PERS case study can be accessed through the website of the Rotman International Centre for Pension Management (ICPM).
3. For more on the financial economics of DB plans, see Bader (2014), "How Does Investment Return Affect Pension Cost?," *Financial Analysts Journal,* Sept/Oct., and Andonov, Bauer, and Cremers (2015), "Pension Fund Asset Allocation and Liability Discount Rates," SSRN.

Chapter 7. Defining Defined-Ambition Pension Plans

1. The World Bank (1994), "Averting the Old Age Crisis."
2. See the article by Jaap van Dam (2014), "Rethinking Investing from the Ground Up: How PFZW and PGGM Are Meeting This Challenge," *Rotman International Journal of Pension Management* (Spring), for more on this project.

Chapter 8. What Are Target-Benefit Plans and Why Should You Care?

1. I have contributed a recent study to this debate titled "Taking the Dutch Pension System to the Next Level: A View from the Outside." It can be accessed via the KPA Advisory Services website.
2. NEST recently announced that it is making progress on the design of an "income-for-life" for the decumulation phase of its investment program.

Chapter 9. Designing 21st-Century Pension Plans

1. For more detail on these ideas, google MERCER LIFETIMEPLUS. Also see Bovenberg and Nijman (2015), "Personal Pensions with Risk Sharing," NETSPAR.

Chapter 10. How Effective Is Pension Fund Governance Today?

1. The complete study is titled "How Effective Is Pension Fund Governance Today? And Do Pension Funds Invest for the Long-Term? Findings from a New Survey," January 2015. It can be accessed via the KPA Advisory Services website.
2. O'Barr and Conley (1992), *Fortune and Folly: The Wealth and Power of Institutional Investing,* Irwin Books.

3. Keynes (1936), *The General Theory of Employment, Interest and Money*, Chapter 12, Palgrave Macmillan.
4. Ambachtsheer, Boice, Ezra, and McLaughlin (1995), "Excellence Shortfall in Pension Fund Management: Anatomy of a Problem," unpublished working paper available from the author.
5. The studies by Clarke et al. are summarized in (2008), "Best-Practice Pension Fund Governance," *Journal of Asset Management*. See also Clapman (2007), "Model Governance Provisions to Support Pension Fund Best-Practice Principles," Stanford University Law School.
6. Clark and Urwin (2008), "Making Pension Boards Work: The Critical Role of Leadership," *Rotman International Journal of Pension Management*, Fall.
7. Ambachtsheer, Capelle, and Lum (2008), "The Pension Governance Deficit: Still With Us," *Rotman International Journal of Pension Management*, Fall.
8. Visit https://www.rotman.utoronto.ca/ProfessionalDevelopment/Executive-Programs/CoursesWorkshops/Programs/Pension-Management.aspx for more information.
9. The "Other" category in Table 10.4 was a mix of multi-employer pension plans, union pension plans, fiduciary managers, and special-purpose organizations such as workers compensation insurers.

Chapter 11. The Evolving Meaning of Fiduciary Duty

1. The two articles are required reading for participants in the Rotman-ICPM Board Effectiveness Program (BEP). The articles as well as information on BEP can be accessed through the Rotman-ICPM website.
2. Collaboration theory and practices is another unique area where Rotman ICPM has invested research monies. See Danyelle Guyatt's *RIJPM* articles, "Pension Collaboration: Strength in Numbers" (Fall 2008) and "Effective Investor Collaborations: Enhancing the Shadow of the Future" (Fall 2013).
3. See the FCLT website for more information on this initiative.

Chapter 12. Pension Organizations and Integrated Reporting

1. International Integrated Reporting Council (IIRC). *The International <IR> Framework*. December 2013. Available at www.integratedreporting.org.
2. *The Australian* (2014), "Superfunds Enthusiastic about New Reporting Regime," July 15.
3. Sentinel Retirement Fund Integrated Annual Report, 2014. Full report available at http://www.1.sentinel.za.com/Annual%20Reports/Sentinel%20Retirement%20Fund%202014.pdf.
4. Ibid., p. 1.
5. Ibid., pp. 2–7.
6. Ibid., pp. 8–15.
7. Ibid., pp. 16–25.

8. Ibid., pp. 26–60.
9. Ibid., pp. 61–81.
10. Drucker (2006), "Classic Drucker: From the Pages of the Harvard Business Review." *Harvard Business Review,* March.

Chapter 14. Measuring Value-for-Money in Private Markets Investing

1. Morgenson (2015), "Hidden Fees Take a Big Bite out of Pension Savings," *New York Times,* May 4.
2. Phalippou and Gottschalg (2009), "The Performance of Private Equity Funds," *Review of Financial Studies.*
3. Dang, Dupont, and Heale (2015), "The Time Has Come for Standardized Total Cost Disclosure for Private Equity," CEM Benchmarking Inc. position paper.
4. CEM's customized private equity benchmarks are based on lagged, small-cap equity indexes.
5. Note that the total reported Dutch costs for 2012/2013 are lower than the pre-2009 costs calculated by Phalippou-Gottschlag. It is not clear at this point whether this is due to Dutch underreporting, whether costs have come down over the course of the last decade, or some combination of the two.
6. A related issue here is "materiality." Given the complexity of some of the fee structures in the PE space, there is a limit beyond which it is not worth going to achieve decimal place accuracy.

Chapter 15. How Pension Funds Pay Their Own Investment People

1. The study could not have been completed without the outstanding support of KPA colleagues Virginia Atkin and Kalia German, and of John McLaughlin of Treasury Technologies International. All data collected for the study were checked for completeness and consistency. In many cases, specific issues were discussed with the respondents. However, KPA cannot guarantee 100 percent accuracy of the resulting database.
2. Dyck and Pomorski (2011), "Is Bigger Better? Size and Performance in Pension Plan Management," working paper, Rotman School of Management, University of Toronto.

Chapter 16. Investment Beliefs and Organization Design

1. Keynes (1936), *The General Theory of Employment, Interest, and Money,* Macmillan.
2. See del Rio and Howlett (2013), "Beyond the 'Tinbergen Rule' in Policy Design: Matching Tools and Goals in Policy Portfolios," Annual Review of Policy Design.
3. See Bernstein (2009), *Capital Ideas Evolving,* John Wiley & Sons.

Chapter 17. Norway versus Yale—or versus Canada?

1. Vasan (2012), "Norway vs. Yale Models: Who Wins?," *aiCIO Magazine,* Feb. 14.
2. Chambers, Dimson, Ilmanen (2011), "The Norway Model," October, SSRN.
3. For example, see "Maple Revolutionaries," *The Economist,* March 3, 2012.
4. I thank Gordon Clark and Ashby Monk for this insight. See their article, "The Norwegian Government Pension Fund: Ethics Over Efficiency" in the *Rotman International Journal for Pension Management* (Spring 2010).
5. The report was produced by the Rowan Task Force, to which I was a principal advisor. The report was titled "In Whose Interest?" and was released in 1987.
6. The two organizations report their returns and management costs somewhat differently. In Norway's case, the "Return of Fund" is a gross return and the "Average Management Cost" includes both external fees and internal investment management expenses. In the case of Ontario Teachers', the "Return of Fund" is net of external fees, and the "Average Management Costs" only represent internal management expenses. However, this different treatment of returns and expenses has no impact on the two "Net Excess Return" calculations, which remain comparable.

Chapter 18. Does Culture Matter in Pension Organizations?

1. O'Reilly and Chatman (1996), *Culture as Social Control: Corporations, Culture, and Commitment,* JAI Press, and Schein, (2004) *Organizational Culture and Leadership,* Jossey-Bass.
2. Lo (2015), "The Gordon Gekko Effect: The Role of Culture in the Financial Industry," prepared for the Federal Reserve Bank of New York.
3. Lewis, Michael, *Liar's Poker,* Norton: 1989.
4. Lewis, Michael, *Flash Boys,* Norton: 2015.
5. See Andonov, Bauer, and Cremers (2015), "Pension Fund Asset Allocation and Liability Discount Rates," SSRN.

Chapter 19. Are Investment Returns Predictable?

1. Brock (2013), "The Logical Basis for Outperforming the Market," SED Inc.
2. Akerlof (1970), "The Market for Lemons," *The Quarterly Journal of Economics,* August.
3. Dyck and Pomorski (2011), "Is Bigger Better? Size and Performance in Pension Fund Management," SSRN.
4. Ambachtsheer and Farrell (1979), "Can Active Management Add Value?," *Financial Analysts Journal.*
5. Ambachtsheer (1977), "U.S. Stock Prices and Interest Rates: A Three- to Five-Year View," *Financial Analysts Journal.*

Chapter 20. Investment Returns in the 21st Century

1. From Chapter 4 of this book. Return to that chapter to learn more about Piketty and the historical background addressed here.
2. Look for a new film titled *Boom Bust Boom* on Hyman Minsky and his Financial Instability Hypothesis. Contact Marja Koolschijn at Cardano for more information (m.koolschijn@cardano.com).
3. Based on research published by GMO LLC.
4. Bernstein (2013), "The Paradox of Wealth," *Financial Analysts Journal.*
5. For more detail, see Lazonick (2014), "Profits Without Prosperity," *Harvard Business Review*, September.

Chapter 21. Long-Termism as the Dominant Investment Paradigm

1. Ambachtsheer (2014), "The Case for Long-Termism," *Rotman International Journal of Pension Management*, Fall.
2. Ambachtsheer and McLaughlin (2015), "How Effective Is Pension Fund Governance Today? and Do Pension Funds Invest for the Long-Term? Findings from a New Survey." The study can be accessed through kpa-advisory.com.

Chapter 22. Investing for the Long Term I

1. Ambachtsheer and McLaughlin (2015), "How Effective Is Pension Fund Governance Today? and Do Pension Funds Invest for the Long-Term? Findings from a New Survey." The study can be accessed through kpa-advisory.com.
2. Focusing Capital on the Long Term (FCLT). "Long-Term Portfolio Guide," March 2015. The complete document can be accessed through fclt.org.
3. Ibid.
4. See, for example, Dyck and Pomorski (2011), "Is Bigger Better? Size and Performance in Pension Fund Management," SSRN.
5. The Guide referenced the article, "Reclaiming Fiduciary Duty Balance," by Hawley, Johnson, and Waitzer, *Rotman International Journal of Pension Management*, Fall 2011.

Chapter 23. Investing for the Long Term II

1. Burgman and Van Clieaf (2012), "Total Shareholder Returns and Management Performance," *Rotman International Journal of Pension Management*, Fall.
2. Mauboussin and Rappaport (2015), "Transparent Corporate Objectives," *Journal of Applied Corporate Finance*, July.
3. Van der Velden and van Buul (2012), "*Really* Investing for the Long Term: A Case Study," *Rotman International Journal of Pension Management*, Spring.

4. I have been a member of the Jeffrey Company's Board of Directors for 23 years.
5. The Jeffrey Company itself stands out as a singular example. See also Ambacht-sheer (2014), "The Case for Long-Termism," *Rotman International Journal of Pension Management,* Fall; and Eccles, Ioannis, and Serafeim (2012), "The Impact of Corporate Sustainability on Organizational Processes and Performance," NBER working paper.

Chapter 24. Investing for the Long Term III

1. Eccles, Ioannou, and Serafeim (2012), "The Impact of Corporate Sustainability on Organizational Processes and Performance," NBER working paper.
2. EIS use the term "Team Production Model" in the paper, in deference to the authors of another paper who first used this term. I converted it to "Long-term Stakeholder Value-Creation Model" to fit the terminology used in prior chapters.
3. Quantitative analysts call this the "low-volatility" effect, which they attribute to the systematic overestimation of earnings growth in "sexier" high-volatility stocks.
4. See the previously cited article, "The Case for Long-Termism," for more on this idea.
5. *Rotman Management*, Winter 2015. The interviewer was Karen Christensen. Used with permission.

Chapter 25. Are Alphas and Betas Bunk?

1. The two *FAJ* articles are (1977) "U.S. Stock Prices and Interest Rates: A Three, to Five-Year View"; and (1979) "Can Active Management Add Value?" (with Jim Farrell).
2. For example, see Ilmanen, Asness (foreword by) (2011), *Expected Returns: An Investor's Guide to Harvesting Market Returns*, Wiley.
3. See Ilmanen (2012), "The Death of Diversification Has Been Greatly Exaggerated," *Journal of Portfolio Management,* Spring.

Chapter 26. Risk Management Revisited

1. Markowitz (1952), "Portfolio Selection," *Journal of Finance.*
2. For example, *Ontario Teachers' Pension Plan* employs 50 people in its risk management group.

Chapter 27. From an Unknown to a Known

1. The Mercer Study can be accessed by just googling its title on the Internet. The study was supported by 16 institutional investors managing a collective $1.5 trillion.

2. Participants in the Paris COP21 Climate Change Conference in December 2015 agreed to target to keep global warming below 2C through country-specific five-year plans that would be peer-reviewed by an independent body. A hopeful agreement, but much remains to be done.

3. A powerful new example of collective action is the case of 886 Dutch citizens suing the Dutch Government for insufficient action on climate change. They demanded new standards requiring a 25 percent reduction in carbon emissions in five years. The judge decided in favor of the plaintiffs. Similar actions are being contemplated in other countries. The other notable target for collective action is COP21, the UN conference on climate change held in December 2015 in Paris.

About the Author

Keith Ambachtsheer has been a participant in the pensions and investments industry since 1969. He founded his own firm KPA Advisory Services Ltd. in 1985. Through KPA, he provides strategic advice to a global clientele in person, and through the monthly *Ambachtsheer Letter*. He is the author of three bestselling books, and has been a regular contributor to industry publications since the 1970s. He was the editor of the *Rotman International Journal of Pension Management* from 2008 to 2014.

In 1991, Keith co-founded CEM Benchmarking, which benchmarks the organizational performance of some 400 major pension funds around the world. In 2005, he played a major role in founding the Rotman International Centre for Pension Management (Rotman ICPM), and was appointed Director of Rotman ICPM and Adjunct Professor of Finance at the Rotman School of Management, University of Toronto. He was appointed Director Emeritus in 2014.

At the start of 2011, he was appointed Academic Director of the Rotman-ICPM Board Effectiveness Program for Pension Funds and Other Long-Horizon Investment Institutions. He has personal governance experience as a member of two corporate boards, and has served as Board Chair of a major medical foundation. He is a member of the Melbourne-Mercer Global Pension Index Advisory Council, the CFA Institute's Future of Finance Advisory Council, the Georgetown University Center for Retirement Initiatives Scholars Council, and Ontario's Advisory Group on Retirement Income Security.

His research, writing, and advice have influenced pension and endowment design, policy, and organizational structure around the world. He has won major awards, including CFA Institute's Award for Professional Excellence in 2011 for "exemplary achievement, excellence of practice, and true leadership," and the EBRI Lillywhite Award in 2010, given in recognition of outstanding lifetime contributions to Americans' economic security. In 2009 Keith was awarded the James Vertin Award from the CFA Institute for his contributions "of enduring value" to investment theory and practice. In 2007, he was honored with the Outstanding Industry Contribution

Award by Investments and Pensions Europe. In 2003, he was named "One of the 30 Most Influential People in Pensions and Investments" by Pensions and Investments in the USA. In 2013, *aiCIO* named him one of the globe's "10 most influential academics in institutional investing," and the globe's #1 "knowledge broker" in institutional investing in 2014.

Index

A

"Absence of Value," 19

Accounting performance, 185

ACSI. *See* Australian Council of Superannuation Investors

Active investing, cost, 18

Adaptive Markets Hypothesis (AMH), 146, 153, 157–158
  realities, 160

Adequacy-affordability-safety conundrum, examination, 50

Affordability, 51

Agents, impact, 82

AIG. *See* American International Group

AIST. *See* Australian Institute of Superannuation Trustees

Akerlof, George, 17
  Lemons thesis, 154

Alignment-of-interests, challenges, 5

ALM modeling techniques, 192

Alphas
  problems, 189, 194
  risk, 200

Ambachtsheer, Keith, 157, 207
  Return Prediction journey, 155–156

American Finance Association, French presidential address, 18

American International Group (AIG), failure, 142

AMH. *See* Adaptive Markets Hypothesis

And-and mindsets, 53–54

Animal spirits, 19

Arbitrage, risk-free test, 43–44

ASFA. *See* Australian Superannuation Funds Association

Asness, Cliff, 192

Asset allocation, 108, 110–111
  total asset percentage, 111f

Asset classes, attention, 204–205

Asset-liability mismatch risk, liability return (contrast), 96f

Assets owner organizations, inertia, 174–175

Assets under management (AUM), 108–110
  categories, allocation, 110–111
  distribution, 109

Australian Council of Superannuation Investors (ACSI), 88

Australian Institute of Superannuation Trustees (AIST), 88

Australian Superannuation Funds Association (ASFA), 93

Average annual rate of pre-tax real
   return on capital (R), 26
   examination, 28
   First Fundamental Law of
      Capitalism, relationship, 27
Average Dutch private equity cost
   experience, application, 104t
Average net private equity returns,
   104t
"Averting the Old Age Crisis"
   (World Bank), 50

B
Balance sheet-related outcomes, 112
Barton, Dominic, 164
Beauty Contest
   investors, 153–154
Beauty Contest (Keynes)
   analogy, 128
Behavioral biases, 171
Benchmarking, 109, 120
   implementation, 173
   practices, 117–119
   processes, portfolio
      strategies/management, 170,
      173
   strategy, 173
BEP. *See* Rotman-ICPM Board
   Effectiveness Program
Bernstein, William, 159
Betas
   problems, 189, 194
   risk, 200
Black swans, 201
Board Effectiveness Program (BEP)
   2014 survey
   CEO satisfaction areas, 76t
   demographics, 74t, 75f
   description/respondents, 74

governance
   findings, 74–80
   respondent comments, insights,
      77–80
   lowest-scoring statements, 77t
   response distributions, 75f
Board of directors
   effectiveness, 187
   involvement, 184
Boesky, Ivan, 142
Bovenberg, Lans, 65
Brock, Woody, 41, 151–153
Business model, 178

C
C. *See* Capital
Canada
   funds, private markets
      internalization strategy, 122
   investment model, 133–134
      comparator, 134
Canada Pension Plan (CPP), 14, 59
Canada Pension Plan Investment
   Board (CPPIB), 133–134, 164
Canada, pension plans (lessons), 16
Canada Supplementary Pension
   Plan (CSPP), 14, 16
CAP. *See* Income capitalization rate
Capital (C), 27
   average annual rate of pre-tax
      real return on capital (R), 26
   commitment, 102
   forms, 178
   markets
      entry, 158t
      examination, 158–160
      function, 160
   transfer mechanism, 65
Capital/income ratio (C/I), 27

Capital in the 21st Century
(Piketty), 25, 160
Capitalism, 4
demographics, 159
environmental risks, 159
first fundamental law, 27
fiscal deficits, 160
gateways. *See* Functional
capitalism.
geopolitical risks, 159
narratives, 159–160
second fundamental law, 27
Carry investors, money making,
183
Caveat emptor philosophy, 7
CDC. *See* Collective
defined-contribution
CDOs. *See* Collateralized debt
obligations
CDSs. *See* Credit default swaps
CEM Benchmarking, Inc., 9
database, average net private
equity returns, 104t
international pensions space,
three-element framework, 94
pension fund database, usage, 20
standardized measurement
initiative, 103–105
value, definition, 94
CFA Institute ("Future of Finance"
initiative), 86
Chambers, David, 133
Chief executive officer (CEO)
responses, 71
satisfaction, areas, 76t
C/I. *See* Capital/income ratio
Client/Beneficiary Value, 19–20
Climate change
accountability, 204

asset classes, attention, 204–205
Mercer climate change study,
203–205
transformation scenario,
achievement, 205
Climate change risk, management,
201
Climate risk
complexity/duration, 205
inevitability, 204
Collaboration strategies, 187–188
Collateralized debt obligations
(CDOs), 142
Collective action strategies,
requirement, 187–188
Collective defined-contribution
(CDC) design, 52
Collective electorates, preferences, 5
Commercial financial services
providers, 66
Commonfund, 195
Communication
impact, 171
technologies, impact, 160
Compensation, 79, 125, 146
average compensation
FTE size, 121f, 122f
location basis, 123f
average total compensation, 113f
compensation to total fund
average compensation ratio,
114f
externally imposed compensation
restrictions, 112–113
levels, 120, 124
practices, 113–117
principles, 108, 111–117
structures, 120, 124
design, accountability, 112t

Compensation, (*Continued*)
  target performance
    Org + Pers/Investment Variable
    Compensation splits, 117f
  target performance, base/variable
    compensation splits, 116f
  variable compensation,
    calculation, 118t
Complete pension contracts, 42
Conley, John, 69
Contribution rate. *See* Target
  contribution rate
  push, impossibility, 45–46
Contributions, 12
Corporate managers/owners,
  alignment-of-interests
  (challenges), 5
Corporate value creation, aspects
  (monitoring), 179
CPP. *See* Canada Pension Plan
CPPIB. *See* Canada Pension Plan
  Investment Board
Credit default swaps (CDSs), 142
Crown Corporation, 139
CSPP. *See* Canada Supplementary
  Pension Plan
Culture
  bad outcomes, 142–143
  good outcomes, 144
  impact, 141
  issues, 146–147
  legal structure, impact, 146
  question, examination, 141–142
Customers, value (absence), 17

D
DA. *See* Defined ambition;
  Defined-ambition
DB. *See* Defined-benefit

DC. *See* Defined-contribution
Defined-ambition (DA) pension
  plans, 38
  challenges, 53–54
  defined-ambition to target benefit
    (DA/TB) pension plan,
    features, 38, 46
  defining, 49
  delivery organization, 39f
  design, 50–51
Defined ambition (DA), term usage
  (increase), 53
Defined-benefit (DB) pension plans,
  6, 33
  balance sheet, exposure, 43
  costing/funding, 41
  designs, 4
    public sector DB plans,
      problems, 38–39
  discomfort, 83–84
  examination, 46–47
  funding requirements, reduction,
    43
  shortfall risks, 57
  unconventional wisdom, 41–42
Defined-contribution (DC) pension
  plans, 6, 33
  designs, 4
  discomfort, 83–84
  employer deposit, 42
Demographics, impact, 159
Dimson, Elroy, 133
Disclosure, emphasis, 184
Dividend yield, definition, 160
DNB (regulator)
  Federation of Dutch Pension
    Funds, interaction, 106
  impact, 104
Dot.com bubble, 152

Double bubble blues era, 158
Drucker, Peter, 54, 92, 177
  fiduciary investment institutions, 155
  high-performance pension investment organization formula, 135
  pension institutions, construction, 155
  pension organization, arms-length legal structure, 58–59
  Unseen Revolution, The (visibility), 190–191
  wisdom/insights, 136
Dutch Pension Act, 83
Dutch private equity cost experience, application, 104t
Dysfunctional pension contracts, win-lose formulas, 191

E
Earnings yield, definition, 161
Eccles, Ioannou, and Serafeim (EIS) study
  design, 184–185
  market performance, 185
Eccles, Robert, 183, 184
Economic growth, physical limits, 5
Economic profit (EP), metric, 179
Efficient Markets Hypothesis (EMH), 82–83, 146, 153
  alternative, 157
  assumption, 197
  creation, 196
  realities, 160
EIS. *See* Eccles, Ioannou, and Serafeim
Either-or mindsets, 54

EMH. *See* Efficient Markets Hypothesis
Employee actual compensation, target compensation percentage, 115f
Employer responsibility, 12
Engagement
  protocols, 174
  strategy, 91
Environmental risks, 159
Environmental, Social, and Governance (ESG)
  considerations, 130, 206
  factors, 171
EP. *See* Economic profit
Epistemic proceduralism, 134
Erasmus University (Rotterdam), defined-ambition pension plan workshop, 49, 52
ESG. *See* Environmental, Social, and Governance
Evaluation/incentives, portfolio strategies/management, 170, 173–174
Ex ante costs structures, 105
Ex ante distinction, 202, 205–206
Excess investment cost, ten-year net value added (contrast), 95f
Excess service score, excess cost per member (contrast), 98f
Ex post costs structures, 105
Ex post distinction, 202, 205–206
Ezra, Don, 65

F
Fair value pricing, maintenance, 18
Farrell, Jim, 155
FCF margins, 173

FCLT. *See* Focusing Capital on the
Long Term
Federation of Dutch Pension Funds,
DNB (interaction), 106
Fiduciary duty
collective responses,
national/global levels, 85–86
court interpretation, pension
board lag, 81–82
interpretation, reasons,
82–84
investment beliefs/policies, 85
legislation, rethinking, 85–86
meaning, evolution, 81
organization design, 84
protection, legal mechanisms
(creation), 85
stakeholder communications, 84
win-win collaborations, fostering,
85
Fiduciary investment institutions
(Drucker), 155
Financial Instability Hypothesis
(Minsky), 145, 157–158
Financial Products Group (AIG),
142
Financial system dysfunction, legal
responses, 83
First Fundamental Law of
Capitalism, 27
Fiscal deficits, 159
Fit-for-purpose pension formula,
35–36
Flash Boys (Lewis), 144
Focusing Capital on the Long Term
(FCLT), 85, 164
action areas, 170
initiative, 169–170, 177
support, 166

Long-Term Portfolio Guide
(purpose), 170
Fortune and Folly (O'Barr/Conley),
69
French, Kenneth, 18, 22
FTE. *See* Full-time equivalent
Fuld, Dick, 143, 145
Full-time equivalent (FTE),
108–110, 120–122
count, 122, 124
distribution, 109
employees, 108
investment-related FTE, impact,
121
size, 121f, 122f
Functional capitalism, gateways, 3
Future makers/takers, 205
"Future of Finance" initiative (CFA
Institute), 86

G
Game theory (Brock), 41
Gateways lecture (London), 3–4
components, 4–5
*General Theory of Employment,
Interest, and Money, The*
(Keynes), 153
General Theory, The (Keynes),
128
Geopolitical risks, 159
GKO bonds, 142
Global finance crisis, 200
Global Financial Crisis (GFC), 83,
85–86
Global pension sector, long-horizon
investing (status), 167t
Governance. *See* Pension boards;
Pension governance
impact, 202, 206

quality, nonfinancial
  considerations, 163
strength, 7
Government Accounting Standards
  Board (GASB), disclosure
  requirements, 105–106
Government of Ontario bonds,
  136–137
Government Pension Fund Global
  (GPFG), 133, 138, 146
GPFG. *See* Government Pension
  Fund Global
Greenberg, Hank, 142, 145
Gurria, Angel, 69

H
Hawley, Jim, 81
Heisenberg Uncertainty Principle,
  application, 192, 194
HFT. *See* High-frequency trading
High-compensation drivers, search,
  121–123
High-frequency trading (HFT), 144
High-performance pension
  investment organizations,
  Drucker formula, 135
High-sustainability (HS)
  corporations, 184
Historical returns, mirage, 62–63
HS. *See* High-sustainability
Human resources (HR)
  principles/practices, 111–112

I
I. *See* National income
ICPM. *See* International Centre for
  Pension Management
IIRC. *See* International Integrated
  Reporting Council

Ilmanen, Antii, 133, 192
ILPA. *See* Institutional Limited
  Partners Association
IMPL (implementation) findings,
  20–21
Implied ERP, definition, 161
Income capitalization rate (CAP),
  130
Income replacement
  outcomes, 92
  rate. *See* Target
    income-replacement rate.
Incomplete pension contracts,
  42–43
Incomplete pension contracts,
  win-lose formulas, 191
Index value, definition, 161
Inflation-adjusted dividends, stream
  growth, 180–181
Inflation-indexed income
  replacement, 50
Institutional investing
  future, 17
  theory to practice process, OTPP
    example, 21–22
  Tokyo speech, 17–18
Institutional investment categories,
  global asset values, 29t
Institutional Limited Partners
  Association (ILPA), 106
Integrated Reporting <IR>. *See*
  International Integrated
  Reporting framework
  concepts, 178–179
  initiative, 87–89
    contexts, 93–94
  presentation, basis, 89
Integrative Investment Theory,
  19–20

Intergenerational fairness,
36–37
problem, 37f
Intergenerational risk asymmetry,
37f
Intergenerational risk-sharing,
absence, 64
Intergenerational wealth-shifting,
38
International Centre for Pension
Management (ICPM), 9
Discussion Forum, 44
research projects, 81–82
workshops, 49
International Integrated Reporting
<IR> framework
content elements, 89
guiding principles, 88
International Integrated Reporting
Council (IIRC), Integrated
Reporting framework
initiative, 87–89
International pensions,
three-element framework, 94
Investee organization
health/effectiveness,
assessment, 178–180
Investing. *See* Institutional investing
cost, 22–23
Investment
allocation/structures, 119–120,
123
behavior, 8
benchmarking, 120
benchmarks, 124–125
fits/misfits, 193–194
goals, 128–129
implications, transformation
scenario (impact), 205

income
monitoring protocol, 181t
production, performance
(comparison), 180–181
investment-related FTE, impact,
121
mandates, portfolio
strategies/management, 170,
174
models, comparison, 133–135
objectives, duality, 120
organizational implications, 132
organizational models,
comparison, 135–136
organization design, 127
program
characteristics, 191–192
redirection, 53
progress markers, 177–178
returns, 157
calculation/equation, 130
predictability, reason, 151
predictable returns thesis,
152–153
risk sharing, examination, 63–64
scientific investment paradigm,
192–193
strategies/outcomes, integration,
92
theories
over-reliance, 82–83
practice, reconciliation,
151–152
Investment beliefs, 127, 128, 146
articulation, reasons, 171
organization design, relationship,
187
portfolio strategies/management,
170, 171–172

rethinking, 157
sensibility, 7
"Investment Horizons," 19
Investment organizations, investing
  cost, 22–23
Investment performance
  absolute target benchmark, 119t
  benchmarking, 108
    practices, 117–119
  calculation, usage, 116, 118
  market-based benchmark, 118t
  peer relative benchmark, 119t
  performance-based variable
    compensation, 116
  variable compensation ceilings,
    118t
Ioannou, Ioannis, 183, 184
<IR>. *See* Integrated Reporting
  initiative

J
Jeffrey, Robert, 180
Johnson, Keith, 81

K
Katsuyama, Brad, 144
Kerviel, Jerome, 143
Keynes, John Maynard, 3, 70, 134,
  183
  Beauty Contest investors, 128,
    153–154
  investor status, 139
  wisdom/insights, 136
Key performance indicators (KPIs),
  124
Knox, David, 65
KPA Advisory Services, pension
  investment pay practices study,
  107–108

asset allocation, 108, 110–111
average compensation, 123f
compensation, 125
  practices, 113–117
  principles/constraints, 108,
    111–116
  structure design,
    accountability, 112t
  structures, 124
compensation to total fund
  average compensation ratio,
    114f
employee actual compensation,
  target compensation
  percentage, 115f
fund characteristics, 108,
  109–110
high-compensation drivers,
  search, 121–123
investment benchmarks,
  124–125
investment performance
  benchmarking practices,
    117–119
  variable compensation ceilings,
    118t
observations, 124–125
organizational/personal
  performance, variable
  compensation ceilings, 117t
organizational structures,
  110–111
  total asset percentages, 111f
parts, 108–119
responding funds
  characteristics, 109t
  size, 110f
risk management, 125
survey

KPA Advisory Services, pension
  investment pay practices study,
  (*Continued*)
  findings, insights, 119–120
  participation, 119
 target performance
  base/variable compensation
    splits, 116f
  Org + Pers/Investment Variable
    Compensation splits, 117f
KPIs. *See* Key performance
  indicators

L
Lamoureux, Claude, 21
Leech, Jim, 33, 34
Lehman Brothers, failure, 143
Lemons thesis (Akerlof), 154
Leveraged buyout (LBO) fund,
  102
Lewis, Michael, 142, 144, 145
Liability return, asset-liability
  mismatch risk (contrast), 96f
Liar's Poker (Lewis), 142
Lo, Andrew, 141
  adaptive markets hypothesis, 153
  framework, usage, 145–146
Longevity
  pooling vehicle, 64
  protection purchase option, 52
  retiree longevity, increase, 37
  risk
    pooling, DB plans (impact), 36
    sharing, examination, 64–65
  within-group/within-time period
    dimension, 36
Long-horizon (LH) investing
  global pension sector status, 167t
  survey findings, 166–168

Long-horizon (LH) return
  compounding instrument,
    usage, 7
Long-horizon (LH) wealth-creation
  capability, 38
  investment
    program, redirection, 53
    strategies, 8
  sustainability, 53
Long-Term Capital (LTCM),
  failure, 142, 145
Long-term focus, 171
Long-term investing, 169,
  177, 183
  change, 182
  effectiveness, 183–184
  results, measurement, 177
  Unilever example, 186
  value creation, 185
Long-termism
  absence, 165
  deductive case, 165
  examination, 164–165
  inductive case, 165
  institutional survey, 165–168
  investment paradigm, 163
  investor stories, threads, 166t
  shift, 163–164
Long-term orientation, 184
Long-Term Portfolio Guide (FCLT),
  purpose, 170
Low-risk liability portfolio, 94
Low-sustainability (LS)
  corporations, 184
LS. *See* Low-sustainability
LTCM. *See* Long-Term Capital
LT TIPS yield
  definition, 161
  material spike, 162

M

Madoff, Bernie (failure), 143, 145

Management fees, impact, 102

Market-based TIPS yield curve, usage, 44

Market equities, emergence, 198

Market forces, impact, 23

Market performance, 185

Markowitz, Harry, 195–196, 198

Material scale economies, 132

Mauboussin, Michael, 179

McNish, Jacquie, 33, 34

Measure, disseminate, and celebrate (M-D-C) strategy, examples, 9

Measurement, emphasis, 184

Member services/benefit administration, value-for-money (measurement), 97–98

Mercer climate change study, 203–205

Mercer LIFETIMEPLUS initiative, 66

Meriwether, John, 142

Merton, Robert, 142, 196

Minsky, Hyman, 145
moment, 157

Modern portfolio theory (MPT)
changes/application, 195
elements, 196–197
helpfulness, 196–197
insights, 195–196
risk, identification, 198–199
simplicity, 197–198
theory/practice, 196–197

Morgenson, Gretchen, 101

MPT. *See* Modern portfolio theory

Mutual fund databases, usage, 20

N

National Employment Savings Trust (NEST), 15, 16
creation, 59

National government initiatives (pension designs), 66

National income (I), 27

National Transportation Safety Board (NTSB), 144

NB Investment Management, 136

NEST. *See* National Employment Savings Trust

Net buy-back yield, definition, 161

Net excess returns, calculations, 137

NETSPAR, DA pension plan workshop, 49

NETSPAR-ICPM workshop, 54

Net value-added (NVA), 95–96

NIMC. *See* Norway Investment Management Corporation

Non-marketable Government of Ontario bonds, 136–137

Norges Bank, 146

Norway Fund, 138–139
Canadian approach, decision, 139
investment model, 133

Norway Investment Management Corporation (NIMC), 139

Norway Model, 138

NTSB. *See* National Transportation Safety Board

O

OAS. *See* Old Age Security

O'Barr, William, 69

Old Age Security (OAS), 14

Ontario Teachers' Pension Plan
(OTPP), 9–10, 14, 134, 138
creation, 137, 155
golden rules, 21
initiative, 66
offerings, 59–60
institutional investing, theory to
practice process, 21–22
Operationally meaningful theorems,
189–190
Optionality, concept, 196
Organizational
competencies/design, 198
Organizational models,
comparison, 135–136
Organizational performance,
variable compensation ceilings,
117t
Organizational structures,
110–111, 146
total asset percentage, 111f
Organization design, 127
Organization design, investment
beliefs (relationship), 187
Outcomes
Eccles, Ioannou, and Serafeim
(EIS) study, design, 184–185
production, improvement,
183–184
Own pocket make-ups, 43

P
PADA. *see* Personal Accounts
Delivery Authority
Pax Americana I/II, 160
Pay drivers, impact, 108
Payment-certainty portfolios, size,
129
Payment safety

goal, 132
instruments, 97
investment programs,
characteristics, 191–192
portfolio, 194
management, 131
purchase capability, 38
Payout yield, definition, 161
Pensioenfonds Zorg en Welzign
(PFZW) PGGM, 44, 52–53
model, 45
Pension boards
compensation, 79–80
composition/skills, 77–79
dilemma, 132
effectiveness, 84
regulatory requirement, 73
roles, management roles (clarity),
73
self-evaluation protocol,
initiation, 73
skill/experience matrix, creation,
72
Pension boards, Board Effectiveness
Program (BEP) 2014 survey
board process, 79
CEO satisfaction areas, 76t
demographics, 74t, 75f
description/respondents, 74
governance
concerns, 80
findings, 74–80
quality, regional variations,
78t
respondent comments, insights,
77–80
lowest-scoring statements, 77t
response distributions, 75f
Pension designs, 84

commercial financial services
    providers, 66
improvement, 3
national/regional government
    initiatives, 66
problems, passive acceptance,
    83–84
realities, implications, 35
single employer/multi-employer
    context, 66
sustainability, 6–7
Pensioners
    annuity balance sheet, 92
    payment security, 7
Pension fund governance
    deficit
        action, recommendations,
            72–74
        understanding, 70–71
    effectiveness, 69
    management, challenges, 72t
    scoring statements, 73t
    survey, 69
Pension funds
    agents, impact, 82
    capitalism, transformation, 6
    characteristics, 108, 109–110
    database, usage, 20
    democracy, 13
    examination, 101–102
    global perspective, 29–30
    growth, 82
    investment theories,
        over-reliance, 82–83
    management, *Capital in the 21st
        Century* (relevance), 25
    model, comparison, 136–138
    organizations, effectiveness, 7–8
    oversight/management, 71t

payments, 107
scoring statements, 73t
sector, institutional investing
    evidence, 18–19
short-term emphasis, 82
thought-leading pension funds,
    119
transformation project, 8–9
Pension governance
    challenge, 54
    organization design, 84
    quality, regional variations, 78t
    research findings, 69–74
    respondent comments, insights,
        77–80
    responses, pension organization
        level, 84–85
    stakeholder communications, 84
Pension organizations
    agents, layers, 8
    biology framework, 144
    culture
        impact, 141
        issues, 146–147
    environment, 145
    group composition, 145
    improvement, 3
    investment beliefs, relationship,
        187
    leadership, 145
    lessons, 187–188
    success drivers, 8
Pension plans
    arrangement, 62
    design, 13, 61–62, 187
        implications, 63
    funding, implications, 63
    future, 11
    governance, 16

Pension plans (*Continued*)
 historical returns, mirage, 62–63
 investment policies, 63
 investment risk sharing,
  examination, 63–64
 longevity risk sharing,
  examination, 64–65
 participants, interests
  (alignment), 7
Pension reform
 book review, 34
 conversation, change, 35, 39
 reasons, 33
Pension Revolution
 (Ambachtsheer), 207
Pensions
 arrangement
  employment basis, 62
  long-term sustainability, 146
 complete pension contracts, 42
 contracts. *See* Complete pension
  contracts; Incomplete pension
  contracts.
  redesign, 72
  win-lose formula, 191
 formula. *See* Fit-for-purpose
  pension formula.
 incomplete pension contracts,
  42–43
 integrated reporting, 87
 intergenerational fairness,
  36–37
 investment
  pay practices, study, 107–108
 management, risk (relationship),
  202–203
 mitigation, identification, 36
 organizations, 87
  culture, impact, 141

 practice, theory (contrast),
  90–91
 value-for-money, measurement,
  93
 providers, 12
 risks
  consideration, 36f
  identification, 36
  management, 84
  measurement, 98–99
 systems, design features, 35
 systems, goals, 7
 target, setting/cost, 35
 value for money, measurement,
  98–99
 Washington, D.C., debate, 33–34
Performance. *See* Investment
  performance
 accounting performance, 185
 benchmarking, 109, 120
 investment income production,
  comparison, 180–181
 key performance indicators
  (KPIs), 124
 market performance, 185
 measurement, 178
  process, 177
 performance-based compensation
  schemes, 184
PERS. *See* Public Employees'
  Retirement System
Personal Accounts Delivery
  Authority (PADA), 15
Personal performance, variable
  compensation ceilings, 117t
PGGM. *See* Pensioenfonds Zorg en
  Welzijn
Phalippou-Gottschalg paper,
  104–105

Piketty, Thomas, 25, 157, 160
  conclusions, 26
  contributions, 30
  order-of-magnitude examination, 29
  phenomenon, 25–26
Plan insolvency, 191
Plowback yield, definition, 161
Polman, Paul, 186
Ponzi scheme, 143
Pooled Registered Pension Plans (PRPPs), 14
Pope Francis, 201
Portability, 13
Portfolios
  management, reorientation, 170–174
  modern portfolio theory (MPT), 195
  payment-certainty portfolios, size, 129
  payment-safety portfolio, management, 131
  reference portfolio, 120
  return-seeking portfolios, 129–131
  strategies, reorientation, 170–174
  theory, usefulness, 190
Post-work financial security, 127
Post-work income stream, target/length, 131
Predictable returns thesis, 152–153
Price discovery, 18
Principal-agent problems, 171
Principles for Responsible Investing (PRI), 9
Private equity fee formula, 103
Private markets

internalization strategy, usage, 122
investment, value for money measurement, 101
  retrospective, 102–103
Productive capital investor, 135
Progress markers (investments), 177–178
Property rights, rule of law (impact), 159–160
PRPPs. *See* Pooled Registered Pension Plans
Public Employees' Retirement System (PERS)
  balance sheet problem, solving, 45–46
  case study, 47
  enhanced balance sheet
    full guarantees, usage, 45t
    reduced guarantees, usage, 46t
  pension plan, 44

Q
QSuper funds, 51–52
  delivery model, 52
  transition plan, development, 52

R
R. *See* Average annual rate of pre-tax real return on capital
R>G inequality, 26–27
Rappaport, Alfred, 179
Rational actors, 144–145
RBC. *See* Royal Bank of Canada
Real return risks,
  within-group/within-time period dimension, 36
Reference portfolio, 120
Regional government initiatives (pension designs), 66

Responsible Investment (RI)
activities, 92
Results, measurement, 177
Retiree longevity, increase, 37
Retirement plans
integration, 13
states, impact, 13
Retirement savings, challenge, 11
Return
prediction journey
(Ambachtsheer), 155–156
short-term return volatility,
193–194
total fund return, importance,
181–182
Return on invested capital (ROIC)
margins, 179
metric/excess, 179
Return-seeking investment
programs, characteristics,
191–192
Return-seeking portfolios,
129, 194
conversion process, 131
management, 130–131
size, 129
RI. *See* Responsible Investment
RIJPM. *See Rotman International
Journal of Pension
Management*
Risk
appetite
matrix, 172T
statement, portfolio
strategies/management, 170,
172–173
categorization, 201–202
climate change risk, management,
201

ex post/ex ante distinction, 202,
205–206
exposure, measurement,
199–200
governance, impact, 202, 206
identification, 198–199
matrix, 172t
management, 91, 125, 195,
205–206
identification, 202, 205
strategic
advice/implementation, 200
metric, 96–97
pension management,
relationship, 202–203
plan insolvency, 191
risk-adjustment process,
118–119
risk-free arbitrage test, 43–44
risk-free investment, payment,
199
risk-taking investment policy,
adoption, 42
time horizon, importance, 202,
206
tolerance, 120, 196–197
ROA margins, 173
ROIC. *See* Return on invested
capital
Rotman-ICPM Board Effectiveness
Program (BEP), 74
Rotman International Centre
for Pension Management
(ICPM), 9
Discussion Forum, 44, 202–203
research projects, 81–82
*Rotman International Journal of
Pension Management* (RIJPM),
163

fiduciary duty, meaning (articles), 83
pension organization boards observations, 70, 82
Rotman Management publication, 186
Rotterdam. *See* Erasmus University
Royal Bank of Canada (RBC), 144, 145
Rule of law, impact, 159–160
Rumsfeld, Donald, 201

S
Samuelson, Paul, 189, 194
Sarro, Doug, 81, 85
Savings rate (S), 27
Savings rate to growth rate (S/G) ratio, 27
Scale economies/opportunities, 132
Schein, Edgar H., 141
Scholes, Myron, 142, 196
Scientific investment paradigm, 192–193
Scientific rationalism, 159
Second Fundamental Law of Capitalism, 27
Securities Exchange Commission (SEC), 143
  Office of Compliance, Inspections, and Examinations, 105–106
Selection criteria, 174
Sell triggers, 174
Senior Investment Professional (SIP), 114–115, 117
Sentinel Integrated Annual Report, 90–91
  steps, future, 91–92

Sentinel Mining Industry Retirement Fund, 88, 89–90
  practice, theory (contrast), 90–91
  report, 90
Separation Theorem (Tobin/Sharpe), 128, 196
Serafeim, George, 183, 184
Service score, 94
SG. *See* Societe Generale
S/G. *See* Savings rate to growth rate
ShareAction organization, 3, 8–9
Shared risks pension arrangement, 58
Shared-risk TB plans, single/multi-employer levels, 58–59
Sharpe, Bill, 128, 196
Shaw, George Bernard, 207
Shiller, Robert, 17
Shortfall risks, 57
Short-term return volatility, 193–194
SIP. *See* Senior Investment Professional
Societal have-have not divide, 5
Societal income, future distributions, 26
Societal wealth
  distribution, inequality (divergence), 26
  future distributions, 26
Societe Generale (SG), 143, 145
Solvency-testing protocols, absence, 64
South Africa, Sentinel mining industry retirement fund, 89–90
  report, 90
Sovereign credit, 192

Stakeholders
communications, 187
improvement, 87
identification/engagement
processes, priority, 184
matrix, integrative
elements, 91
solidarity message, 125
term, usage, 58–59
value-creation model, 185, 187
features, 184
Standard & Poor's 500 (S&P500)
examination, 160–162
fundamentals, transition, 161t
nominal returns, 62
Structural changes, 152
Success, defining, 93–94
Success drivers, 7–8
confirmation, 16

T
Target benefit (TB) pension plans,
38
benefits
examination, 55–56
financing, 56
commercial solutions, 59
defining, 55, 60
employers, impact, 57–60
government initiatives, 59–60
shared-risk TB plans,
single/multi-employer levels,
58–59
target, defining, 56–57
Target contribution
rate, 38
Target income-replacement rate, 38

Target performance
base/variable compensation
splits, 116f
Org + Pers/Investment Variable
Compensation splits, 117f
TB. *See* Target benefit
Ten-year net return, liability
return/asset-liability mismatch
risk (contrast), 96f
Ten-year net value added, excess
investment cost (contrast), 95f
Ten-year value-for-money
investment results, 95–96
Ten-year value-for-risk investment
results, 96–97
Third-party risk underwriter,
requirement, 199
Third Rail, The (Leech/McNish),
34, 39
Thought-leading pension
funds, 119
Time horizon, importance,
202, 206
Tinbergen, Jan, 7
two goals-two instruments
principle, 128
Tinbergen Pension Model,
update/applications, 65–66
Tobin, James, 128, 196
Total fund return, importance,
181–182
Trailing earnings, definition, 161
Transparency, 13
Transportation technologies,
impact, 160
Treasury Inflation-Protected
Securities (TIPS)

LT TIPS yield
  definition, 161
  material spike, absence, 162
  real return, 28
  real yield curve, 42
  yield curve, usage, 44
  yields, 161
Trend-following herding instincts,
  193
Trust-building, emphasis (increase),
  53
Turner Commission, 16
2 and 20 haircut, avoidance, 20
Two goals-two instruments
  principle (Tinbergen), 128

U
Unilever, long-term investing
  example, 186
United Kingdom Pension
  Commission, 15
United States, pension plan lessons,
  16
Universal coverage, 12
Universal, Secure, Adaptable (USA)
  Retirement Funds Act, 12–13
Unknown known, 201–202
Unseen Revolution, The (Drucker),
  54, 155
  visibility, 190–191
Urwin, Roger, 141

V
Value
  CEM definition, 94
  creation, 179, 185
  unlocking, 170

Value for money (value-for-money)
  excess service score, excess cost
    per member (contrast), 98f
  functional measurement,
    elements, 94
  measurement, 93, 94–99, 101
    changes, 103
    future, 105–106
    member services/benefit
      administration, 97–98
  standardized measurement, CEM
    initiative, 103–105
  ten-year investment results,
    95–96
  ten-year value-for-risk investment
    results, 96–97
  test, 17–18
van Buul, Otto, 179–180
van der Velden, Alex, 179–180
Variable compensation, calculation,
  118t
Viceira, Luis, 202–203
Vilgan, Rosemary, 51

W
Waitzer, Ed, 81, 85
Wealth
  capability. *See* Long-horizon
    wealth-creation capability.
  concentration, laws, 27–28
  creation
    instruments, 97
    sustainability, 163
  definitions/relationships, 27
  distribution, dynamics, 26
  intergenerational wealth-shifting,
    38

Wealth (*Continued*)
  paradox, 159–160
  power, equivalence, 30
Weapons of mass destruction
    (WMDs), possibility/risk, 201
Whitmarsh, Theresa, 163
Win-win collaborations, fostering,
    85
Wiseman, Mark, 164
WMDs. *See* Weapons of mass
    destruction

Workers, pension systems, 7
World Bank, 50

Y
Yale University, investment model,
    133

Z
Zero-sum beauty contest game, 154
Zero-sum game, 134–135